Please remember that this is a library book,
and that it belongs only temporarily to each
person who uses it. Be considerate. Do
not write in this, or any, library book.

WITHDRAWN

CARY LIBRARY
VERMONT COLLEGE
36 COLLEGE STREET
MONTPELIER, VT 05602

WITHDRAWN

WITHDRAWN

W9-CDA-901

LOST BOSTON

Jane Holtz Kay

Houghton Mifflin Company, Boston, 1980

974.461
K231L
1980

Copyright © 1980 by Jane Holtz Kay

All rights reserved. No part of this work may be reproduced or transmitted in any form by any means, electronic or mechanical, including photocopying and recording, or by any information storage or retrieval system, without permission in writing from the publisher.

Library of Congress Cataloging in Publication Data
Kay, Jane Holtz.
  Lost Boston.
  Bibliography: p.
  Includes index.
    1. Architecture — Massachusetts — Boston — Mutilation, defacement, etc.   I. Title.
NA735.B7K39   974.4'61   80–16056
ISBN 0–395–27609–8

Printed in the United States of America

M   10   9   8   7   6   5   4   3   2   1

Book design by Larry Webster

Front end leaf:
View from East Boston, 1848.

Back end leaf:
Environs of Boston from Corey Hill, Brookline, Mass.

Frontispiece:
Federal Street Church and its residential and streetscape in 1858.

Title page:
View of Boston on the masthead of Gleason's *Pictorial.*

Opposite:
Decoration on Shoe and Leather Building by Hartwell and Richardson

To Stephen,
Jacqueline,
and Julie

Acknowledgments

THIS WORK, not unlike the city that it represents, is a collective undertaking, drawn from and dependent upon the labors of formal and informal "students of the streets." Whether impassioned lookers or scholars, they are the city's best friends — and for months were mine.

Robert Bayard Severy, who believes in an afterlife for buildings, has done his best to ensure the ghostly preservation of the architecture he knows so exhaustively through his research and photographic contributions to this volume. I am in his debt above all others.

I am grateful to those who read through the whole or portions of the manuscript, especially to John Coolidge for his provocative and insightful comments; and to Frederic Detweller, David Hall, James O'Gorman, Nina Meyer, Cynthia Zaitzevsky and, finally, to Martin Robbins for labors in behalf of this book's lucidity.

I also stand indebted to countless antiquarians and historians whose texts describe the landscape of Boston in a long and fascinating tradition, from the nineteenth century to Walter Muir Whitehill's *Boston: A Topographical History.* The works to which any student of Boston's buildings must refer range from quaint guidebooks to the proceedings of the Bostonian Society, from political biographies to *Old Time New England* and more standard works. But Boston architecture is undergoing still more thorough examination from those who focus closely on its neighborhoods and periods of design. Their labors must, or soon will, appear in print. Some of those whose published or unpublished texts, reminiscences, or knowledge of the city and its architecture proved helpful were: John D. Bryant, Richard Card, Margaret Henderson Floyd, Richard Heath, Arthur Krim, Morgan Phillips, and Margaret Supplee Smith. Buckminster Fuller's taped notes on early-twentieth-century Boston supplemented the memories of other elder Bostonians.

The pictorial collections of Boston's libraries and historic institutions are overwhelming. One could have drawn ample photographs from any one of them — the Bostonian Society, the Boston Public Library, the Boston Athenaeum, or the Society for the Preservation of New England Antiquities, all of which gave me access to their riches. I am especially indebted to the Bostonian Society's librarian, Mary Leen, and its director, Thomas W. Parker, for making the Old State House a sometime home; to Jack Jackson and Sally Pierce of the Boston Athenaeum; to Sinclair Hitchings, curator, and Eugene Zepp of the Boston Public Library's print department and Florence Connolly, curator, and Theresa Cederholm of its fine arts department; and to Elinor Reichlin and Margaret Ziering of the Society for the Preservation of New England Antiquities. George Collins of the Boston *Globe,* Kathy Flynn of the Peabody Museum, Massachu-

Interior of St. Mary's Church by Patrick C. Keeley.

Acknowledgments

setts Bay Transportation Authority librarian George Sanborn, and
Captain Albert A. Swanson of the Metropolitan District Commission
Library and Norton D. Clark also directed me through and
to much material.

Boston has a tradition of first-rate architectural photography. The
nineteenth-century views of Boston architecture by Josiah Hawes,
T. E. Marr, J. D. Black, Baldwin Coolidge, A. H. Folsom, Soule
Photo, and others comprise works of arts rendered into fresh prints by
Salvatore Lopes and Lee Nadel, who coaxed even dog-eared photographs
to life, and by Jackson Smith, whose care is apparent in his
copywork. Some of the most poignant photographs here came out of
the files of living photographers who, unwittingly, were contributing
to the record of vanished architecture over the last three decades. I
am grateful to Irene Shwachman, Jules Aarons, Steve Rosenthal,
William Clift, and Leslie Larson, among a tribe of building watchers.

My gratitude to my editor, Anita McClellan, is endless. Her astute
and enthusiastic response sustained this project at every step. My deepest
appreciation to Alan Emmet for her dogged research and to Margaret
Nash DeLaitre and Amy Rule for their help. A thanks to
Carolyn McCloud for rendering scribbles and squawkings into manuscript
form. Larry Webster's patience and talent went far beyond
what an author can expect from any book designer.

On a more intimate level, I am grateful beyond words to my extended
family for personal support; to my sister Ellen Goodman for
her ongoing counsel, to Jeanne MacLaren for her myriad contributions
to all the facets of my life, and to Victoria Puglisi for bracing
my labors. Finally, thank-you beyond all others goes to my husband,
Stephen Kay, who made this book possible.

Original train, Boston and Lowell Railroad.

A Personal Preface

THERE IS no clock of common memory: my Boston is not your Boston, is not John Winthrop's or Paul Revere's Boston, not Oliver Wendell Holmes' or James Michael Curley's. Yet, we share a sense of Boston — a place that is, above all, memorable; a city that feeds all the routine senses of touch, sight, sound, but especially, a city that is a sight for the eyes. Boston, as planner Kevin Lynch put it, is "imageable." Bostonians inhabit a landscape of loveliness and livability; we pace our hours amidst an architecture of special worth.

For me, this Boston was not always a city upon a hill. Only slowly did Boston's graces seep into my consciousness. A child of the Hub, I enjoyed the city's urbanity long before I saw or appreciated the architecture that bred it. To a youngster growing up a trolley ride from downtown's splendors, Boston was a place of smudged but endearing glamour. In the 1940s and 1950s, Boston meant streetcar trips downtown with Mother to shop for buttons or nubby winter coats. It was lunch defaulted for a Bailey's sundae, walks through alleys and curving streets, and rides up a creaking elevator to my father's Devonshire Street law office.

In my youth, Boston was theater and the Opera House, now long gone, where from a fifth-tier seat one had a glittering if periscoped view of *Madame Butterfly* or descended to join a dance recital's fantasy of life upon the wicked stage. Boston was infinite riches: it was Chinese food on streets inscribed with a foreign calligraphy; meals of spaghetti just off the crowded byways of the North End. It was Beacon Hill's antique purple windows or Christmas carolers in Louisburg Square.

Boston was a maze of masonry and greenery, unwinding endlessly as a child's vistas unwound. It was the swan boats, where you leaned over the edges of the Public Garden lagoon at your peril, and it was the spiral ramp leading to the circus at Boston Garden where the smell of elephants added to the clammy odor of concrete. It was domestic memories too — sitting on the stoop of a two-family house blowing bubbles from pink Popeye-the-Sailor soap or posing against the "family tree" in Franklin Park to record my year's growth in inches. It was Sundays at the Aquarium and, graduating from rainbow-hued fish, rainy afternoons with the full color range of the Museum of Fine Arts' impressionists.

When does a child realize that the frame for all these splendors is architecture? For me, the sense of Boston's richness and diversity in urban design and neighborhoods came in the 1950s. As a teenager I traveled through the wildly mixed landscape of the Tenth Congressional district. My father's political campaign took us from the tree-shaded houses of Jamaica Plain to the tenements of Mission Hill, from the row houses and apartments of the Back Bay, Roxbury, or the Fens to Dorchester, with a last stop for the election eve ritual at the G&G Delicatessen on Blue Hill Avenue, now, too, long gone. I would like to think my sensibility to architecture and urban values grew from following his defense of the shopkeepers and tenants driven out in the renewal-cum-removal of the old West End. Its Urban Villagers became Herbert Gans's classic losers in a benighted era.

I suspect that my view of Boston's art and urban design developed slowly like Boston itself and that my "education of the eyes" came in a barely conscious way, fostered by the city's visual delights and civilized aspect. The city as a work of collective art went beyond those single "artistic" episodes called architecture: Boston evolved through the shared sense of humanity and urbanity of many designers over many years and was transmitted to so many wayfarers here. In long residence or not, they learned to love its architecture.

Not all are so sensitive, I slowly recognized. Years later as architecture critic for the Boston *Globe,* I doggedly pursued the threats to many buildings; success and failure marched apace. Especially, I remember tracking down Hap Kearn, the crusty publisher of the Boston *Record-American,* to ask whether he had any notion of what would happen to his environs once the paper left. Did he have any feeling for the Italianate structure that housed his bankrupt newspaper and the small square of open space that fronted it? I inquired. His response — part gruff, part genuinely questioning — was short: "What architecture?"

I am afraid the question continues to come from those who should know better. Planners and the larger populace who still let old buildings fall where they will confirm the ignorance of what architecture means to their city's life. The streets made toothless by parking lots and rendered hostile to human life by high-rises attest to our failure to appreciate the built environment. The lively neighborhoods and prize buildings now visible only in photographs reveal the vast wealth of Boston's vanished architecture and the thoughtless sacking of its cityscape.

In 1980, Boston reached an awesome anniversary: three and a half centuries, ten generations, 350 years. Throughout that span, builders have made their mark within the city's annals and upon its soil, but never, I suspect, so fast as now; never with such reckless abandon as in our own generation. So much of historic Boston is gone. So much is lost beyond the power of photography to recall. For all Boston's enduring elements, the scars on the city's profile are sharp and real, its architectural heritage clearly impaired.

The time of anniversary is also the time of expansion. Again the city is in flux and once more the question concerns those who cherish their cityscape: Will the lost Boston chronicled here be an epilogue of past losses or a prologue to the vandalism of a future day? The sensibility to Boston's urban values, the comprehension of the grace and comfort and dignity of its building is an awareness lost along with much of its architecture. Although understanding grows, the pressure also mounts — pressure not only to maximize the value of every site and structure but to ignore the neighborhood, the scale, the sense of the old city and to build ahead by the meanest dictates of the purse.

Change, the narrative of Boston's building shows, can be a creative act: It can be a manifesto of the joy in city-making. The eighteenth century gave way to a still more splendid Boston in the nineteenth, for Victorian builders responded to the city and its citizens. Our twentieth-century builders do not: When nineteenth-century architecture falls, it falls for naught. We of the twentieth century seem most adept at paving paradise to put up a parking lot.

You will find many such "paradises" within these pages; they come as reminders of a glorious heritage in a remarkable city, I believe, but above all, they come to plead for the salvation of the splendors left intact.

Lion's head, Somerset Club.

Iron lighthouse on Minot's Ledge.

Contents

St. Mary's Church, razing.

Lost Boston

CHAPTER 1

The City Upon a Hill, 1630–1680

The Church hathe no place lefte to flie into but the wilderness.
—JOHN WINTHROP, 1629

IT WAS A New England that drew the first Americans, but it was not a new landscape. Long before the Puritans broached the shores of Boston the glaciers had carved its hills and enfolding waters; had formed sand, gravel, and boulders into its tadpole shape. Eons of ice floes had churned the soil of Boston into a bubbling terrain — clay above, bedrock of slate or puddingstone below — to create the Puritan's "city upon a hill."

The Atlantic finished the job of the glaciers. Ocean and bay ringed the coming city, lapping round its 789 acres and washing over the skinny neck that tied the peninsula to the mainland. When the seas flooded this fragile link, the meaning of the shape of Boston showed: It was no longer a mere tadpole but a sealed and fortified island, a land mass like an isolated village, "invironed . . . with the Brinish flouds." A tight little island, said one early witness, "a heart naturally situated for fortifications" with three hills "like over-topping towers" to guard it from its enemies. Boston's bay, sheltered by thirty-eight islands, made more than a snug harbor; it made the walls of a medieval town.

All things to do, as in the beginninge of the world. Buildings, fencings, clearings, breakinge up of ground, lands to be attended, orchards to be planted, highways, and bridges and fortifications to be made.

So the first governor of the Massachusetts Bay Colony, John Winthrop, recorded the creation of a new world in his journal. And yet the land he viewed was neither untouched nor unseen by visitors. Other ships had slid past its rocky headlands, poked into the reedy marshes, surveyed the tidal basin, and scouted the profuse forests beyond the deep-set peninsula: Indians as long ago as 2500 B.C.; then, Norsemen, trailed in time by traders and fur dealers, fishermen and would-be farmers. Stragglers and eccentrics from the sixteenth and early seventeenth century's Great Age of Exploration had traded here and there around the Boston Bay. Adventurers and promoters from the Old World chronicled the first Boston long before Winthrop's religious zealots fled Europe's "fleshpots" for the Promised Land.

Captain John Smith was chief among them. The explorer-adventurer first mapped Boston's shoreline, plotting the coast between Cape Cod and Cape Ann as "New England." It was Smith who returned to England to publicize the place as the "Paradise of all those parts" and name the Charles River for his prince. With others, Smith drew the cheerful maps garnished with sea monsters and mermaids. They limned the shores threaded with the sea and depicted the ragged coast penciled with countless rivers and streams. Other visitors extolled the new Eden across the sea. Displaying equal parts of

Detail of Captain John Smith's map of New England.

Overleaf:
The Indian weathervane carved by Shem Drowne that spun atop the Province House cupola in the seventeenth century.

artifice and art, they told of the New World's wild turkey, beaver, marten, porcupine, and otter, of its lynx and gray fox. They wrote poems to a land of plenty — with cod so abundant it would fertilize the fields, and lobster infinite in store. Clams were bedded down in such number, Captain John Smith assured all England in 1616, that they were scattered to the swine. Massachusetts was a primeval Eden, promoters wrote, where the loon and great auk greeted the visitor and "the herring schooled so prolifigately that the [Savages] compare their store in the Sea to the haires of their heads." As for the sky, it was a bounteous gift of heaven, chaste and new above them. "A sup of New England air is better than a whole draught of Old English air," another booster wrote in *New England Prospects:*

> *The Kingly Lyon, and the strong arm'd Beare.*
> *The large lim'd Mooses, with the tripping Deere.*
> *Quill darking Porcupines and Rackcoones be*
> *Castell'd in the hollow of an Aged tree.*

The situation did not quite fulfill these prospects. Sailing with the *Arbella* and three sister ships on March 22, 1630, John Winthrop came upon no Eden north of Boston. A landscape with barely three hundred planters greeted him at his first stop. "Salem where we landed pleased us not," his Puritan colleague Thomas Dudley wrote. There the Puritans had had to dig into the very earth to survive and Winthrop did not tarry long. Charlestown, his next destination to the south, produced no more of the predicted plenty: "Sickeness . . . befell against them, so that almost in every family, lamentation, mourning and woe was heard, and no fresh food to be had to cherish them . . . And that which added to their present distresses was the want of fresh water."

It was not plenty that brought the new settlers to their final home in Boston, then, but happenstance; happenstance in the form of William Blackstone.

The Reverend Blackstone was an oddity in an age of eccentrics, a hermit who had fled the Old World's irritations for the isolation of the New. A bookish loner, Blackstone had chosen a peninsula no larger than an ample farm for his home in 1625.

To this hermit, solitude was Boston's redeeming virtue along with the ample waters of the spring that earned the name *Shawmut,* or "living waters." There, atop today's Beacon Hill, he passed his days under Boston's first colonial shelter, a thatched roof, tending his flowers and fruit and vegetables, hunting game or fish, minding his pigs and cow, reading his three Bibles, ten manuscript volumes, six large

3

books in Latin, six in English, and 159 smaller works. "There had been books on the slope of Beacon Hill when the wolves still howled on the summit," the literary critic Van Wyck Brooks would write.

We can still score Blackstone's first path on the city map (crooked as his cow's path, some say); fix his house upon the sunny side of Beacon near Spruce Street and picture his view across today's Boston Common with its young elm tree. The Great Elm, native to a swampier Shawmut, was a landmark that aged through Indian wars and independence. Citizens of Boston's Age of Athens and soldiers of the Civil War walked under its monumental umbrella. Blackstone's land would itself become the Puritan Common — and eventually the shared open space of an expanding town.

Despite his joy in isolation, Blackstone's invitation to the floundering Puritan community is well documented. "He came and acquainted the Governor with an excellent spring there, withal inviting him and soliciting him thither." So Winthrop crossed from Charlestown, settling his flock near the spring of today's Spring Lane and in the North End. For himself, he chose a site near the Great Cove, at the head of today's State Street.

The Reverend William Blackstone's House.

Whither the frame of the Governor's house, in preparation at this town, was also (to the discontent of some) carried; where people began to build their houses against winter; and this place was called "Boston."

"Boston!" At last the wandering tribe had sealed the site with the name chosen long ago to echo the east coast town that launched their enterprise in England. Derived from the patron saint of fishing, St. Botolph (a contraction of *Bot,* meaning "boat," and *ulph,* meaning "help"), Boston was a good name — a symbol of the ocean-sent theocracy of the past and the ocean-linked town to come.

Together now against the wilderness, the lord brethren began to build their model Christian community. The merchants, traders, and fishermen settled near the docks; the main body of farmers on plots to the west and south; the principals near the center of market, church, and Governor Winthrop's house by today's State Street. It was a settlement that linked their physical and moral well-being intimately, a close plan that bound the first Bostonians physically and spiritually "with the notables — the Governor, the elders of the church, the artillery company and the captain of the artillery company, and the most needful of the craftsmen and artificers of the humble plantation; and at a short distance . . . the meeting-house, the town-house, the school-house, and the ever-flowing spring of

pure water."

From the first, Boston's narrow peninsula would not support the whole Bible Commonwealth, however. Footpaths leading from the center became lanes and lanes grew into highways. Within a decade Tremont Street was fixed upon the streetscape; the axes of travel to "the Great Highway to the Sea" (State Street) and to the mainland "the Highwaye to Roxberre" (Washington Street) crossed at the heart of the settlement. Water became a major highway too. Boats and ferries took the first Bostonians outward to tend their oxen, cows, sheep, and swine and to gather wood or farm in Cambridge, Winnissimmet (Chelsea), Mount Wollaston, Muddy River (Brookline), Noddle Island (East Boston), and the harbor islands.

"Whatsoever we stand in need of is treasured up in the earthe by the Creator," Winthrop declared, "and is to be fetched there by the sweatt of our browes." Long before Ben Franklin's Poor Richard uttered his axioms, the Puritan work ethic bound old Boston. Barely sheltered, the community had built its first defenses atop Fort Hill, constructed the windmill atop Windmill (Copp's) Hill to grind out rich yellow Indian corn, framed a meetinghouse, cleared market space at the Town Dock (Dock Square), and defined its roads. In less than half a decade, the earliest Bostonians had built the dock to secure the economic lifeline to England. And, more importantly, had named the first schoolmaster to secure a still more vital link — the link of the next generation to the Almighty through the reading of His scriptures. From the first, mind and matter had shelter here. In 1635, the Boston Latin School began and, in 1636, Harvard College opened across the Charles in Cambridge (to take Latin School graduates, alumni would later boast). A year later, the first press came from England and printed the first native almanac.

Season following season, the buildings multiplied. The soil made farming marginal, but purchases by countless new immigrants supplemented the colonists' lean fare. Ships, wharves, and docks multiplied to serve the sea. In the next four decades Massachusetts would build 730 ships. In turn, sea life called for still more docks, ropewalks and ironworks to make chains and anchors, and shelters to house the looms to weave the sails. Although farming remained the staple, the stony soil and the endless boatloads of newcomers to clothe and house made the Hub a nexus for marketing. As the town grew, both the landscape and seascape dictated that the thoughts of Boston's first citizens were oceanbound.

From the first, too, Bostonians tampered with their natural environment. The tides used to power the gristmill and sawmill in the North End made it necessary to widen and deepen Mill Creek. Bridges, a drawbridge, and a refurbished dock showed Boston's urge to conquer its watery turf — to become more than defensive outpost or religious enclave. A miracle, the author of *Wonder-Working Providence* declared as early as midcentury:

The chief Edifice of this City-like Towne is crowded on the Sea-bankes, and wharfed out with great industry and cost, the buildings beautifull and large, some fairly set forth with Brick, Tile, Stone, and Slate, continuall inlargement presages some sumptuous City. The wonder of this Moderne Age that a few years should bring forth such great matters by so meane a handfull . . . but now behold, in these very places where at their first Landing the hideous Thickets in this place were such the Wolfes and Beares nurst up their young from the eyes of all beholders, in those very places where the streets are full of Girles and Boyes sporting up and down, with a continued concourse of people.

For the most part, farms and houses filled out the landscape. Upon landing, the settlers threw up impromptu shelters. Some resorted to caves or casks; others settled for tents, rude huts, and the bent saplings and bark or thatch-domed Indian huts called English wigwams. Soon, however, the transplanted English men and women re-created the architecture of their East Anglian source in harmony with the new land. The wealthier Puritans could afford more than mud houses, and dwellings reflecting Elizabethan or Jacobean England replaced the crude and flimsy hovels of early days along the highways and roads. The colonists had left a medieval England of wooden cottages and long narrow streets, of timber houses and barns. They brought its image to New England, where their carpenters and sawyers transplanted it to these shores.

Though the colonial house was a simple one, its wood-frame structure of plaster and thatch would soon give way to clapboard and shingle and its single story would expand to two. However rustic, sentimentalists warm to its rough form. Scholars laud its rugged texture and "well-nigh barbaric" massiveness. Handhewn logs, some eighteen inches across, were felled to frame the house and joined by mortise and tenon with clay or brick nogging tucked between. With its north side chimney protecting the family from wind and weather and its ease in allowing additions, the house adapted to both nature and the needs of the fast-growing town. The familiar pitched roof, the narrow leaded casement windows and the oversailing second story and looming chimney characterized seventeenth-century America's domestic architecture. With the passing years, the blossoms near the dooryard, the elms aging gracefully overhead, and the softening of nature brought a comely look to the staunch house of tradition.

The Reverend John Wilson's church of 1632.

Inside, the chimney and its hearth both sheltered and symbolized home life. The chimney was functional; it heated two floors and two rooms to either side. It was almost organic; for the house grew, it pulsed, from the stocky shape. Whether built of wood, stone, or brick, the chimney was as ponderous as the frame — sometimes four feet deep and twelve feet wide, spanned by an equally long oak lintel. The chimney boasted a mammoth fireplace. Blazing with fire and radiating warmth, it was big enough to hold a fleet of cast-iron pots and a brick nook to bake the steamy loaves of bread. You could build a small house from such an immense chimney, the nineteenth-century author of *Porter's Rambles* would affirm after seeing the quantity of bricks in a North End house taken down in his day.

Family life, those Puritan "cells of righteousness," clung to this hearth. Furnishing their rooms as best they could, Boston's first families made their homes "at the same time more richly elaborate and more starkly primitive than we realize," historian Abbott Lowell Cummings has observed. Hens hopped about the kitchen a cluck away from velvet tapestry. Straw or rush thrown upon the wooden floor formed a rude contrast to the quilt and brocade hung above. The strange mix of "wheat with bedding, carpenters' tools with pewter flagons, and cushions with a still," provides a clue to "the seventeenth century attitude toward the home as a 'machine for living' in a much more real sense, perhaps, than even our most progressive designers in the twentieth century have ever envisioned," Cummings writes.

Many of these goods had withstood the hard Atlantic crossing to serve the new Americans. The oblong- or diamond-shaped panes of glass that fit into small sashed windows, the oriental carpets that covered some tables, and the wrought iron that hinged the door came by ship with the loads of immigrants, but the "roughcast" (stucco) covering of clay and wood, the furniture that filled the house, the clapboard that covered the exterior, and the building were largely native work.

The house-raising was a local holiday: It was a call to sharing for a neighborly people. It was the embodiment of community for settlers joined against the wilderness in the service of a harsh God. For generations — for centuries — New Englanders would heed the call, streaming in to help, slotting and bolting and heaving the enormous frame into the upright posture of a stout house, "knowingly engineered."

In the passing years, most such houses and shops were felled by ax or fire. Yet the ones that lasted into the nineteenth century lasted well. Sturdy structures like the Old Feather Store with its roughcast plastering endured "in such a manner that this great lapse of years has made no perceptible effect upon them," a witness almost two centuries later found. This particular gabled landmark had held on for 180 years. Only the determined wreckers in the Victorian building boom wiped it out. Other relics of antique Boston like Julien's restaurant or the Triangular Warehouse lived long enough for the nineteenth century to admire and engrave.

Boston's bridges and the windmills on its hills had equal sturdiness. It took a deft artisan to fix the mobile windmill to withstand the gusts of winter and no mean mechanical skill to ford and harness the North End's soggy Mill Creek or find firm footing around marsh and bog. To protect the fledgling colony from seaside invasion, forty-one Bostonians subscribed to the building of a 2200-foot defensive barricado in the harbor (along today's Atlantic Avenue) in 1673. Other Boston builders designed some of America's earliest bridges and, in the case of the Great Bridge of 1662, constructed the colony's longest span, across the Charles River in Cambridge on the site of today's Larz Anderson bridge. Boasting stringers of almost twenty feet, it was the only link to the northern bank for more than 125 years.

Bostonians created a public space as well as public structures. With the common purchase of Blackstone's field in 1634 they established a great precedent and reinforced it. From the first, the "equall Right of Commonage" and the order that none of the Common's land would be released "without consent of the major part of the inhabitants of the town" shaped the use. The Common soon became more than a lot for "Milch Kine" (cows). As early as March 30, 1640, a town order forbade the granting of its land "for house plotts or garden to any person." Through the years, the swatch of land endured as fairground and countryside, as picnic place and space for military training. It was a shared space, a place so contained and agreeable that visitors noted it as a

small but pleasant Common where the Gallants, a little before sunset, walked with their marmalet-madams, as we do in Moorfields, till the o'clock bell rings them home to their respective habitations, where presently the constables walk their rounds to see good order kept, and to take up loose people.

Despite "good order" and short curfews, the Puritans' drab garb and darkened countenance is as much a myth as the notion of a joyless public life. We see a truer portrait in the gold cuffs, lace collars, and bright wardrobe of dress portraits. Though seventeenth-century Bostonians would not adorn their architecture needlessly, it too showed "style." An overhanging second story could have the tear-drop ornament called a pendant, a bit of embellishment at either end. Brackets, handcrafted finishes, plastered surfaces, or a roof looked quite picturesque. Plain but well proportioned, the early house stood: a weathered hulk against the new land's brooding sky.

If the Puritans built a plain architecture in their domestic life, they dictated it in their spiritual one. Spare, even spartan, the meeting-house outlawed graven images, for nothing should intrude in the building where a sinner sat before the Almighty. No carvings of saints, no stained-glass windows, no sensual lures — no visual matter whatsoever — might throw a curtain between the churchgoer and the Lord. The meetinghouse was the architectural embodiment of the Puritan theocracy; it was political as much as sacred, secular as much as religious. Notices of daily life (sales, legal declarations, and the like) festooned its doors; its interior was partitioned into an elaborate hierarchy of seats. Sometime school, sometime town hall, the meeting-house demanded the right locale. Its siting was the most sensitive subject in the Boston and New England town plan. A "meetinghouse devil" was said to stalk debates on where and how to place the house-hold of the Lord in New England. Bostonians argued heatedly on whether the market or the green best fit.

To create plainness in the seventeenth-century church caused no less work than shaping a complex structure; to fulfill both a theo-logical and architectural role was an arduous task. The plan of the blunt, often "four-square" structure must confirm radical beliefs and refute ancient habits: Never would it follow the Anglican altar mode; its pulpit was on the west or north; its main door opposite. Its members would not kneel; a tilted stoop gave them some upright support. Only later would a bell tower or spire dare to stretch to the sky.

Though seeking shelter more than splendor, the Puritan meeting-house had much appeal. We now find it graceful in its proportions, ample in its barnlike size, and aesthetically pleasant in its oak and pine construction, its hipped roof and windows. We appreciate its spartanness and overlook a cold so intense that the fires of hell and brimstone couldn't warm its congregants or loose the coins frozen to their communion plate. Huddled as best they could against the New England chill, the Puritans faced a harsh environment. A severe ar-chitecture was its evidence. The plain style prevailed as the first Bos-tonians axed the wilderness into ready soil and framed the ancient trees into settled homes.

State of Mind

The spires that dominated Boston's first skyline, and the bookstores and schools that distinguished its streetscape told much of the spirit of the city. "In New England they have done it they do do it they will do it and they can do it in every way in which education can be thought about," wrote Gertrude Stein, describing the city's intellectual and spiritual life.

As early as the Great Fire of 1711, Increase Mather counted seven bookstores servicing the "People of the Book." "It being one chief project of that old deluder, Satan, to keep men from the knowledge of the Scriptures," the Puritans commanded that a town of fifty householders had to appoint a master and that one of one hundred must set up a grammar school from the first. As with schools, so with churches. Both proliferated beautifully until our day, when the very universities and religious bodies that created them, idly watched them die.

Spires to God

The landmark Brattle Square Church (left above), designed by patriot-architect Thomas Dawes, was the house where a veritable *Who's Who* of the American Revolution worshiped. It held John Hancock, John and Sam Adams, Joseph Warren, and bore the mark of a Revolutionary cannonball like a medal of honor. Later historians called Dawes's 1772 design "one of the crowning architectural achievements of eighteenth century Boston." The Central Congregational Church on Winter Street (left below), broodingly elegant behind its Corinthian columns and deep portico, lent dignity and even mystery to its residential neighborhood from the 1840s. Asher Benjamin's First Church, on Chauncy Street looking to Summer Street (right), settled as compatibly into the streetscape of nineteenth-century Boston as it did into the course of its citizens' lives. Built in 1808, it meshed with the urban pattern for decades. All three churches fell when their congregations moved to the Back Bay.

"I did not know how much I liked the great gloomy old thing till I saw her windows bursting and the flames running along the old high pews," the Reverend Phillips Brooks testified to the somber granite dignity of Trinity Church of 1829 on Summer Street. Designed by architect George M. Brimmer, it was consumed by the Great Fire just as its congregation began the Copley Square successor.

Italianate, Romanesque, shingled, or Queen
Anne, a ring of churches around Boston
paralleled the inner-city ones for new
congregations of suburban dwellers in the
latter nineteenth century. In a wooden
idiom, Cambridge's handsomely shingled
Cornerstone Baptist Church at 2114
Massachusetts Avenue (above) showed
Italianate vestiges of its 1854 architect,
Alexander R. Estey, and its Queen Anne
remodeling by Van Brunt and Howe in
1885. The Eliot Congregational Church
at Newton Corner (below), a Byzantine
Romanesque building by architect George F.
Meacham, welcomed its suburban congregation in 1889. The Newton church burned
in 1956 and the Cambridge one on Hal-
loween night 1979.

Schools and Universities

Reading, writing, and 'rithmetic of the late eighteenth century went on in Mrs. Rowson's private school for girls on Washington Street near the Roxbury line (above). Later it became a resort known as the Washington House, and was finally demolished. Scrubwoman Mrs. Dennis, who stands stolidly before her flock at the Gibson School, Dorchester (below), kept cows on nearby Harvard Avenue at the time this picture was taken in the 1880s. Built in 1857 from plans by Gridley James Fox Bryant, the building was first moved, then demolished.

The Romanesque arch of Roxbury High School on Warren Street (above) and the schoolyard of the Eliot School, North Bennett Street (below), frame some of the generations of students taught there. The Roxbury High School by city architect Charles J. Bateman was built in 1885 and torn down in 1976. The Eliot School, second only to Boston Latin in longevity, was spanking new about the time this Civil War picture was taken. It became a model for other city schools and served the venerable Eliot School until the Depression.

"The architecture should be such that a student on entering it will be impressed and elevated, and feel a pride that such a place is free to him," a contributor to the first Boston Public Library on Boylston Street near the Common declared at its opening in 1858. Architect Charles Kirby's exterior — a red-brick and sandstone facade with huge arched windows crowned by a heavy cornice — was outdone only by his Bates Hall interior with its Corinthian columns, tile floor, and handsome furnishings. "Do you let bare-foot boys in this reading room?" Matthew Arnold asked in wonder at the library's democratic policy. Reading room and all were sacrificed when the library moved uptown. Today the Colonial Theater sits on the site.

A landmark in education, the new brick and freestone Massachusetts Institute of Technology (right) offered early courses using the laboratory method and held the Lowell Lectures and Handel and Haydn Society rehearsals in the Rogers Building on Boylston Street. Though the design came from architect William Gibbons Preston in the Civil War era, a witness to its demolition in 1939 still found it "very imposing." An insurance company building took over the site after MIT moved to its Cambridge campus across the Charles River.

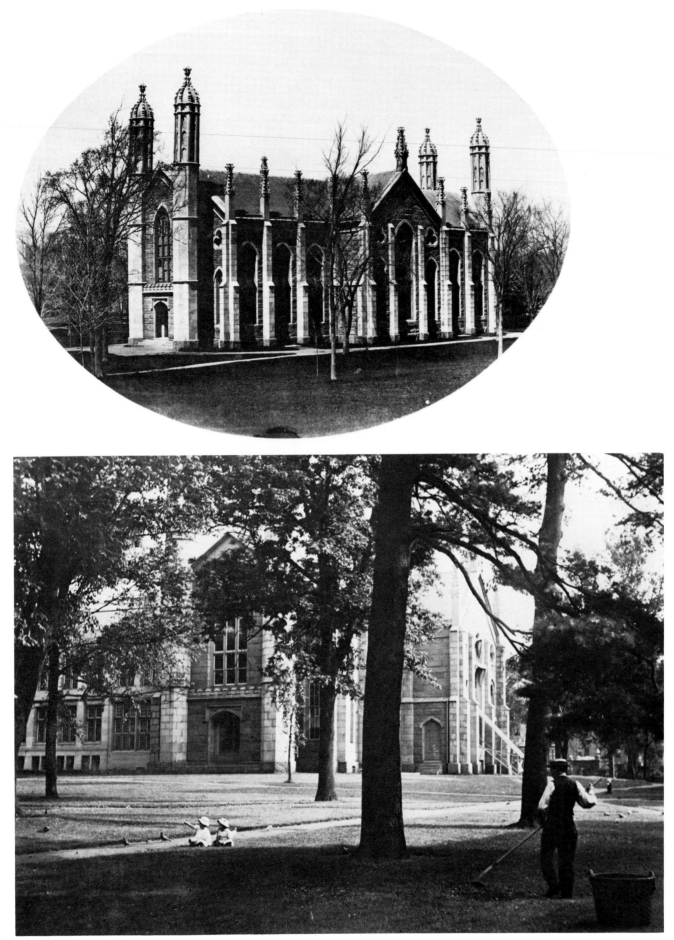

18

With the churchlike Gore Hall Library to serve the mind, Harvard students and professors set the stamp on Boston's intellectual life from across the Charles River. Gothic Gore, designed by Richard Bond in 1838 (above left), and expanded in 1874 by Ware and Van Brunt (below left), stood on the site taken for the Widener Library in 1913.

Coal grates were a treat and sofas and lamps a fine embellishment for Harvard students in Little's Block near Holyoke House in the 1870s. The brick mansard roof structure just across from Harvard Yard on Massachusetts Avenue, Cambridge, gave way to a high-rise administrative building in 1961.

Ennobling its small interior through vaulted ceiling and classical columns, the Mayhew School made the most of a small urban site in the design of architect John Lyman Faxon in 1897. Such appealing touches did not suffice for the educators who declared the school unfit shortly before this picture was taken in 1959. The building on Poplar and Chambers streets saw its last in the destruction of the West End.

Wellesley College's College Hall by Hammatt Billings offered the amenities of handsome architecture and palm-filled foyers from the 1870s. The building burned in 1914.

Four walls filled with desks do not the only schoolrooms make. The bookstores and printing and publishing places tucked into Boston's streets enriched the city's intellectual life beyond the formal classes. On Cornhill and Washington Street small storefronts housed a myriad of book shops (left) and, along Tremont Street, Gleason's Publishing Hall (right) turned out its influential *Pictorial*. Gleason's building, which began as the Boston Museum and Gallery of Fine Arts in 1841, was replaced by Horticultural Hall in 1865. The last of Cornhill's bookstores was the Brattle Book Shop shown here fighting its futile battle against urban renewal in 1962.

CHAPTER 2

Geography Is Destiny, 1680–1730

Their houses are generally wooden, their streets crooked, with little decency and no uniformity.

— THE ROYAL COMMISSIONERS, 1665

When we consider the small Number of the first Settlers and coming from an old Cultivated Country, to thick woods, rough unimproved Lands, where all their former Experience and Knowledge was now of very little service to them: They were destitute of Beasts of Burden or Carriage; Unskilled in every Part of Service to be done. It may be said: that in a Sort, they began the World a New.

— REVEREND JOHN ELIOT'S GRANDSON, 1748

LET THE good commissioners huff. Let latter-day historians sniff.
The grandson of the Puritan divine, John Eliot, was right: in
little more than a generation there was a new Boston. Visitors
who had known the early days of the Massachusetts Bay plantation
would marvel at how this straggling village had bloomed into a
town.

By the end of the seventeenth century, corn fields grew where Indians once roamed and "frequented wayes" plunged through the old
lair of wolf and bear. Two ferries crossed the northern waters, while
orchards flourished on once wild land. True, "noisome swine" roamed
the filthy lanes, nibbling their way through the carcasses of trashed
animals while a motley array of chickens, horses, cows, ducks, and
geese meandered about. Yet, signs of a genuine colonial culture had
also begun to appear.

By 1680 seven or eight hundred houses sat near Boston's shores. If
few resembled Governor Winthrop's second house, with its five
rooms, porch-entry, garden, and assorted outbuildings, others had
grown beyond the early chimney-bound size. The expanding population and the booming trade kept builders busy. Carpenters, brick-
makers, limeworkers, sawyers, and masons had an ever longer construction list, of mill and dock and well; of coffeehouse and tavern; of
farm, barn, shed, and a miscellany of shops to serve the emerging
town.

The Boston whose 6000 citizens celebrated their first half-century
in 1680 seems tiny to us now, but it equaled many of the world's

Overleaf:
An allegorical view of Boston from Cam-
bridge painted on a nineteenth-century fire
engine shows the three peaks of Beacon
Hill (left to right, Pemberton Hill, Beacon
Hill, and Mount Vernon).

A certificate depicts the South Battery, a
wooden wall filled with earth to protect
Bostonians in 1666, surrounded by buildings
on the long-gone Fort Hill.

greatest seaports. In all the English colonies, Boston was first in publishing and schooling, and much noted for its commercial life. No wonder the rising merchants and provincial squires began to model themselves more on the Old World's mixed forms than on the austere monotheism of their Bible Commonwealth. Though the harsh winters and the ungiving soil produced a slow yield, trade swelled the town. Prosperity split the Puritan Commonwealth into social and economic classes. Prominent among these parts a city-building merchant class arose — a peacock rich ready to spread its wings in a new architecture.

Consult Samuel Sewall, the Pepys of Boston. In his diary, Judge Sewall sniffed at the carryings-on of the wealthy. Though himself a man of substance, Sewall blasted the fledgling airs of the Anglophiles, jeered at their lice-ridden wigs, and jotted down his scorn of party-goers who

stop and drink Healths, curse, swear, talk profanely and baudily to the great disturbance of the Town and grief of good people. Such high-handed wickedness has hardly been heard of before in Boston.

The clergy clearly agreed: the Heavenly City was no more, they railed. The great fires of 1676 and 1679 that leveled the growing town convinced some that they were right.

Some, but not all. Many saw the consuming flames as a God-given chance to space out the crowded streets and build afresh. Bowing to another priesthood — the priesthood of the opulent merchant class — Bostonians had more pride in the earthly present than fear of future doom.

The second half of the seventeenth century saw Bostonians fill in the two ends of the old town. Contouring close to their living-working houses, the townsfolk fashioned the North End near Copp's Hill where Winthrop first landed, and added to the South End between the Town Cove and Boston Neck where the others of his flock had settled. Then, and forever after, Bostonians have clung to such neighborhoods. From the first, the landscape of hill and sea insisted on it. When the ocean swelled Mill Creek, the neighborhoods were sometimes literally cut in two. Three bridges eventually spanned the watery enterprise that separated the two ends of town. Each neighborhood, north and south, held separate docks and separate housing, separate private and public spaces. By the time of the next century's Great Awakening, the galvanic preacher George Whitefield would preach to two separate congregations in new North Church and the Old South Meeting House.

The two ends of town, divided into North End and South End gangs as well as environments, were devilishly combative. The toughs of colonial days fought with an intensity greater than that of their heirs recorded two centuries later by that other Boston neighborhood boy, Henry Adams, in his *Education*. In fact, only the War of Independence and a peacemaking dinner organized by John Hancock persuaded the fighting spirits of North End and South End to link hands rather than smash heads. On Pope's Day, an early American cross between Guy Fawkes Day and Hallowe'en, the enmity reached a pitch of violence more intense than many of the mob gatherings of the Revolution. Rival floats paraded on home turf until dusk when they met on middle ground at Union Street. There, the pugnacious "Hatter's Squarers," "Fort Hillers," or "Wheeler's Pointers" engaged in mock, and sometimes not so mock, battles to capture the foe's "Pope" and sport it off to kindle in their open space: their *separate* open space.

For the North End, the open space was Copp's Hill. The high burial ground with its sea breezes gave Bostonians a fine view and the surroundings supplied a splendid picnic grove. It was to the North End what the Common was to the settlements south and west: a pleasure ground and meeting place. So, too, the thoroughfare of Hanover, Middle, and North streets was to the North End what Cornhill, Marlborough, Newbury, and Orange streets (jointly forming today's Washington Street) were to the south: The North End's central thoroughfare wound north from Pemberton Hill over the bridge to the North End peninsula and the sea; the South End's curled south to the isthmus of Boston Neck and the Roxbury line.

The two old Bostons aged apart and took on separate flavors. The North End was the "court end" of the town, the home of Mathers and merchants, and especially of seafaring souls. It was the spicier and brinier, the place of adventure for Boston boys like Ben Franklin and Paul Revere. No matter how confined or crowded, houses on the waterfront kept Boston childhoods in rhythm with the sea the whole year round. In good weather, the lives of North Enders were secured to its breezes and moods. The tidal pond and salt marshes, sluices and creeks were the streets of North End life. The harbor was the highway to the wider world. An island within the near-island of Shawmut — waterbound by Town Cove, Mill Creek, Mill Pond, and Boston Harbor, and populated by the prosperous merchants and roughs of the sea town — the North End was wharfed out in ever-shrinking space; its pastures gradually giving way to the pungent mix of shop and sea, garden and grime.

The South End was less salty, but more spacious. "The best part of the town," Sewall wrote in his diary. On the lanes just off the Town

Cotton Mather's house in the North End.

Home of Thomas Dawes, Jr., in the South End.

The Triangular Warehouse at Town Dock.

House (the site of today's Old State House) pleasant homes with gardens of fruit and flowers rolled down to the sea, their small shops sometimes housing storekeepers and artisans above. Just north of where Governor John Winthrop (as well as his nemesis, Anne Hutchinson) had set up house and garden, dock and meeting-house, shop and market at Dock Square, the bay dominated and commerce began its long rule. Near there, the streets seemed to pave themselves in the pattern left to posterity from Cornhill (Washington Street) through the crooked "H" shape of today's School, Milk, Court, and State streets, which took on their modern outlines. Finally, Great (or King) Street pushed from market to sea, foreshadowing its later fate as State Street, the counting kingdom of the merchants.

Beyond the North End and South End, the hills and pastures of the peninsula housed only a few settlers atop a rise or in farms among the fields. Farther south and out of town, settlement ended abruptly in the pinched and narrow corridor of Boston Neck. Soggy in summer, snowbound in winter, the slim strip of Neck land gave a hard welcome to visitors — a welcome made even harsher by the forbidding town gate, stark brick fortifications and menacing gallows. A somber greeting warned the traveler: Put on your town manners in God's Own Capital.

Still they came. The burdened oxen and the bulging wagons, the beasts pulling sleds and the horses knee-deep in high-tide waters, the farmers rolling back and forth across the isthmus with goods for town. And the ships, the countless brimful boats, adding to the tally. By land and sea, the ships and beasts arrived; together they made Boston the trading center of all New England. Fish, furs, cattle, wood, and grain entered an ever bigger port and fattened Bay Town larders. Long before its centennial, Boston was a compact and prosperous hub, a gateway to the world, and a populated seaport.

This urban density was no accident. No one has ever labeled it Manifest Destiny but, in a way, it was: Boston's posture as a city was preordained, in part by the growing trade, in part by the Puritan dogma. With its demand for a close community of saints — house close to meetinghouse, meetinghouse to common or square — the lofty aspirations of the leadership and the basic needs of the congregation linked on the landscape. So the theocracy commanded, so commerce reinforced, so Boston obeyed for its first century.

But Boston's closeness was also ordered by a set of natural dictates. With water on all sides and hills enclosing land, the topography yoked the town. Each natural bay, each ancient rise bound its inhabitants in a way beyond any building code or Puritan call for community. "If we could only plot with certainty the seventeenth century location of rocky outcrops, marshes, sinkholes and firm ground, the rambling pattern of streets in central Boston might turn out to be a sophisticated bit of organic planning," the urban historian John Reps has observed.

The three hills dominating early Boston loomed largest in the path of construction. To the north, Copp's Hill rose 50 feet and steep as cliffs; to the south, Fort Hill, 80 feet upright and fearsome from the harbor; and, above all, the Trimountain rose majestically to the west. Though made of three peaks — Sentry (or Beacon) Hill, named for a defensive beacon, and two spurs, Cotton (or Pemberton) Hill and West (or Mount Vernon) Hill — the Trimountain rolled into one hulking shadow 150 feet above the town.

While such hills held Boston from outward growth, the penetrating waters of the sea conditioned its inner form. Deep inlets punched into the shore — the great Town Cove at the center, South Cove (today's Chinatown), and Mill Cove (Mill Pond) between Haymarket Square and North Station. Their waters joined tidal marsh and creeks to dictate the direction of every spade that hit the soil and every roadway laid.

So it was that then and in all times the land made Boston. Compare the Bay State capital to its sister colonies of Virginia and the Carolinas. There, an environment that was warm and fertile and as sultry as the southern rivers opened itself to the rice and tobacco plantation systems. The plantation culture swept across the palmy southern soil, pushing the slave economy far into the interior. In the South, the gently spreading landscape with its penetrating rivers allowed settlers' ships to trade inland with ease, dropping cargo. The Southerner had no need to carry goods to one market, hence no compulsion to collect in one snug town or medieval hamlet.

In Boston, it was otherwise. The lands of New England were granite-bound, ice-packed, and sterile. "Little more than the sinews of a merchant marine," it was said. They made farming difficult but, more important, fought against a sprawling settlement. The map that led the first settlers to think they could cross the continent along the waters that began in Boston was a tease. The Charles River stopped short. Other Bay State rivers like the Merrimac gave scant access. Inland from the once tempting coast, the hills of central Massachusetts and the Berkshires beyond the Connecticut River created still another overpowering obstacle. The Bay Town would grow "thick and firm" indeed before any settler ventured west.

At the very least, the tight landscape shaped Boston's building pattern. It pushed more people into less and less space. No wonder colonial Bostonians shared the nation's first party walls, by some accounts. The early duplexes had to arise in such close confines. Scant surprise that the colonists' descendants would crop the hills and fill the bays to get more land in America's most heroic earth-engineering acts. Some would flee to nearby Charlestown, Roxbury, Watertown, or Cambridge in the earliest days, and "plant dispersedly." But to be a true Bostonian you had to stay shoulder to shoulder in the crooked and narrow streets of a cohesive town. The landscape framed Boston's intimate dwellings and made its urban ways imperative.

Captain John Bonner's map of Boston in 1722.

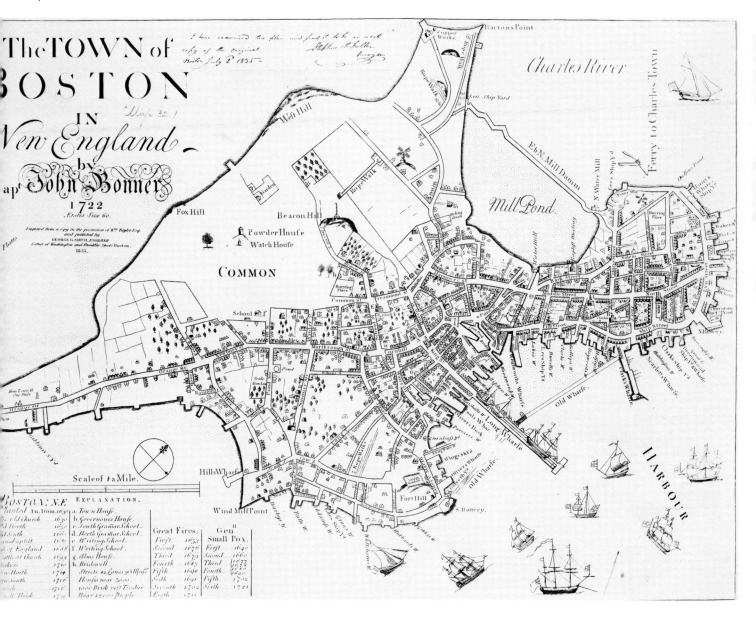

The Sway of the Land

Bostonians were always taking the view, surveying the scene, and rhapsodizing over the landscape below. From the heights, they gained a sense of themselves and their irregular surroundings, rough contours that accounted for the famous crooked and narrow streets of the old town. While other places boasted of their broad boulevards and uncluttered vistas, Bostonians idled happily within the organic contours of their winding streets. They found pleasure in the curving path. Sometimes called courts (though little about them was regal), sometimes alleys (though they need not be small or grimy), the intimate or meandering roadways offered elements of surprise and joy lost in the ruthless straightening of the twentieth century.

Viewing the City

"To live on such a hill was like living on the roof of the world." So the twentieth-century author Francis Russell described the view from a Dorchester hill much like this earlier view from Dorchester Heights, South Boston (left).

Southeast prospect from Beacon Hill overlooking the Common with its Great Elm and Dorchester Heights in the distance.

Boston rose to the occasion to view the city from the first balloon in 1860. Aloft in this fragile structure, the photographer immortalized the downtown district destined to be wiped out by Boston's Great Fire a dozen years later.

From on high, the West End always offered
a view of packed streets and animated roof
detail whether in this 1950s view from
North Station (left) or one taken from the
State House a hundred years earlier (right).
Only the Massachusetts General Hospital,
the Charles Street Jail, and a fraction of the
buildings survive from the older scene.
About half the buildings in the twentieth-
century view were destroyed to make way
for luxury apartments.

Crooked and Narrow Streets

"More often than not I would prefer to walk in the rear alley," Lewis Mumford wrote, "precisely for all those little hints of life, activity, and transition which the placid visual arts of suburbia did their best to suppress or politely disguise." The Clough House (circa 1697) and its early-nineteenth-century brick neighbors formed one such alley, Vernon Place in the North End (above). Change Avenue (right), squeezed between State Street and Faneuil Hall Square, was another. Despite preservationist clamors, the Clough House was removed in 1931. The last remains of Change Avenue were obliterated in 1971.

Tremont Street once meandered its way from Scollay Square to the South End of the city, twisting and changing guises and architecture along the way. Its curve lent a sense of mystery and its mixed architecture made for changing vistas. The section toward the south (above) was widened and straightened just after the Civil War; that to the north (below) between King's Chapel and the Park Street Church spire lost its buildings in piecemeal fashion over the years.

The narrow confines of Boston's old streetscape gave an intimate, almost backstage air to the old city. Picturesque Province Street was laid out in 1715 as Governor's Alley (right). Province Street lost all its right-hand buildings in an early-twentieth-century street widening. Later attacks erased the other side of the street beyond the stone wall of the Province Steps.

The BLOODY MASSACRE perpetrated in King — — Street BOSTON on March 5th 1770 by a party of the 29th REGt.

Engrav'd Printed & Sold by PAUL REVERE BOSTON

BUTCHER'S HALL

Unhappy BOSTON! see thy Sons deplore,
Thy hallow'd Walks besmear'd with guiltless Gore.
While faithless P——n and his savage Bands,
With murd'rous Rancour stretch their bloody Hands;
Like fierce Barbarians grinning o'er their Prey,
Approve the Carnage, and enjoy the Day.

If scalding drops from Rage from Anguish Wrung,
If speechless Sorrows lab'ring for a Tongue,
Or if a weeping World can ought appease
The plaintive Ghosts of Victims such as these;
The Patriot's copious Tears for each are shed,
A glorious Tribute which embalms the Dead.

But know, Fate summons to that awful Goal,
Where JUSTICE strips the Murd'rer of his Soul:
Should venal C——ts the scandal of the Land,
Snatch the relentless Villain from her Hand,
Keen Execrations on this Plate inscrib'd,
Shall reach a JUDGE who never can be brib'd.

The unhappy Sufferers were Messrs. SAML. GRAY SAML. MAVERICK, JAMS. CALDWELL, CRISPUS ATTUCKS & PATK. CARR.
Killed. Six wounded two of them (CHRISTr. MONK & JOHN CLARK) Mortally.

CHAPTER 3

Growth to Independence, 1730–1780

A stranger at Boston, soon remarks the industry of its inhabitants; and their attention to business. While he laments that so noted a town in the . . . page of history, were not regulated by a better police. It is under the controul of select men, as indeed all the other towns of the commonwealth are: but their powers, are too much abridged by reason of their town meetings, to undertake any thing of efficiency, without having recourse to the opinions of a multifarious assembly. Few lamps assist the passenger through the streets by night, and if ever they were necessary in any place, they certainly are in this. For the streets are crooked, and narrow; paved from side to side with round stones, extremely disagreeable, and inconvenient to those who walk them: and for this reason, strangers are more apt to ride about this, than any other town on the continent. In many streets there are no railings or posts, to defend one from the carriages, which are incessantly traversing them. Carts, waggons, drays, trucks, wheelbarrows, and porters are continually obstructing the passage in these streets: While, the people concerned in this kind of business, are not apt to put themselves out of the way, for the pleasure of conferring favors. They seem so conscious that all men are equal, that they take a pride in shewing their knowledge of this principle upon every occasion.
—From *The Letters of John Drayton*

THE CENTURY of the Revolution dawned brightly. Down at the waterfront, by the crowded market, along the crooked and narrow lanes, the town swelled into the trading capital of America. Within the first decade, Long Wharf thrust almost half a mile into the harbor in a broad and spacious welcome to the flourishing trade. The masts of ships "make a kind of Wood of Trees," a Londoner declared. True, six churches commanded the loyalties of 6700 Bostonians, and the whipping posts and stockades of *Scarlet Letter* fame still stood at stern attention in the Puritan citadel, hovering straight and ominous near the Town House where the laws were made. A step away, however, the taverns served less puritanical thirsts. A London bookseller who lodged in the neighborhood at the turn of the century found "less of punishment than of downright drunkenness — men who seldom go to bed without muddled brains."

That was not all the bookseller, John Dunton, brother-in-law of Daniel Defoe, noticed as he traveled about Boston. Dunton saw Cotton Mather at the prestigious Harvard College, dropped in at the thriving Blue Anchor Tavern, and attended the churches crowded with the godly and ungodly company for Sunday sermons. Dunton observed a congenial town and numerous travelers shared his view. They described the expanding landscape: its dwellings, "some joined," its streets, "some paved," and its "stately edifices" on the chief High Street, "the buildings like their capital women, being Neat and Handsome. And their Streets like the hearts of their Male Inhabitants are Paved with Pebbles."

At all hours, day and night, weekday or Sabbath, this busy village was aclatter. Bostonians were hammering up wharf and warehouse, private dwelling and public house. At services in Increase Mather's Second Church (the first Old North Church) the pastor damned the profanation of the Lord's day and, again, he blamed a fire — that of 1711, the town's eighth great blaze in sixty years — to the scorn of Sunday churchgoing. "Burnings Bewailed," the Reverend Mather titled the sermon that described the fire that ravaged Cornhill, the Town House, and 100 buildings from Meetinghouse to School Street. With harsh words, he dragged the Almighty's wrath down upon the frightened shoulders of his congregants:

Has not God's Holy Day been profaned in New England? Have not Burdens been carried through the streets on the Sabbath Day? Have not Bakers, Carpenters, and other Tradesmen been employed in Servile Works on the Sabbath Day?

The townspeople shuddered, it was said, but just as quickly set to lugging the rubble of the fires to fill Long Wharf. Upon completion, the

Overleaf:
Paul Revere's engraving of the 1770 Boston Massacre shows the Old State House and landscape of long-gone brick shops.

impressive wharf measured 2000 feet from today's State Street into the bay. The workers shaped the docks to hold the ships to bring the goods to fill the houses to hold the parties . . . that no midcentury preachings could ring shut.

Pre-Revolutionary merchants had the coinage, and good times flowed. Colonial grandees began to mimic Europe's finest, and not the least in fire-scarred Cornhill where the chance to build the Town House and first church afresh inspired new brick buildings and broader sunnier streets. In 1712, a new Cornhill and church rose out of the ashes: the building destined to hold the Old Corner Book Store soon appeared, and, two years later, Bostonians installed a new brick Town House with spacious and costly glass windows. "Let this large transparent, costly Glass serve to oblige the Attornys always to set things in a True Light," Samuel Sewall wrote in his diary.

A generation later, even this well-lit space would not suffice. In 1742, prosperous Peter Faneuil's splendid structure, the Faneuil Hall Market, rose two and a half stories high with an arcaded market below and assembly hall above. By midcentury, some 3000-odd houses and 300 shops helped fill the landscape of bell, book, and candle. A Southern visitor who viewed the buoyant town exclaimed that he "saw not one prude while I was there." But the clergy took less joy in "Shoe toes pointed to the heaven in imitation of the Laplanders, with buckles of a harness size."

Such sighs could scarcely stop the town's change in garb, whether sartorial or architectural. New buildings flaunted their means with pomp and circumstance. Wealthier Bostonians could pay for architectural elegance and had the patrician zeal to match their means. They tacked a more lavish style on to the old frame house. Neither blunt box nor skimpy vegetable patch would do — not for a Hutchinson or a Hancock. For a Vassall or Faneuil, a Sargent or Bromfield, it must be mansion and grand garden, elaborate trim and fancy façade.

The town did not yet disown wood. Contrary to our visions of the pre-Revolutionary landscape in red brick, only one of every three dwellings of the eighteenth century was built of masonry. Brick, the staple stone of Boston, came slowly, more slowly than the fire laws shrilly sought as "the masterless flames" leveled section after section, eight times in six decades. "The wonder to me is that the whole city has not burned down, so light and dry are [these houses]," a European visitor observed. Time and again, the selectmen legislated. They ruled that buckets of water should be set by every door. They ordered chimney sweeps at certain times. They demanded a fire engine, and — most dramatic of all — insisted on an end to all wooden houses. As early as 1649 the General Court had ruled that no dwelling house in Boston "shall be errected and sett up except of stone or bricke, and covered with slate or tyle . . ." The official demands for stone and brick created the first building codes in the New World.

To no avail: law was one matter, enforcement another. When the ruling hurt the poor it was allowed to lapse; when fire struck, the ruling was re-enacted, off and on in similar words through the years.

This court, having a sense of the great ruins in Boston by fire, and hazard still of the same, by reason of the damage and loss thereby for the future do order and enact that henceforth no dwelling-house in Boston shall be erected and set up except of stone or brick, and covered with slate or tile, on penalty of forfeiting double the value of such buildings . . .

Nonetheless, for generations Bostonians built with wood and it is a sign of new wealth and a new way of life alike that the sunny brick that we call Georgian took hold even in that era's modest form.

It was not so much the *substance* of the city that changed in the Georgian period, then, as the *style.* Boston's architecture followed the time of the Georges. "The staccato of the medieval gable slowly gave way to the Legato of the classic cornice," as architectural historian Fiske Kimball puts it. No longer content with the old East Anglian ideal, wealthy Bostonians parroted Mother England's new language of academic forms and its merchants' flights to more modish dwellings. Boston's builders borrowed British phrases — "a window architrave, in one case, a level cornice with modillions in others, a hip-roof, or a gambrel," for their more pretentious houses. The English uncovered the styles of the ancient world and the Americans adopted their reclaimed neoclassical accents.

One hundred years before, Governor Winthrop had scolded his deputy "that he did not well to bestowe so much cost about wainscotting and adorning his house." New times and new saints came and ornament became a virtue. God, as the moderns would put it, was in the details: in quoins (corner blocks) bounding up the edges; in pediments over doorways; and, of course, in the classic orders — in the Ionic and Doric columns or, on occasion, in the high-flown Corinthian. The beauties of Rome via English precedent came to Boston's affluent class and many a merchant at Clark's (North) Square now boasted an elegant mansion.

The Hancocks had the greatest flair and hence took on the new aesthetic of the suburban ideal. Thomas Hancock, thirty-two, founder of his famous nephew's fortune, and his wife, Lydia, determined to bring the graceful British life to Boston. They bought an acre of Beacon Hill pasture with a fine prospect of hill and water, and set out to lavish it with the luxuries of English country life. From across the Atlantic came the Hancocks' seeds and bulbs — the walnut, mulberry, cherry, pear, plum, peach, nectarine, apricot, and gooseberry trees (for which New England horticulture was indebted) plus marble hearths, a clock with carved figures, and flocked wallpaper, not to mention a crest of arms in silver, gilded copies of Cato, and other sumptuous if smuggled goods.

The design was not all decoration and decorum, not all mimicry and no energy. Boston builders hadn't dismissed crude functionalism to adopt mere piecemeal appliqué. Their notions of space and formal organization, of order and balance were full and complex, not the mere afterthought of applied parts. While the carpenter-builder might show tact, even obsequiousness, in copying design details from his picture books, he had a sense of the commodious whole; the seemingly rude builder framed an ample mansion with a light-dappled parlor and elegant chambers for an appreciative gentry.

Symbolically enough, one chimney and one fireplace no longer heated the home from dead center, looming above the roofline like some gargantuan idol. The blaze from its one huge hearth, that primitive flame of life, now might split into two, three, or four slim and politely mantled fireplaces, scattered about the more stately dwelling. Dignity of a robust sort prevailed. From pillar to post, from portico to balustrade, from glazed transom to central hall, these houses and estates had as much presence as their owners. Did the colonial grandee take on a lordly manner in life? So then in his architecture. Did he acquire courtly airs or a Renaissance-modeled architecture? There need be no raison d'être for the parapet poised whimsically atop a roof or the balustrade lined up for display. Form for form's sake. Dormer windows gave extra light and halls permitted privacy, but what purpose had the broad stairs that rolled into the hall? What need for all those twisted fancy banisters and elaborate mantels? Those fancy sweeps served no end but sculpture.

Those of middling means could not indulge in the Hancocks' extravagance, of course. The 1750s saw harder times, and the population leveled off. The old two-story structure with a lean-to still survived and many a simple wooden house stood on a plot just large enough to grow the household vegetables. For the truly impoverished, home might be barely a box tucked into a back lot with the whole family jammed into a single room, or a rickety structure standing forlornly on the muddy outskirts of the town. Even the dwelling of many a solid artisan squatted above his shop, and, rich or poor, all endured the chill described so graphically by Cotton Mather: "Tis dredful cold. My standish is froze and splitt in my very stove. My ink in my pen suffers a congelation."

For the new aristocracy, however — the well-coifed-and-costumed Boston presences who look out from the portraits of John Singleton Copley — the surroundings had to fit their apparel. The latest roofs lost their timebound pitch, the casement windows breathed deep and spread into a sashed affair or took wing in the Palladian butterfly. Status-seeking merchants custom-ordered interiors and fine wares from an artisanry of carpenters, upholsterers, glaziers, painters, chair-makers, joiners, and cabinetmakers. With the wealth wrung from trade, they adorned their houses with imported objects, covered white plaster walls with rich tones, draped their windows in fine English fabrics, and filled their rooms with elegant Chippendale furniture. At night, candles cast a glow over dancers who swirled by the paneled walls and shadowed the Georgian mantels. The carved scrolls, acanthus leaves, flowers, and fruit complemented the banquets in their midst. Well-groomed guests eyed glazed cupboards bursting with imported wares, stood tall in the high-ceilinged rooms and relished the ancestry implied by the prints of Roman ruins.

"While the new community was hardening from gristle into bone," the Puritan spirit held sway, a historian has observed. Now the corpulent leisure class coveted the goods of the English gentry. And what they coveted, they commanded. The American merchant family, like its English country cousins, had only to buy a book of English patterns to find the design of the hour. Almost one hundred of their so-called pattern books reached the New World, where a drawing by Inigo Jones or James Gibbs supplied the ideal from across the Atlantic.

In part, that ideal was the pastoral motif. The landed aristocracy in the New World called for a villa or country place just as it did in the Old World. The would-be lords and ladies of the Bay State ringed the Hub with Georgian mansions, building estates atop Boston's hills or in the adjoining towns of Roxbury, Cambridge, Dorchester, and Milton. A handful of enlightened "amateurs" created such houses. As early as 1723, mapmaker William Price used his drafting skills to design Christ (Old North) Church in the North End; the royal governor, Sir Francis Bernard, drew Harvard Hall; and the colonial artist John Smibert, who painted the portrait of the high-living Peter Faneuil, supplied a drawing for the brick Faneuil Hall. Similarly, portraitist John Singleton Copley cast a trained eye to architecture. When he spied a "peaza" that he liked in New York he mailed directions home to his Boston builder: make the "peaza" like "the cover over the pump in your yard," he wrote. The artist misspelled *piazza* but his instruction made clear that he knew its use — "so cool in summer and in winter break off storms somewhat."

No professionals, in the modern sense of the word, shaped the architecture that was slowly dappling the landscape of Boston; talented housewrights arose to do the job. A skilled shipbuilder could muscle up a seaworthy wooden vessel or sculpt its figurehead. In the shipyards, craftsmen shaped oak into curved frames with graceful hulls; they fashioned seaworthy ships lighter and tighter than any house. So too the carpenter or housewright could carve a broken-scroll pediment or sheathe a building. Now, as later, town life whittled such woodworkers into semispecialists with a flair for everything from framing a house to copying a flower or fruit from *Swan's British Architecture.*

Travelers from Europe's masonry cities were astounded that mere carpenters could transform crude Maine timber into such polished forms. Scholars praised the "modesty and economy" of the Georgian style so fitted to the American landscape of wood. What matter that New Englanders lacked lime to seal the brick that was à la mode in English building? The thicketlike forests of oak and pine helped keep the pragmatic New Englanders facile with lumber for centuries. Wood, not stone, would do — in fact, would *out*do the Old World in furnishings. The elegance of even the grandest stone house in America derived from its wood trim.

Some master builders whom we would call architects and some buildings which we would call public architecture did appear as Independence neared: the Town House and Smibert's Faneuil Hall, soon to ring with patriot cries, qualified as "public design"; so did the stone jail destined to hold Captain Preston of the Boston Massacre. In such structures, the citizens who would earn a worldwide name as Children of the Enlightenment in philosophy or politics showed they were not stepchildren in the most public art of architecture. In the mid-eighteenth century, the dozen or so churches that rose from the streetscape to serve the growing town of 16,000 had the grace and charm of England, modeled on the work of James Gibbs or Sir Christopher Wren, the genius of postfire London.

Slipped into a similar urban landscape of tiny, lopsided sites, hemmed in by close-packed buildings, the Boston churches would similarly start to emphasize the steeple. No longer the bluff four-square meetinghouse, the new church had a spire and its needle tapered high above the town. Christ Church in Boston or Cambridge "might as probably have occurred in Yorkshire as in Massachusetts," an English scholar notes. These churches stemmed from the outlook of London's Wren as clearly as the political doings within descended from the mind of Sir John Locke.

King's Chapel on Tremont Street, the most impressive of Boston's churches and the first large cut-stone structure in New England, came from the man whom some have called America's first architect. Decades before Thomas Jefferson brought full-blown neoclassicism to America, Peter Harrison's 1749 church was a forerunner of the mode. Some said its vaulted ceiling had an effect unparalleled in any church of the time.

Harrison, who lived from 1716 to 1775, was a Quaker youth from Yorkshire who grew into a gentleman-designer with a taste for pomp and a mastery of Palladian forms. Like other so-called amateurs, the gifted architect acquired the proper design skills while absorbing the crafts of the sea; learning navigation, shipbuilding, drafting, woodcarving, cartography, military engineering and construction, commerce and agriculture gave him lessons in design. Harrison eloped with a woman who was wealthy enough to indulge his talent and taste for fine building, and made his way from Newport to London; there, he feasted on the buildings laid out like a banquet upon the city's streets and dipped into literary sources to learn how the English built with brick. This knowledge plus a coterie of cultivated friends enabled him to execute splendid buildings on the Newport townscape and brought his name to the attention of the church builders of Boston's leading Anglican congregation, among them Charles Apthorp, the grandfather of Charles Bulfinch, who would be Boston's greatest architect at the close of the century.

Great buildings depend upon architects. But early and late, Boston's great buildings have depended upon good clients too — upon clients conversant with the art. Somehow Bostonians had acquired a language of form sufficient to carry on design discussions with Harrison by correspondence. King's Chapel was planned through the mails. "We do not require any great Execution of Ornament," the church building committee wrote, "but chiefly aim at Symmetry and Proportion."

Harrison never came to see the empty site, yet — save for a missing steeple — the architect was content with what his mail-order clients wrought. So might be countless others. The unsung engineers and carpenter-builders who executed his paper plans and the stonecutters who split the first Quincy granite ever used into four-foot blocks for the building had performed an impressive feat. The grand exterior, the vaulted ceiling, and the handsome wineglass pulpit told the world of a church-building vogue fortified by keen design intelligence. In

days to come, the King's Chapel bells would ring and the structure would bear its portico. And later still, in the twentieth century, the hero of Santayana's *The Last Puritan* found inspiration in the

Georgian elegance of the interior, all white plaster, shining mahogany, and crimson damask. In those high-walled pews, with their locked doors, every worshipper might pray in secret as if in his own closet.

Long, long before Independence then, the citizen of Boston could witness fine architecture, and the homeowner find a craftsman so capable that "every joint he ever framed/he knew would pinch a hair." Few of their houses survived in even a gnarled and butchered form. A still greater loss was that of the routine skill and everyday comprehension of the colonial citizenry who created them — the untutored art of city building.

Did the townscape as a whole share in this small-scale Renaissance in architecture? There was little true urbanity in Boston's total urban design. The roads and streets were scrambled lanes, the crooked and narrow streets of later fame. The squares barely deserved the name. Church Green, blessed by little more than a patch of land, was no "green" at all. Buildings or groups of buildings tended to grow in a random way within the topographical framework: indeed, the expansion from path to lane to street to highway over the years before Independence almost seemed to pattern itself. Lacking the power, time, or wealth to be conquerors, the new Americans mostly made do with the given landscape for their first hundred and fifty years. Where Blackstone trod, they trod. Celebrating the city's two hundred and fiftieth anniversary years later, a nostalgic writer in Winsor's *Memorial History* could still record the crabbed growth during that quarter of a millennium fondly:

Thus, the narrow, winding streets, with their curious twists and turns, the crooked alleys and shortcuts by which [Blackstone] drove cows to pasture up among the blueberry bushes of Beacon Hill or carried his grist to the windmill upon Copp's Hill Steeps, or went to draw his water at the spring-gate, and the highways, worn by his feet and established for his convenience, remain after two centuries and a half substantially unchanged, endeared to his posterity by priceless associations.

There was little planning and scant proof that the main streets were formally laid out. Not until 1708 did the selectmen give the irregular paths their proper names. As with streets, so with buildings: they were placed for the sake of economy and convenience. The selectmen harrumphed that these structures wandered every which way, stealing land from the streets. So what? The streets reciprocated by stealing land right back again from the buildings, and from the pedestrians too. As for sidewalks, not one lined the streets before the Revolution. Most walkers held to the center of the road. Once in a while, a post and chain scored a pedestrian path out of harm's way. Time after time the town ruled on the need to repair the mucky streets or protested the holes left ragged and dangerous. Despite this sorry state, Boston was called the cleanest, best-paved city in Georgian America, and by some accounts "the best governed town in the colony."

The village blossoming into the full-flowering colonial period was becoming a crowded town, a trading town. Visitors were describing the old bay port as the Georgian Boston alive in today's imagination — a packed town, an English town with a paper-doll parade of brick and wooden houses. Starting to crowd the North and South ends, filling both sides of the streets, reaching skyward in the masts of its sailing ships and the spires of its churches, Boston was maturing. It was moving toward the urbanity of Independence.

Ask a sailor or merchant prince to pick his patron in the eighteenth century and you'd hear "Hancock" or "Mammon" long before the good "St. Botolph." Just try to cross the busy streets and the carts, drays, wheelbarrows, horses, and random animals would time your steps. As early as 1711, the protest of cramped citizens had led the selectmen to widen Common (Tremont) Street to twenty feet. It wasn't wide enough. Many a building owner still had to plant a roadside post to keep the thumping, bumping vehicles from ramming into his walls. The millstone, today's Boston Stone, standing at the old "point zero," or the center of the city, was set into a house on Marshall Street to fend off such rambunctious vehicles.

Even the Common's shared soil, the rolling fields where cows grazed, soldiers drilled, and citizens took the air, would have been carved into petty house plots if the advocates of trade had had their way. Stubbornly the selectmen said no and no again, repeatedly forbidding incursions. By defining public space as sacred for more than a century, Boston officials formed the outlines of America's first park.

While the earliest town meetings had dealt summarily with intrusions on the Common, colonial Bostonians also took a more positive step: They began to improve the Common's acreage. Starting in 1723, private citizens planted trees in a line along Tremont Street; then, in 1734, the town fenced in the eastern side and added a second row of trees to complete a 1400-foot mall. For years, this arching processional of trees would shade passersby. The selectmen also ordered more fences to prevent the "herbage spoiled by means of Carts,

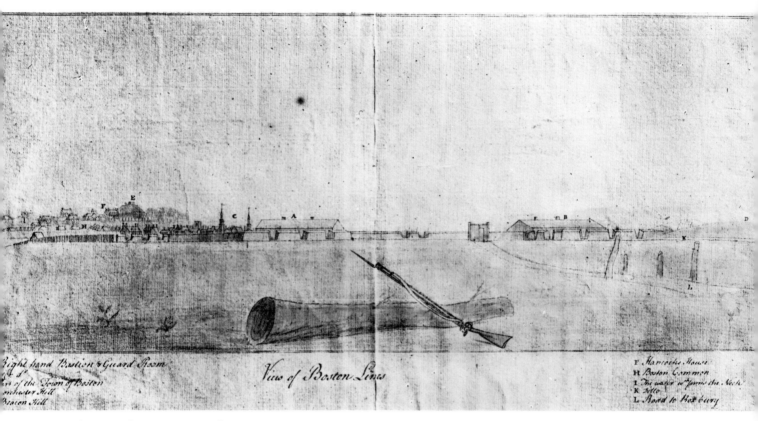

Right hand Bastion & Guard Room
... of the Town of Boston
... chester Hill
... eacon Hill

View of Boston Lines

F *Hancocks House*
H *Boston Common*
1 *The water w forms the Neck*
K *Ditto*
L *Road to Roxbury*

View of Boston from Boston Neck.

Coaches, Etc. passing and repassing over it"; they also raised a mound near today's Beacon Street to spare the grass from the rivulets gushing down off Beacon Hill.

Public life — from executions to open-air religious services, from holiday tents crowded with cakes and oranges to military parades and meetings — centered on the Common. There, Bostonians practiced their impulses to beautify the public grounds. Thomas Hancock, John's distinguished uncle, planted lime trees where his Beacon Street property touched the Common. Prosperous Adino Paddock brought in English elms in 1756, grew them at his country estate in Milton and planted them along the walking grounds before the Granary Burial Ground. Not content to leave well enough alone, Paddock sallied forth to defend his lovely imports from the small boys who dared to molest them. More plantings, more fines, the process continued here, on the Boston Neck, and elsewhere as town folks tried to green their pleasure grounds.

Bostonians and other chroniclers found a rude and handsome order in many quarters of their seaport town. The rolling hills surmounted a lovely urban village. The bay and ocean created a water vista, its sights and sounds visible from every side — east with the sea just beyond the Town House and docks; north with the bustling shipyards; west with the bay a sparkling sheet at the Common's edge; and round about with wetland and creek. The Views and Prospects drawn in the period show a graciously enfolding landscape, curving to the sea, legged with wharves, punctuated with windmills and rising spires.

Countless such Views depicted the expanding town. By the time Boston had taken its first formal survey in 1722, artists were making maps to depict the town and record such numerous structures as twenty-seven shipyards. Some fifty-eight wharves, forty-two streets, thirty-six lanes, and twenty-two alleys were drawn by mapmaker Captain John Bonner. "Houses, near 3000; 1000 brick, rest Timber. Near 15,000 people," he scribbled in the margin of his map. The map itself was a sign of urban conciousness; it showed a graphic self-awareness of great significance — of parallel importance to the buildings blocked along the coast in the clean black lines of the engraver. Year by year, straining to self-government, the town began to change and, year by year, its self-conscious citizenry updated such maps. "In the light of this pictorial evidence, there is no doubt of the real and rapid growth of metropolitan America," historian Carl Bridenbaugh has written.

"Metropolitan America," the phrase evoked by Bridenbaugh's classic *Cities in the Wilderness,* rings strangely modern to our ears, as "modern" as the cries for separation that the new age of liberty would usher in. Conditions in Boston were "as truly urban as any known to their age," the historian maintained. They incubated the seeds of the Revolution. "More like a long-established town of the Continent than a country," a contemporary French visitor confirmed. An independent town, we now would add.

The hundreds of such Views of Boston that rolled off the presses as booster prints in the half-century before Independence traveled through America and then sailed off to England to display the New World's achievements. Ruled by itself, built by itself, Boston had a pride in this progress and urbanity. Not surprisingly, such self-confidence would not long tolerate intrusion from afar. On the eve of rebellion Bostonians had knowledge of the arts and sciences, philosophy and culture. According to Sam Adams, the very word *caucus* came from the caulkers in their midst. Boston had ninety-two booksellers and five or more printing presses. It had three thousand houses, and clubs, societies and taverns to house the inhabitants' political-social dialogue. It had a court to gather a rough cosmopolitan population and Harvard's nearby college to refine that roughness and sharpen those politics. And all about, it had the citified shoulder-to-shoulder lifestyle that would intensify the call to liberty.

There is one final view of pre-Revolutionary Boston that endures today. In it, Paul Revere has depicted the opening chapter in the tale of the American Revolution played out in Boston's environs. The artisan of the Revolution engraved the town with its old houses and wharves, the roofs, "pointed, hipped, and gambreled," the tortuous streets, all as they were then. But in this last view, a fresh presence is seen. Revere now fronted his portrait of the city with a fleet of ships: the city stands behind a cage of foreign masts. The masts stem from the vessels brought by the British troops — the enemy troops that carried the sounds of war a town too headstrong, vital, and independent to tolerate this view.

A VIEW OF PART OF T[...]

1. Beaver   5. Mermaid   On fryday Sept.r 30.th 176[...]
2. Senegal   6. Romney   a Spring on their Cable[...]
3. Martin   7. Launceston an d Train of Artillery[...]
4. Glasgow   8. Bonetta   playing, and Colours [...]

Landscape of Revolution

Boston was the backdrop for the Revolution. The city of twisting streets, sturdy bricks shops, frame houses, and bustling waterfront and marketplace was a stage set on which the events leading to the War of Independence were played out. It was, however, *only* a stage set to the restless builders who followed the heroic generation. In rapid succession, they knocked down vast numbers of such landmarks. "Ghosts," said Henry James, "belong only to places and suffer and perish with them." Boston and the nation are poorer for the loss of such ghosts.

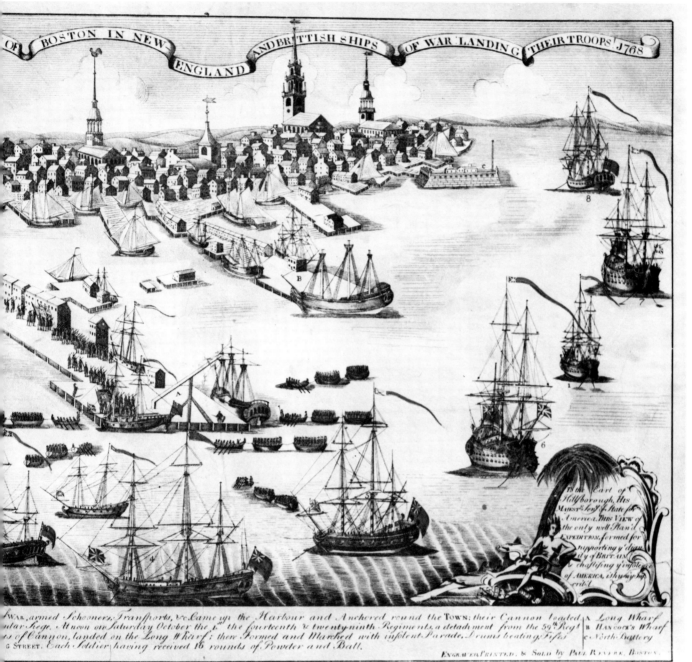

OF BOSTON IN NEW ENGLAND AND BRITTISH SHIPS OF WAR LANDING THEIR TROOPS! 1768

...WAR, armed Schooners, Transports, &c. Came up the Harbour and Anchored round the TOWN; their Cannon loaded... Long Wharf
...ular Siege. At noon on Saturday October the 1st the fourteenth & twentyninth Regiments, a detachment from the 59th Regt. B HANCOCK'S Wharf
...s of Cannon, landed on the Long Wharf; there Formed and Marched with insolent Parade, Drums beating, Fifes... C North Battery
...G STREET, Each Soldier having received 16 rounds of Powder and Ball.

ENGRAVED, PRINTED, & SOLD by PAUL REVERE, BOSTON.

...SIMILE of Paul Revere's Picture of ONE HUNDRED YEARS AGO is issued by Alfred L. Sewell, Publisher of The Little Corporal Chicago Ill.

Of the close-packed houses, shops, and wharves seen in Paul Revere's "Landing of the British Troops" (1768) only the tiny landmarks of the Old State House at the head of King Street and Christ Church (the Old North Church) on Salem Street in the North End remain intact. Long Wharf, the chief wharf of eighteenth-century Boston, begun in 1710 and thrusting out into the harbor here, succumbed to such incursions as the nineteenth century's Atlantic Avenue, and is now largely a roadway and parking lot.

Heroes and villains of the Revolution inhabited the sometimes grand, sometimes diminutive structures of the seventeenth- and eighteenth-century town. The simple clapboard house on Milk Street where Ben Franklin was born in 1706 (above left) burned in 1810. The Hutchinson House in North Square adorned with an arch and filled with Roman busts (below left) held the controversial Royal Governor. It was sacked by a Revolutionary mob in 1765 and destroyed in 1834. The John Hancock House (right) built of hand-hewn stone by his affluent uncle in 1737, stood to the left of the State House on Beacon Hill. "No stranger who felt the patriotic impulse failed to pay it a visit," a nineteenth-century Bostonian wrote. Despite one of Boston's first preservation efforts, officials removed the building in 1863. "I . . . used to sit at the window of my play-room and watch the men slowly pry off one block of stone after another, for the masonry was so solid that it could be accomplished in no other way," a character in the novel *The Chippendales* declared.

View of Faneuil-Hall, in Boston, Massachusetts.

Some say the American Revolution brewed in the tavern—forum, and social club for Bostonians—long before the urge for independence took on a more public voice in Faneuil Hall. Above its market stalls, the Hall, the vaunted Cradle of Liberty, held the fiery debates on the Molasses Tax and other "bloodless battles" of the Revolution. Designed by painter John Smibert in 1742 and rebuilt after a fire in 1761, the Faneuil Hall shown here disappeared in Charles Bulfinch's 1805 enlargement, which stands today. The Green Dragon (below left), a mansion built in the mid-1600s, was a "nest of treason" to the British and "headquarters of the Revolution" to Daniel

Webster. This meeting place of Adams, Otis, Warren, and Revere came down for the widening of Union Street half a century after the Revolution. King's Head Tavern, on Fleet and North streets (below), another popular gathering hole, lasted until the Civil War decade pictured here. The more mythical Hancock House (above), a "place of resort" for Benjamin Franklin, Talleyrand, and Louis Philipe, was razed for an office building between State Street and Faneuil Hall Square in 1903.

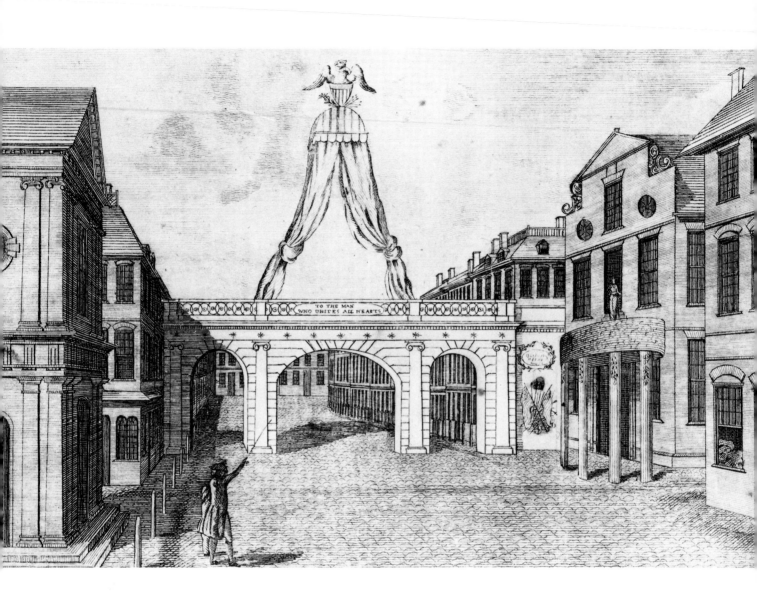

The city holds the collective memory of humankind. Its symbols, both designed and accidental, make that memory visual. In the glory days after the Revolution, Bostonians honored the visit of George Washington with this temporary arch and colonnade designed by Charles Bulfinch (left). The Liberty Tree (above), which held effigies of the loathed stamp collector, was taken down by the angry British and turned into fourteen cords of wood. Brick buildings and a plaque on Washington Street at Essex mark the spot where this seventeenth-century dwelling stood beside the famous tree. Sculptor John Francis Paramino designed the bas relief to record the British soldiers leaving Long Wharf (below). The plaque, mounted at 148 State Street during the tercentenary celebration in 1930, has vanished just as completely as the British.

SITE OF
THE HEAD OF LONG WHARF
BUILT BY THE CITIZENS OF THE TOWN 1710
FROM WHICH THE BRITISH EMBARKED
ON THE EVACUATION OF BOSTON
17 MARCH 1776

PLACED BY THE CITY OF BOSTON
1930

CHAPTER 4

Federalist Foundations, 1780-1800

Again the harbor was whitened with the sails of merchant ships, once more the trades began to flourish with their old activity in shop and ship-yard, and the old bustle and movement were seen anew in the streets; but there was much weary work to be done before the ravages of war could be repaired. Ten years elapsed before the population reached the point at which it stood before the Revolution.

— HENRY CABOT LODGE, *Memorial History,* 1880

Boston was the child of my father and he did pretty much as he pleased with it.

— FRANCIS VAUGHAN BULFINCH

THE CRADLE of liberty had rocked. The "shot heard round the world" had grazed the town. Just across the Charles River, the British had torched Charlestown into ashes during the Battle of Bunker Hill. The sister town still bore "a melancholy prospect" to visiting Abbé Rodin. Boston proper, the Shawmut peninsula, suffered no such total disaster. Still it suffered: "There was near as many houses in it destroyed during the War as were burned in Charles Town," Elias Boudinot noted in his *Journey to Boston.*

The North Square church where Mathers preached fell to fuel British fires. Fences, barns, outbuildings, and about one hundred large wooden structures joined the list — "demolished and distributed for firewood," said a report. Wharves went up in flames; so did John Winthrop's homestead, then serving as the parsonage for the Old South Meeting House, along with its shading butternut trees. The cramped peninsula had always lacked wood. When blockades kept out lumber, the British simply hacked buildings like forests, ships and trees like logs. With glee, they downed the Liberty Tree and, though they spared the Common's great elm, they stoked their fires with the wooden railings round it.

No *single* year of siege laid the town low, nor any one side's belligerence, however. During the decades when Boston cradled the pursuit of liberty, rebel and royalist alike struck out at enemy walls as if they were the foe. The innocent townscape, like its innocent inhabitants, suffered, if only from neglect. "The distress of the troops and people of Boston exceed the possibility of description," wrote one fleeing citizen, "the inhabitants and troops literally starving with cold. They had taken the pews out of all the places of worship for fuel; had pulled down empty houses, and were then digging up the timber of the wharves for firing."

In the prelude to the Revolution, American patriots had wreaked vengeance on or enjoyed the pillage of Tory mansions and official quarters. The Sons of Liberty sacked and demolished the office of Andrew Oliver, distributor of the loathesome revenue stamps. They looted the house of Lieutenant Governor Hutchinson, destroying its historic documents and damaging its splendid architecture. Even before the Battle of Bunker Hill, the Americans had denuded East Boston and leveled its dwellings to keep the British from finding shelter or a command post there. Nothing would do but to burn every emblem of Old England: on July 17, 1776, the lion and unicorn on the east gable of the Old State House came down in honor of the reading of the Declaration of Independence.

The British invaders began their 1775 occupation in the same spirit, leveling Boston Neck houses to build their line. By order of General

The burning of Charlestown.

Overleaf:
Dorchester Heights and the harbor.

64

Gage: "Houses, fences, trees pulled down," a diarist wrote. The elegant Province and Hancock houses stayed intact to provide luxurious quarters for the English; so did the trees planted by Tory sympathizer Adino Paddock. The Hancock house was almost untouched, save for some sword marks on its fence, nor were the spacious houses of the North End abused. Poorer houses suffered more. The modest dwelling of Samuel Adams on Purchase Street near Church Green was mutilated and disfigured "past his slender means of restoration."

The vandalism to the Old South Meeting House where the Boston Tea Party brewed was pure mischief, and especially painful. Only one fine pew was saved. (Better extinction, patriots fumed, than its ignominious use as a Tory hog sty!) British officials toasted good healths from a bar in the Meeting House gallery. "Gentleman Johnny" Burgoyne's dragoons pranced about on horseback on the dirt and gravel spread upon its hallowed floor and practiced leaps over a barrier. Elsewhere, Burgoyne relaxed a bit more graciously in the mansion vacated by James Bowdoin.

Finally, the British beheaded West Church. By removing its steeple, they sought to prevent the Americans from signaling to forces in Cambridge — thereby stopping rides by any future Paul Reveres. The makeshift barracks inside West Church were typical. Everywhere houses of God served military men: the Hollis Street and Brattle Square churches lodged Redcoats, and the Old South Meeting House held their horses. Soldiers seemed quartered on every corner, taking pot shots at old gravestones, staging theater in Faneuil Hall (a specialty was Burgoyne's "Blockade of Boston"), digging trenches and staking tents on the Common and Fort Hill, putting distilleries in sail lofts.

Outside the Hub, the farmers on the Neck suffered too. During their siege of 1775, the Americans dug into the hills of Roxbury. They razed the mansion of Puritan governor Dudley and used its brick basement walls as entrenchments from which to bombard the British. Much worse seemed possible in those dark days: "Boston, I fear, must be given up for the common safety," General Washington wrote his secretary. Some say only the lack of gunpowder and cannon saved the town. At long last evacuation came on March 17, 1776, but the British in their hasty exodus leveled and looted Castle William, and the shot that hit the Brattle Square Church from American cannon in Cambridge was a landmark for generations. Fifty years later, Edward Everett Hale still saw the marks of the British encampment on Boston Common's Flagstaff Hill.

The traces of neglect were even more visible, so visible that Boston's master architect Charles Bulfinch would begin his career a decade later with the "houses of some friends, all of which have become exceedingly dilapidated during the war." Though Boston was less damaged than most war towns, empty lofts, rotting storefronts, and barren docks scarred the landscape. Not every patriot returned to nothing but four walls, but all returned to a shrunken townscape.

At war's end, much of Boston's citizenry had left. Many of them were the noblest, some affirmed. First, the revolutionaries with the British "Wanted" branded on their heads had fled; then, the vanquished Tories packed their goods and their skills and scuttled off to safety in Halifax. Some said only scum with no stake in the soil were left: "Fellows who would have cleaned my shoes five years ago now ride in chariots," one old aristocrat groused. "Those who five years ago were the 'meaner people' are now by a strange revolution become almost the only men of power, riches and influence," another groaned. "I have been credibly informed that a person who used to live well has been obliged to take the feathers out of his bed, sell them to an upholsterer to get money to buy bread," a third lamented.

Shoe cleaners or swells, featherbedded or breadless, by the time peace was signed the number of Boston's inhabitants had dropped to one third of the preceding decade. Boston was not much larger in population than the seaport Salem to the north, and, as the postwar depression set in, it was smaller in trade.

The Revolution had left not just a vacuum of power, however, but a vacuum of place. The seats of Tory affluence, of Oliver and Hutchinson, were sold to the newly affluent. The so-called Country Aristocracy from the North Shore bought into the patrimony of the Crown's children. The Tory heraldry of money and power passed on to Essex County rulers — the Cabots and Lowells, Grays and Gerrys. With their past wealth from privateering and their coming wealth from maritiming, the out-of-towners entered the war-thinned list that topped colonial society. Vigorous trade with China and maritime fishing activities multiplied their fleets almost ten times and fattened their purses. They looked for new places to establish their supremacy on the crowded land. New places clearly required a new architecture.

History tells us that post-Revolutionary Boston would slowly lose its political and economic hegemony, that its politicians would become parochial, its arts conservative. Its path lay far off an American mainstream whose course was the manifest destiny of the Louisiana Purchase. In a way, that is true. But what is a city's true destiny? As an architectural showplace and designed landscape, Boston would lead the new nation. If Washington would exhibit the grander architectural aspirations of the new Republic, Boston would become the handsomer place. For the greater part of the nineteenth century, this sidestreet town would be a model in the art of citymaking.

Charles Bulfinch, the man who would be the prime placemaker of Boston's new epoch of building, was what we would call a dilettante, a gentlemanly designer who never had a day of tutoring in his chosen field. Creator of Boston's State House and rebuilder of Washington's capitol, framer of the Boston Common and Boston squares, shaper of the Federalist style — Bulfinch never earned enough from his architecture to make it more than "amateur." Unselfish to a fault, the architect would create Federalist mansions for patriots with polished boots and polished ways; he would bless their less lordly heirs with a town that had become a city. Twice bankrupt, he was once jailed for it. Housed in an ever descending spiral of "small dwellings," unpaid as designer and underpaid as head of selectmen, police, and education, Charles Bulfinch brought Boston into its post-Revolutionary age. In the end, limping from a fall on the steps of the Faneuil Hall he had enlarged (without personal profit), the architect was called to rebuild a Washington he never loved so well. Meanwhile the town that bore the look of his labors grew on without his work.

At the start of Bulfinch's work, such a career seemed unlikely. Trade had stilled in the aftermath of war; weeds grew in the once lush gardens, and cold winds swept the once busy wharves. Bulfinch's town had few jobs to offer a young architect. Not for long. For a generation, the townscape had stayed locked in place while its dwellers burst their neighborhoods. War and trade restrictions had left an economically stagnant city; the fire of 1760 had left a ravaged landscape. Nonetheless it was a physically crowded one. Some 680 dwelling houses and tenements were jammed into the North End and Dock Square. The houses stood so close they gnawed each other's sides, the townsfolk joked. Add 700 structures as the century turned. Record 70 vessels in port on just one given Monday in 1791, double the population in a generation and the flow of traffic mounted. The crowd could sweep you out to sea. With Independence, the signing of the Constitution, and the maritime explosion, came an awakening spirit for local growth and a major period of building.

Slowly, the old peninsula began to finger beyond its narrow shores toward the mainland. Some scoffed at the Bostonians who incorporated to build the Charles River Bridge to Charlestown in 1785: Imagine trying to span 1503 feet, shore to shore, over water deeper than London's Thames! Might as well joust with windmills, old-timers said. Unmoved by such naysayers, John Hancock and his colleagues funded the "Quixote enterprise" and, in 1786, the nation's longest wooden bridge linked the two towns. The thirteen-gun salute to celebrate the event matched the fireworks for the adoption of the Constitution the next year. Within a quarter of a century, the prosperous enterprise spawned three other bridges built by private corporations. "All very well contrived," contemporaries said. Enormous constructions in their day, they joined Boston to the larger land mass in Cambridge by the West Boston Bridge in 1793, to South Boston by the South Boston Bridge in 1805, and from Leverett Street in the West End to Cambridge's Lechmere Point by Craigie's Bridge in 1809. Pedestrian Boston began to expand; its vehicles increased. Stagecoach service between Cambridge and Boston followed a year after the building of the West Boston Bridge. In 1803, the Middlesex Canal added to such engineering enterprises by hooking up to the North End.

Again, naysayers thundered when more trees, fill, grading, or gravel went to repair and beautify Boston Common in 1784. "A luxurious outline of the country's ruined," that crusty old democrat Sam Adams sputtered from his nearby home on Winter Street. First of the patriots, last of the Puritans, Adams' voice was lost in the winds that powered a new wealth, strength, pride, and era of growth. In the thirteen years of plenty between Jay's treaty of 1794 and Jefferson's embargo of 1807, Yankee merchants set sail in the trade that made them world famous. The hulls of the *Constitution* and *Essex,* wrapped in copper by Revere, ranged the world's oceans. The China Trade made the word *Bostonian* synonymous with the word *American* in ports across the seven seas. On the ocean, the Boston merchants doubled and quadrupled their wealth, trading from Oregon Country to India. At home, with the same impetus to grow, they multiplied their structures on the landscape of the town.

The winds of change had blown earlier, of course. The "vile luxuriance" of English nobility and a more grandiloquent architecture had always had appeal. A "box in the country" — the romantic country estate — had always loomed large in the dream of the Anglophiles. Would-be squires had set up the first suburbs earlier than we think in towns that became parts of today's Metropolitan Boston: in Cambridge close to Harvard, with liveried oarsmen to row their owners back to town across the Charles; in Roxbury, a walk or carriage ride across the isthmus; in Milton, Medford, Dorchester, and Charlestown. In such towns, the gentry began to fit the English pattern early on: city by day, country by night — town house and country house even then. In fact, the house of Thomas Hancock on Beacon Hill had stood aloft at such a commanding height that it bore the look of a country mansion.

68   Distance from dense workaday Boston attracted those who wanted

space between work and play. It pleased a number of citizens in this "nation of farmers" who never took to urban life. "Who can study in Boston streets?" farmer-statesman John Adams had asked. He compared seaport Boston to rural Quincy nine miles away and found it wanting:

I am unable to observe the various objects that I meet with sufficient precision. My eyes are so diverted with chimney sweepers, sawyers of wood, merchants, ladies, priests, carts, horses, oxen, coaches, market men and women, soldiers, sailors, and my ears with the rattled gabble of them all, that I cannot think long enough in the street upon any one thing to start and pursue a thought.

Add another third — 10,000 citizens — to the city every ten years of the early nineteenth century, and the earthy smells, the constant sounds, the whirlpool sights impinged still more. Add bridges, add vehicles, and the chance to flee increased.

It is pleasant to picture Boston's Town Cove as a walking, working center with space for market and retail shops in that intimacy of daily life and trade we now so value. Yet the picturesque pump at Cornhill made something less than music morn to night. The ropewalks, twine factories, tanneries, sugar refineries, copper smelters, and smoking brick kilns of the colonial metropolis were not ideal neighbors. The chocolatemaking factories, gristmills, and sawmills of the North End, the clocks and candles, cardboard and soap, shoes and meat packing shops, the thirty distilleries and seven sugar refineries operating by the end of the eighteenth century were scarcely rustic company. Such times and such cities prompted Thomas Jefferson's classic utterance that "the mobs of great cities add just so much to the support of pure government as sores do to the strength of the human body" — the words, no doubt, of a man with a keen distaste for urban life. Even that old city lover, the transplanted Bostonian Benjamin Franklin, had his doubts in Philadelphia. "The din of the Market increases upon me. And that with frequent interruptions has, I find, made me say some things twice over." So saying, Franklin moved to the town's outskirts.

In Boston, it was much the same and would grow more so as the nineteenth century advanced, doubling the town's population every decade and doubling that attack upon the senses. The last few mansions near the North End wharves were squeezed by the swelling sea trade and the retail center succumbed to subdivision to allow the growth. House gave way to business, garden plot to road, orchard to building. More dust fell upon the rough streets. The everlasting putrid smell of tannery and wharf, the threat to life and limb, the filthy

swine and roaming dogs, the oxen and the mongering clamor to
"move on, move on . . ."

Downtown had indeed lost its charm for some. The visiting president of Yale, Timothy Dwight, complained that

*The streets strike the eye of a traveler as if intended to be mere pas-
sages from one neighborhood to another, and not the open handsome
divisions of a great town, as the result of casualty and not of con-
trivance.*

To some, the 170-year-old town was respectable but a trifle quaint.
"Heavy, antique and incommodious," a British traveler complained.
The pale ghosts of Puritan clapboard and the noisy haunts of commerce hounded the postwar plutocracy. They shared their builders'
urge for something more.

Some date the "new" Boston that ballooned across the hills and
marshes and settled upon the very sea from the return of Charles
Bulfinch — from the day the "sensitive and enthusiastic young man
arrived home from the Grand Tour with a collection of architectural
books and a portfolio of drawings." Charles Bulfinch arrived at the
appropriate hour and place, his head swimming with the urban imagery of England and France, his heart set upon creating a city in
their image.

To the returning native, Boston of 1787 must have seemed a
drowsy town, slumbering under a patchwork quilt of styles, its pebbly
lanes a sad contrast to the brick sidewalks of New York. The picturesque seaport of the Revolution, the pleasant enclave of midcentury,
lay dormant. It was the twilight of the old style and must have looked
a dim one at that. To one conversant with Georgian London's orderly
town house rows and Paris's city planning, the architecture in Boston was out of date, the fashions frumpy and eccentric. Why, the
very hair upon the American ladies, a spectacular bit of engineering
"raised and supported upon cushions to an extravagant height," was
passé across the Atlantic — "somewhat resembling the manner in
which the French ladies wore their hair some years ago," the Parisian
traveler Abbé Rodin observed.

Bulfinch would have his chance to update the dowdy old regime.
The congregation of the old Hollis Street Church obliged first; Bulfinch's wealthy friends soon followed. These merchants with their
seaborn riches sought more spacious houses. In Bowdoin Square on
the perimeter of the town, former farmland would supply the land
for their estates. In the fields of his grandfather's old pasture and his
own birthplace, Bulfinch planted the attenuated neoclassical forms
of England's Robert Adam. The rural land of West Boston became

Charles Bulfinch.

"the very center of aristocracy." Golden days came to Bowdoin Square. Across the town the same glorious design reshaped the countrified South End. Here on a quagmire of old Shawmut, another set of mansions and urban projects awaited Bulfinch. "No greater change has taken place in Boston than the conversion of that swamp into useful ground," as a guidebook of the period described the firming of today's Franklin Street.

The architect who created these wonders stares out at us languidly in an early portrait. With his powdered wig, his full lips, and long lordly face he seems sedate, and so he described himself. The serene demeanor matched the title "Charles Bulfinch, gentleman," recorded in the town directory. Still, the style was not the whole man. Bulfinch had set his sights on larger things. If the young bridegroom idled at the gentlemanly art of architecture in his early balmy days, at twenty-seven he took on his first public post with the town selectmen. In short order, plans for trees and promenades on the Common issued from that office. In 1789, the design for the triumphal arch to honor George Washington appeared and soon Bulfinch was pushing for a domed state capitol for the Commonwealth. Clearly, the man with the mild visage had bold ideas.

One of the first of these notions had been to replace the ramshackle old beacon of Beacon Hill. High above the crest of the town "unsightly timbers" still held the grisly black tarpot used to light warning fires in years before. A grim relic, it was "not but a remnant of things that had been." In post-Revolutionary Boston, it had neither use nor beauty and, when fortuitous winds blew it down in 1789, Bulfinch offered to replace this sorry pile with a handsome column. Why not a modest replica of Europe's monuments for the aspiring Republic? Bulfinch designed the column, launched the subscription to raise funds, and helped devise the inscription on its pedestal. Made of brick and stone encrusted with cement, the sixty-foot Roman Doric column stood on an eight-foot-wide base on the loftiest peak of the town, joining past and future in one soaring stroke. It was the architect's most conspicuous piece of sculpture. It was both a memorial of the glory days of revolution that Bostonians had left behind and a portent of the prospects that he and they were ready to create.

To Market, to Market

"The more barrels, the more Boston," wrote Henry David Thoreau. "The museums and scientific societies and libraries are accidentals. They gather around the barrels, to save carting." Certainly the sea was Boston's marketplace and good earth. The clipper ship, her ocean going manifesto, stood as high as six stories, more prominent than many a building — "the highest creation of artistic genius in the Commonwealth," Samuel Eliot Morison declared. "The lines of their hulls were quick and virile as those of a living tree or of a column of the Parthenon."

The city also required Parthenons of a more commercial sort; buildings for business and industry lined the waterfront and city streets. The stunning stone structures that filled the nineteenth-century city reflected the days when "Merchant" bore the word "Prince" as its surname and "Palace" applied to "Palaces of Trade." The architecture of this era neither stinted nor showed off with unneighborly design. It has suffered more abuse than any other in the ruthless claims upon downtown sites.

Down to the Sea in Ships and Wharves

Two of Boston's major wharves, Long and Central, spanned the waterfront before a panorama of sailing vessels. Long Wharf, once a veritable Wonder of the World, stretching 2000 feet into the harbor in 1710, was severed by Atlantic Avenue in 1868. Only a portion of Central Wharf remains.

"In her, the long-suppressed artistic impulse of a practical, hard-worked race burst into flower," wrote Samuel Eliot Morison. "The *Flying Cloud* was our Rheims; the *Sovereign of the Seas* our Parthenon; the *Lightning* [shown here] our Amiens; but they were monuments carved from snow. For a brief moment of time they flashed their splendor around the world, then disappeared with the sudden completeness of the wild pigeons."

Boston's waterfront had its seedy and its sumptuous sides. Finished in 1883, T Wharf (left) had its days as the turn-of-the-century headquarters of the fishing fleet. Its life extended in the lively artists' and writers' colony thereafter, but finally vanished from the harbor, courtesy urban renewal. Fitted out with all the splendor of winter drawing rooms or summer cottage porches, streamers like the *State of Maine,* which plied the New York–Fall River route, offered Boston seagoers opulent interiors for their brief life upon the ocean sea.

75

Houses of Commerce

Picturesque but sturdy, the early commercial buildings of Boston colored the townscape. The Old Feather Store (left), built in 1680 in Dock Square, remained until its demolition in 1860, the novelty of its gables and roughcast plaster surface added to its appeal. "A modern Ovid might describe it as a petrified old Gentleman — petrified as a punishment for old fogeyism," Ballou's *Pictorial* sentimentally observed. Nonetheless, this monument to "the fidelity with which our forefathers constructed their houses for business and for habitation," came down for a brick Victorian replacement.

When Boston was still the center of New England trade, the Cattle Fair attracted hundreds to the Brighton Market at Washington and Market streets in today's Brighton section of the city. The 1830s wooden hotel with its two-story portico lasted until 1898. The cattle run lasted well into the twentieth century.

Bulfinch's Boylston Market (1809) served the old South End of the town on Washington at Boylston Street until it fell in 1888. Its tower survives atop the Calvary Methodist Church in Arlington.

The mighty Merchants' Exchange (left) faced State Street where a daily throng passed through its majestic facade of six pilasters, each forty-five feet high and weighing fifty-five tons. The cornerstone of the building by Isaiah Rogers was laid in 1841. The elegant interior (above) is decked out to mourn the death of President Garfield in 1881. This lofty example of Greek Revival granite stood strong enough to stop the Great Fire of 1872 only to be pulled down for Peabody and Stearns' Exchange Building (below) of 1891 which housed a second grand interior hall, also lost.

Bound to the landscape of Boston, their smokestacks rising to the sky, the early industries of the city created large complexes for their time. The American Flint Glass Works on West Second Street in South Boston (above) rose phoenixlike from two disastrous fires in the early 1850s to produce a quality of glass unsurpassed elsewhere in the country. The Riverside Press (below), bought by Henry Houghton from Little, Brown in 1867, published books by the edge of the Charles River in Cambridgeport. No trace of either building remains.

Oak Hall — by some accounts America's largest clothing store — sold its wares within this wooden American Gothic concoction of 1840 (above right). A renovation of a still earlier structure, the inside may have resembled a medieval tomb, but this engraved view of the exterior on North Street has a cheerful air. The large blocks of granite used in the Union Bank (below right) predicted the coming of age of granite. The stone was destined to cover the rest of State Street and much of the city. Oak Hall went for a more up-to-date structure in 1898; the Union Bank vanished in 1925.

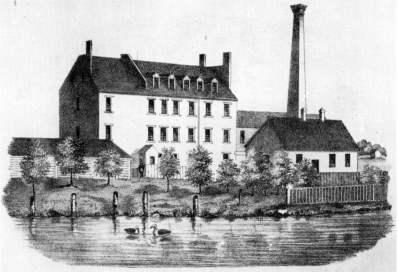

No fortresses ever looked more formidable than H. H. Richardson's Romanesque Ames Building of 1882 or the later castellated Boston Storage Warehouse by Chamberlain and Whidden on Westland at

Massachusetts Avenue. The Richardson
store at Kingston and Bedford streets
burned in the Thanksgiving Day Fire of
1889. The robust warehouse was smashed
down for a parking lot in 1955.

Small was beautiful, or, at any rate, endearing, in the diminutive buildings of old Boston that housed fledgling or specialized businesses. George Davis Dodd sat in his four-story brick and granite early-nineteenth-century store at 130 Milk Street where he plied the fur trade (above and below left). A grocery store on Warren Street in Roxbury (above) used its shop windows to display canned goods and the sidewalk to advertise cheap coffee and tea. The Massachusetts Whip and Saddlery Company's panel brick building on Portland Street (below) displayed harness and saddlery goods and an early tricycle. The fur store was torn down after its owner died in 1917; the grocery and saddlery stores went in urban renewal demolitions in the 1950s and 1960s.

Beneath pointed or rounded arches, Boston's business buildings stood in splendor on the streetscape. The marble Sears Building (left), a showstopper by architects Cummings and Sears in 1869, boasted Boston's first elevator. The Cathedral Building (above right) by Gridley J. F. Bryant replaced Bulfinch's Holy Cross Cathedral on Franklin Street. The Bell Telephone Building on Milk Street (below right), a Romanesque design of the 1880s by Carl Fehmer, had a ponderously handsome front. The Cathedral Building burned in the fire of 1872. The Sears and Telephone buildings were casualties of the twentieth century; the first was replaced by a high-rise office building in 1967, the second fell in 1972.

Palaces for the business enterprises of their day, commercial buildings of the 1870s and 1880s showed a pride of place. Downtown had the Castor Building at 517 Washington Street by the master architect H. H. Richardson (above) and the anonymous Boston Directory Building with its richly eclectic neighbors on Franklin Street (below) from 1874. In the Back Bay, the Romanesque S. S. Pierce Building by S. Edwin Tobey in 1887 (right) spoke of the attention to design in workaday architecture. All the buildings were flattened into oblivion: the Castor Building and Directory by the World War I era replacements of the White and Chamber of Commerce buildings, S. S. Pierce for a parking lot in 1958.

Boston shops display the period panache of
their early-twentieth-century remodelings
at 1 Park Street (above left) by architect
James Purdon, and two shoe stores, Clyde's
(below left) in 1929 at Summer Street on
the site of the start of the Great Fire of 1872
and Wilbar's (above) at 455 Washington
Street between Winter Street and Temple
Place. Not a trace remains of any of the up-
to-the-minute facades.

—CHAPTER 5—

Splendors by the Shovelful, 1800–1820

So much of this once elevated spot has been carried into the sea that the tops of the chimneys are not now so high, as the sod were over which in your youthful days, you strolled to enjoy the richness of the surrounding scenery. Should you again visit this place, you would look in vain for that commanding eminence, Beacon Hill, once the pride of Bostonians.

— SHUBAEL BELL

In Boston I found great progress in their new Buildings, & much ornament from the new style of their Brick Houses & Stores. I was assured upon the best authority that Boston never knew a time of so many buildings as at present. The value of real estate is increased greatly & increases constantly . . . Building never was more brisk in Boston than in the past year.

— WILLIAM BENTLEY, 1803

AMERICANS, the bold inscription on the east side of Bulfinch's beacon declared:

WHILE FROM THIS EMINENCE
SCENES OF LUXURIANT FERTILITY
OF FLOURISHING COMMERCE
AND THE ABODES OF SOCIAL HAPPINESS,
MEET YOUR VIEW,
FORGET NOT THOSE
WHO BY THEIR EXERTIONS
HAVE SECURED TO YOU
THESE BLESSINGS

"Luxuriant fertility . . . flourishing commerce . . . social happiness," the chiseled phrases barely suggest the growth to come to Beacon Hill and the city at its base. "Cutting Down the Hills to Fill the Coves," historian Walter Muir Whitehill has called this bold chapter in Boston's topographical history. These were the times and this was the way that builders, speculators, and developers sought to enlarge the compacted Bay Town. Allied for a generation, the architectural genius of Bulfinch, the boundless energy and tenacity of builder Uriah Cotting, the visual and financial astuteness of developer Harrison Gray Otis and others would reshape Boston's map. Funded by the merchant princes who ruled the sea and town, they would stake out new acres across the town and build on every compass point of land. Jutting fingers of fill and docks would poke farther off the tight-fisted peninsula. Firm soil would replace marsh, wood succumb to brick, and elegant architecture would sit atop former wastelands.

By the time Boston formally declared itself a city, barely one of the three hills of the old Trimountain would survive intact. In a frenzy of fill and building Bostonians would transform wetland and farmland, hill and cove into the foundations for its splendid buildings. Powered by the drive for space by artificial means, the city of 1822 would have a much-altered land mass to match its much-altered urban form of government.

The nineteenth century was not the first to shovel dry soil on wet. Bostonians had always tampered with the topography. Looking for more soil, the Puritans had sent the colonists great distances to farm and establish other towns where they could. A colonial order of 1697 allowed them still more room for growth by granting rights to all land up to the tide's ebb. "In all creeks, coves, and other places about and upon salt where the sea ebbs and flows, the proprietor of the land shall have proprietory rights to the low water mark." The law spelled out the so-called riparian rights. With

Overleaf:
Bulfinch's Colonnade Row of 1812, a "harmonious frame" for the Common on Tremont Street.

Harrison Gray Otis.

these rights, land-hungry builders could dig canal and deepen creek, could mount wharf and dock atop the sea itself.

Now, however, the grasp for fresh footage quickened and the shovels swung at quadruple time to make firm land from wet. Down came pieces of Copp's Hill and Beacon Hill to fill the North End's fifty-acre Mill Pond. Out came hunks of Mount Vernon to form Charles Street. Land came down to create nine acres at South Cove and to make the rugged coastline straight and proper for its ever stretching docks. The shovels flew and the wagons rolled and a few houses crept up the slopes, taking hold on Fort Hill and Mount Vernon as they had on Beacon. Still needing more space, the shovels flew again. Where else could 700 extra houses fit in the first decade of the new century? How else could the new affluent merchant display the profits of the sea? Developer Otis planned away; builder Cotting moved on many fronts; Bulfinch dreamed and drew; and the topographic fist of Shawmut bulged on every side.

For a time, the old landscape held its own. Boston's stunning site defined the look of the land and the designs of Bulfinch or the excavations and developments of Otis, Cotting, Jonathan Mason, Thomas Dawes, William Scollay, and others only added to the "prospect." On Fort Hill, high above the waterfront, the rich dwelt beneath their elms. The fashionable mansions were grazed by the summer breeze that swept east across the harbor, sprayed the shore and "caught up and mingled with its saltiness the spicy breath of the roses, honeysuckle and borders of box," as one hilldweller wrote. Nearby, stately houses rose on High and Pearl streets, gardens flourished and the clear and flowing wells slaked their owners' thirst. The West End no longer dozed round sleepy gardens, mansions, stables, and spreading trees. Yet the traffic to and from the new Charles River Bridge was no roar. Many a fine country seat still lent a rural air to the ample houses or hotels sprouting up by the modish Bowdoin Square. On all sides, the watery vistas, the looming hills, and the graceful countryside seemed beyond the power of mortal earth movers to reshape.

On Beacon Hill, it proved otherwise. Here Boston's builders showed their mastery of the land. They tamed the giant rise of old Shawmut, decapping the majestic elevation that had dominated Boston and the Trimountain for more than a century and a half. The hill they tackled was no hillock either. Even the town surveyor had never ventured to say just exactly how high Beacon Hill really rose, guessing at some 150 feet. Town boys who braved the wooden slide run from the Common — a harum-scarum trip that zoomed them toward the Charles River Bay — shunned Beacon Hill's steep ride. North Enders could picnic on middle-sized Copp's Hill and walkers might promenade atop Fort Hill. Builders even lined their slopes with houses. But there was no easy way to frolic on or gain access to Boston's most forbidding rise.

No matter: neither the pitch nor the Bulfinch column at the crest could save the historic summit now. "Patriotic exertions" be hanged! In 1811, the column honoring the Revolution shared the fate of the earth beneath its base. The soil went to supply the gravel to fill Mill Pond. The monument fell to ruin. It was a "unique and unrivaled ornament," the architect's granddaughter, Ellen Bulfinch, mourned. "But the times were hard, embargo and commercial restrictions had crushed the trade and dampened the spirits of the community," and most of all, she wrote, "the liberal and public-spirited individual through whose agency the monument had been erected had fallen a victim to the derangement of the times, and in the enterprise of Franklin Place, had made shipwreck of his fortunes."

Franklin Place had promised better. On an unmarked tract of Barrell's swampy lot, between today's Milk and Summer streets, Bulfinch had plotted two curves of row houses around a tiny park in an exquisite piece of urban design. In execution, the builders straightened one curve but the other retained its bend. The arched palace whose name lingers in today's Arch Street gave fine housing to the fashionable plus space for the Boston Library Society and the Massachusetts Historical Society. The civic-minded designer also gave to Benjamin Franklin the urn in the park's center and indeed donated the semioval park itself.

Franklin Place's name and appearance are unfamiliar now. Its architecture is lost; its contours are a mere curve in today's Franklin Street. But it was Bulfinch's — and, in a way, Boston's — first piece of urban architecture and it came at a crucial time. The development, sometimes called the Tontine Crescent, was a landmark in Boston's urban planning. Here, as much as anyplace, row-house Boston began; Boston of town house, park, and city palace became the ideal. More than that, the mesh of Franklin Place within a total neighborhood, both functionally and aesthetically, stood as the model for the town. As Bulfinch added the Federal Street Theater, Holy Cross Cathedral, market and nearby dock, the remarkable square became the center of an urban neighborhood. Hancock Row was earlier and Cotting's Cornhill development was similar in design dictates, but it was Franklin Place where the notion of the full block and the city-as-a-conscious-work-of-art became the Boston mode. Cushioned for the future with protective covenants to preserve the park "for the accommodation, convenience, and beauty of the houses of the square," and deeded against encroachment, Franklin Place and its

A tea party that took place inside the Tontine Crescent was the subject of this painting (*The Tea Party*) by Henry Sargent.

covenant became standards for the city and the squares to come.

The Tontine Crescent was a gift for the future, but it was a curse on the present. It plunged the architect and his family into a bankruptcy so deep that three years later friends still noticed Bulfinch's forlorn state. His wife wrote of the depths of their disaster in her diary:

Let me not be too anxious how these tender objects of my affection shall be cloth'd and fed, or repine that my infant should be born in poverty and myself with my Husband and other little ones now eating the bread of dependence.

Nonetheless, the same year of financial failure pushed Bulfinch further into the design of the State House. It ended the early work of Charles Bulfinch "gentleman" and began the career of Charles Bulfinch, public architect. Despairing, Bulfinch took on the post of chairman of selectmen and superintendent of police. "Although this performance was irksome and little suited to my taste or character," the architect wrote, "I undertook to discharge its duties, and it enabled me with my personal attention as Architect to support my family in respectable simplicity."

In accepting this informal post of chief of public works, Bulfinch took on the role of town planner before the phrase was known. Every street that opened, every sidewalk laid, marsh filled, road cobbled over, every new public and private building, every street light and wooden sewer line installed would now pass under the eyes of a servant of the public environment. A man to whom both personally and professionally no aspect of the built world was either trivial or irrelevant took command. True, Uriah Cotting joined in such labors; Cotting's energy and engineering skill had vast significance. His plan to harness the Back Bay's tidal waters for industry and build a western road in 1819 was a daring stroke with momentous impact for the future Back Bay. True, too, the loquacious eloquence of Harry Otis and the determination of countless developers moved Boston through its "milestones on the road of progress from country town to the Great City." Still, the urban eye of Charles Bulfinch oversaw the polishing of the old town in ways no scholar has observed.

Hardly a bowfront building, a classical motif from Pompeii or Herculaneum, a swag panel or recessed arch has been recorded without giving credit — sometimes due, sometimes not — to this architect. Every spiral staircase, oval dining chamber, vaulted ceiling, or iron grillwork in Boston's environs is said to be "by Bulfinch." And yet no one has really told the human story of the early period of town-building: how did the "neurotically self-effacing" architect who was

97

Charles Bulfinch; "the irrepressible social lion" who was Harrison Gray Otis; and the "indomitable" dynamo who was builder Uriah Cotting transform the town? How did they work together, this architect with his "purity of character" and his "temperate philosophic turn" and these profit-seeking developers with their instinct for the purse? Was Bulfinch more forceful than the architects of our day? Were Otis and Cotting more civic minded than the rapacious developers who succeeded them?

The personal story of their work together has few scribes but the visible saga of their most massive and permanent building project, Beacon Hill, is well recorded. Here the labors lasted longest and here many narrators chronicled the first streets that took form in the Hancock and Copley pastures. They drew views of the workmen who dug away at the back of Beacon Hill and told of the land gnawed away in endless dump-car loads.

The State House that Bulfinch was asked to build had indeed turned Boston's eyes to the area. The cornerstone laying on July 4, 1795, was a fit fanfare for the day, the State House, and the work still to come. A team of white horses heaved the cornerstone up the steep hill and Governor Sam Adams aided by Paul Revere, who would later supply almost four tons of copper and 789 pounds of nails for the dome, led the ceremony. It was an impressive launching of both the State House and the Hill. Historians Henry-Russell Hitchcock and William Seale create a vivid picture of the team of fifteen white beasts, one for each state of the union, pulling the massive cornerstone in a truck decorated with ribbons, with a colorful foot parade behind:

Prominent merchant walked beside former patriot; city man lined up with rural dignitary; and the bright feathers and cloaks of Indian chiefs flashed among the dark robes of judges. Governor Samuel Adams delivered an oration. Paul Revere, Grand Master of the Grand Lodge of Masons, conducted the ceremony. Far down the hill on the Common and way up to the memorial column, picnics were spread through hayfields, cows foraged along the fence of the Hancock mansion, armies of dogs and children played everywhere. The citizenry of Boston were celebrating the beginning of a new State House and the nineteenth anniversary of the Declaration of Independence.

Bulfinch's State House, modeled on Somerset House, England's great government building, would be the nation's popular symbol of statehood for more than 150 years. It would define Boston's landscape and create an enduring image of the city.

The Mount Vernon proprietors made the most of the new look of

Bulfinch's India Wharf.

Beacon Hill. While Bulfinch limned Boston's dome-softened skyline, they tended to a more earthbound task, naming the roadways of the Hill. For some streets they chose the names of patriots, for others trees. The awkward, if appropriately labeled, Mount Hoardom became Mount Vernon: "We are taking down Mt. Whoredom," the ebullient Otis wisecracked to a friend. "If in the future you visit it with less pleasure you will do so with more profit!"

Cleaning up the offending red-light district on the north slope of Beacon Hill was nothing compared to the developer's next task, however — taking off the crest of the hill. For this labor, a task like emptying a grain bin with a sugar spoon, the developers planned novel means: They devised a relay of carts descending the steep hill on rails. The wagons that slid along these tracks in the opening decade of the nineteenth century merit a claim as the first railroad in America. They were scarcely less astounding to the early onlookers than a moon launching, as historian Samuel Eliot Morison records:

A little railroad carried gravel from the condemned hilltop down across the future West Cedar Street to the river, where branches distributed the fill to make Charles Street. This primitive gravity railroad, on which the laden cars, attached to the empties by a cable running through a pulley on the hilltop, hoisted them back up, attracted such crowds of idlers and small boys that Otis humorously remarked that one would think it an engineering feat equivalent to Bonaparte's building a road across the Alps.

The host of buildings throughout the town — the rows on Park and Tremont streets, India and Central wharves, and the development of Brattle Street and Cornhill — seemed similar prodigies. "The great number of new and elegant buildings which have been erected in this Town within the last ten years, strike the eye with astonishment and prove the rapid manner in which the people had been acquiring wealth," a returning Boston Loyalist declared in 1808.

The wealth of the Seven Seas bought India Wharf, a grandiose four stories of brick arched like a castle. Central Wharf, a quarter mile long, and Cotting's mile-and-a-half western causeway and Mill Dam (Beacon Street) came from sea wealth. Yankee traders were swapping chisels for furs, furs for tea, and tea for money in a period "without parallel in the history of the commercial world," Henry Adams wrote. The Chinese called the foreign shipmasters moored in their ports "flowery-flag devils." Making their way to Oregon Country, Hawaii, the Far East, and back again; selling ice or Baldwin apples to those who had had no need of either before the Yankee ships appeared, the captains made trades as fantastic as the exotic seas

99

they sailed. Construction flowed from this affluence; so did the dedication to full speed at almost any price. At home, the enterprising Bostonians lacked neither drive nor cunning. They gave fill and took land. They gathered acreage in payment for the acreage they created, making new land in marsh and cove to build their docks, shape their squares, and line the Common's edge. Yet despite the boom in real estate, a notion of the public weal survived. Developers like Cotting defined "great improvement" as more than improvement to their private purse and, above all, the chief of selectmen ruled.

The commanding figure in an era when an address on Bulfinch-designed India Wharf was currency around the world and a Bulfinch mansion currency all over the town, Charles Bulfinch used his power well. "Over and over again," his biographer writes, "we come upon incidents which testify to the soundness of his mind, to his practical wisdom, and to his moral integrity, devotion to the common good being the dominant motif." Earlier selectmen had legislated a brick and stone city: none had a Bulfinch to enforce the rule. This time when a law declared that buildings over ten feet high must have four walls of masonry and a roof of slate or tile or similar noncombustible material there was Bulfinch the town architect, Bulfinch the chairman of selectmen, and Bulfinch the head of police to enforce the building code.

Bulfinch managed to coax his wealthy patrons to fund the promenade from Beacon Street to Charles, to gravel-over Boylston Street, and to spruce up the boundaries of Boston Common. He defined the Common's borders with rows of buildings, lining Tremont Street with Colonnade Row and filling the steep slope of Park Street with brick row houses. Such projects became the walls of a civilized city and a frame for the historic open space. It was no accident that the same year that saw Charles Street created for private developers also saw a fence finish off the western edge of the Boston Common; no coincidence that the crest of Fort Hill with its fine view was fitted out with Cotting's enclosure of Washington Place; or that Church Green was blessed with a new Bulfinch church to become a place finally worthy of its name.

Bulfinch could be sensitive to the work of former architects. He enlarged Faneuil Hall along the model of the past; nearly duplicated Dawes' Hollis Hall of 1763 with his Stoughton Hall; fitted University Hall into Harvard's eighteenth-century environment; added Peter Harrison's portico design to King's Chapel and a new steeple to Christ Church. He could still be innovative, refining his private design and making fine public plans. His square atop Beacon Hill blended his sense of grandeur with concern for the total neighborhood. Atten-

The *Flying Cloud*.

Church Green, at the juncture of Summer and Bedford streets near the harbor.

tion to the city's schools reflected the same care for the minds of the citizenry as his oval dining rooms did for the satisfaction of their luxury-loving bodies.

Bulfinch's own record of these years was self-effacing. His diary, a scant one thousand words, never noted tedious meeting after meeting where the chairman heard out the would-be scalpers and professed saviors of Shawmut and judged between them. Nor did it detail daily tasks: the badge to a chimney sweep, licenses to hacks, street paving, or the ruling that no cart or carriage should go faster than a walk. Bulfinch's term of office saw the town's first real police, board of health, municipal court, system of education, budget and tax collection. His own practice graced the area with court houses; McLean Asylum and Massachusetts General Hospital; Boylston Market; and a list of schoolhouses, banks, almshouses, insurance offices, and a prison. Where private building ended and public began never entered his designs for the town he loved and launched in countless undertakings. Like the Emperor Augustus who bragged that he found Rome in brick and left it in marble, Bulfinch might well have boasted that he found Boston's civic architecture in wood and left it in stone.

Was it any wonder that when President James Monroe swooped Bulfinch off to Washington in 1817, the architect uttered his classic misprophecy on the future of the town? So little was left to be done in the way of public building here, Bulfinch advised his sons, that "he hardly thought a young man could make a living as an architect."

The word *architect* certainly applied to few, perhaps a dozen, of Bulfinch's successors. Yet the simple dignity of his style eased the way for numerous housewrights to copy the Boston house. Soon, the word *Bulfinchian* began to describe much of the granite, brick, and iron-grilled architecture of the period. By the booming 1830s, Bulfinch's youthful collaborator Solomon Willard and other designers like Alexander Parris, Peter Banner, and Asher Benjamin would finally adopt the label to describe the work that established red brick Boston. For professional or for amateur, Bulfinch had set the mold.

Asher Benjamin, one of the finest of the former, showed his predecessor's influence. Benjamin had written *The Country Builder's Assistant* in 1797. A look at Bulfinch's emerging town showed in his second book. *The American Builder's Companion* broadcast the rudiments of Boston's shifting design fashion — the leaner, cleaner, refined Federal style of Bulfinch's Boston. Benjamin was architect of West Church, the Charles Street Meeting House and some homes on Beacon Hill, but the 30,000 or more copies of his books in circulation in the northeast a half-century later attest to his greater impact. Boston was Adams-inspired, Bulfinch-built, and Benjamin-expounded.

Independence and the rise of the Republic changed the fashions in all the arts and crafts. Paul Revere forsook his deft way with rococo. He adapted an Adamsesque purity for clients who now commissioned "stately urns, straight-spouted teapots, usually oval in shape" — the same shape as the ballrooms and spiral staircases in their houses. "A little dry, unimaginative, too pure," Esther Forbes, author of *Paul Revere and the World He Lived In,* called the post-Revolutionary mode. "The earlier [style] is more convivial, less concerned with its own respectability. One is suited more for the hand and the other for the sideboard."

A more affluent Boston had leisure for the sideboard style. The shops of Boston boasted Genevan velvet, Irish linen, and Prussian bonnets in vivid colors. Slumbering industries slowly roused themselves and manufacturers added still other goods for new needs — not the least of these the needs of architecture. Glass need no longer come from England; Medford alone made 14 million bricks a year; and the villages around Boston began to look to their waterfalls to supplement hand labor. At Waltham, the Boston Manufacturing Company introduced the first power loom to America in 1813. Mills soon turned out everything from wagons, shoes, and stoves to paper and wall hangings. Not just copper nails for the state's capitol came from the Revere works but the sheathing for her ships. Countless kilns cooked their own brick in a spectrum of reds: pale salmon, pinkish orange, or red burned to purple — a purple as black as the sides of the kiln itself. They gave Shawmut's buildings a roseate glow.

Federal Boston was no more a monochrome town in Bulfinch's day than in Revere's. Its buildings bore a rainbow of colors. Given his choice, Bulfinch might have opted for dressed stone in the London style or used more of the Chelmsford granite that pleased him so at Massachusetts General Hospital and University Hall. With meager Boston budgets, the architect had to paint brick or stucco to get a stonelike look and protect the porous surface. Yellow, not today's red, covered his State House and Park Street, by some accounts. The Tontine Crescent was gray, Long Wharf a pale white, and the Old State House ocher trimmed with white.

Returning natives spoke with awe of the burgeoning capital. Once less than three miles wide, Boston was now "united by bridge with Charles Town and Roxbury, together one Continued Street, of at least five miles," Elias Boudinot noted. The traveling diarist recorded two dozen places of worship plus

The Joy Building on Washington Street, destroyed in 1880.

State House, the Court House, Concert Hall, Faneuil Hall, Two
Theatres, Gaol, Alms House, Work House, Bridewell, Powder Maga-

*zine, The Athenaeum, The Museum, The Fish Market, Glass House,
and to crown all, the Exchange Hotel, a monstrous building containing 212 rooms . . . seven free Schools having about 900 scholars
. . . upwards of thirty benevolent, useful and Charitable Societies
. . . five Banks and Six Insurance Offices.*

"On the whole," Boudinot jotted in his log, "this is one of the most
flourishing Towns in the United States: The Inhabitants seem to have
established more of a National Character, than any other Town or
State in the Union."

Not every one of the inhabitants of Federal Boston agreed with
these superlatives. "From 1790 to 1820 there was not a book, a
speech, a conversation, or a thought in the state," one young man
said. Ralph Waldo Emerson wandered through these streets, looked
askance at a growth in matter but not mind, and expressed this literary and intellectual skepticism.

Getting and spending, politics and building, the adornment of self
and surroundings had left scant time for the higher arts. "Who reads
an American book?" The question of the day was more than just
rhetorical. Few in Boston did. True, Harvard was nearby and the
Boston Athenaeum, the Handel and Haydn Society, the *North
American Review,* and the Boston *Daily Advertiser* were founded in
the first quarter of the century. Timothy Dwight of Yale praised
Boston as a literary incubator where "knowledge [was] probably
more universally diffused than in any other considerable town in the
world." Still, theatergoing was infrequent, art a hit-or-miss affair.
"The arts except those that respect navigation do not receive much
encouragement here," a foreign visitor felt. "They think of the useful
before procuring to themselves the agreeable." Where the great
portraitist John Singleton Copley had labored long and fruitfully to
capture the elite of colonial Boston a generation before, Gilbert
Stuart found less work. His biographer records how he lolled away
the twilight hours of his career painting the pomaded sons of Yankee
traders, those comfortable but smug gentlefolk. Although Stuart's
study of John Adams pleased the world, the fading artist presented
Faneuil Hall with a portrait of "the most wooden horse since Troy,"
one critic wrote. Boston's untutored citizenry promptly took the
meager work to heart. For Stuart, painting the patrons of Bulfinch,
the Yankee merchant class, was a comedown in a town of diminish-
ing importance. Boston was a "cage," he felt. "A grocer will make
more by buying a cargo of molasses in a day than my labor can make
in a year," Stuart said. He refused to exhibit his pictures because they
had been so badly hung.

Who could guess that a young Emerson, Hawthorne, Longfellow, and a galaxy of New England reformers were pacing these streets? Despite the fierceness of local politics, government was centered in Washington and commerce churned faster in New York, which gradually overtook the town's supremacy at sea after the War of 1812. Even in cultural matters, Philadelphia surpassed the Bay enclave "for most of the comforts and some of the elegancies," Henry Adams testified. In short, the compass of power no longer pointed straight to Boston. Under conservative politicians Shawmut clung to the label *town* and had yet to mesh its new urban designs in an urban form of government.

Nor could the new brick buildings cloak the poverty of life for some. Boston was not Europe's "confined theater of cupidity," and a post-Revolutionary visitor "saw none of those livid ragged wretches that one sees in Europe, who solicit our compassion at the foot of the altar, seem to bear testimony against Providence our inhumanity and the order of society." Nonetheless, while Bulfinch was designing his mansions, the tax assessors found ninety-nine families living in single rooms. The architect himself languished in jail for debts in July 1811.

Despite such hard times, Bulfinch had shaped his vision: Colonial Boston boomed into a Federal town. "Let us conquer space," John Calhoun had told the country, and Boston had done that too. Its citizens had settled a vast acreage through the most heroic means. On the eve of municipal government, the town's building types reflected a more urban life. Consciously and unconsciously in two long and arduous centuries, the Bible Commonwealth had acquired a fluency in the most worthy art of city-building.

Maritime Bostonians liked to think of their town as a seagoing Athens, a crossroads on the transoceanic routes; but the period from peace to the cityhood of 1822 had also transformed the town into a kind of democratic Athens, and the coming age would transform it into still another Athens — the cultural Athens of Boston's greatest renown.

The new age dawned quietly. Too big to follow the village form of government, Boston changed from a town to a city government and installed the first mayor, John Phillips, with little stir in 1822. Two years later, though, the city staged the largest celebration in its history to greet an old friend. In August 1824, thousands turned out to welcome General Lafayette on his first trip to the post-Revolutionary city. Forty years had passed since that old friend of Independence had borrowed money from American merchants to buy shoes for his weary troops . . . thirty years since the victorious colonial town had lit the streetlamps to honor the handsome French benefactor. Now, the prosperous Federal city had another kind of glitter with which to celebrate his coming. A jubilee week was proclaimed.

Joyous Bostonians welcomed Lafayette as he came into town in a barouche chariot drawn by four white horses. "All noise that bells, cannon and human lungs were capable of producing" accompanied a festival of past and present with every length of ribbon and bunting twined around every building. Visitors from near and far crammed beneath a twenty-five-foot gold-lettered arch on the site of the old Liberty Tree stump. Church bells rang for more than three miles and 101 guns saluted in the air.

It was a festival of visual delights as well, the joys of its fresh architecture. It was Bulfinch's new Faneuil Hall in which Lafayette dined, Bulfinch's new Armory house in which he slept, and a refurbished Common enclosed by a new Colonnade Row by Bulfinch from which the aging Dolly Hancock (Scott) waved and Lafayette, "hand placed over his heart, made a graceful obeisance." A battalion of light infantry formed on Park Street mall and two governors donned their continental uniforms to flank Lafayette on the balcony before the crowd. Again it was the balcony of Bulfinch's superb State House on which they stood.

On Sunday morning Lafayette attended services at vintage Brattle Square Church, sat in Governor Hancock's old pew and dined with John Adams in the afternoon. Adams, now almost ninety, was not the vigorous witness of the patriotic era who saw "thirteen clocks strike as one" and Lafayette could not fail to record the changes as the hours wore on.

"That was not the John Adams I remember," the general commented sadly during the lengthening day.

"That was not the Lafayette I remember," Adams was later to recall.

The old days had given place to new. The Revolutionary capital wore only faded images from the heroic past. In their stead, a new landscape appeared. The Boston of the Revolution had become "the most perfect architectural city in the nation," some said, and no more beautiful concourse in the Republic could be found.

Shaping the City

Some cities grow within the bounds of their topography. Others push far beyond them. Boston simply tailor-made its town. As much as Venice or Amsterdam, Boston was a self-made city. In less than a century, the press of commerce and its posture as the Hub made the town of 789 acres more than triple its size. Shovelful by shovelful, Bostonians filled oozy salt marshes, tidal estuaries, and coves with the tops of its three hills. With great boldness, they carved into the existing landscape. Then they made their heroic maneuvers a constructive act of city-building through the creation of squares and enclaves, framing public spaces, and shaping elegant rows of private houses. The finished product was a work of art and health and pleasure. "Such breathing holes in our large cities are as necessary as auxiliaries to the public health and comfort, as they are orna-

mental to the localities where they are placed," Ballou's *Pictorial* put it in the mid-nineteenth century. Thus did the citizens soften the ruthlessness of any land grab. They patterned a humane and delightful environment that contrasted with the wind-swept plazas, faceless buildings, and helter-skelter development of their heirs.

Heroic Acts of Landscape

"Such persons would sell a family grave," an eighteenth-century Bostonian had complained when his fellow citizens first cut into the 150-foot Beacon Hill. In the fourteen years after 1810, the peak of Beacon Hill came down still more. Almost 60 feet filled some 50 acres of Mill Pond taking with it Charles Bulfinch's column.

The leftovers look raw as an apple core in this chromolithograph based on sketches by J. R. Smith (left). Bulfinch's column fell in 1811 and his State House itself changed greatly with the addition of several wings.

"A dreary waste of gravel flanked by bare foundations, a stump here and there of once noble elms, are all that is left of Fort Hill," a contemporary described the leveling of the harborside elevation around High and Oliver streets (above). "Sic Transit," he concluded. The twenty-acre, fifty-foot-high rise — the last major Boston hill to tumble in pursuit of solid footing and the only one to totally disappear — came down between 1866 and 1872. Its earth reclaimed land for Atlantic Avenue and the Town Cove and raised the soggy soil of the Church Street district.

House-moving was "one of the sights to stare at," the English chronicler Frances Trollope wrote in the 1830s. Dickens, too, told how he "met a dwelling coming down hill at a good trot!" Such was the movable state of the Hotel Pelham (above). Designed by Alfred Stone in 1857, it slid off its Boylston and Tremont streets corner for a street widening in 1869. Similarly, the soggy soil on Fayette Street at the corner of Church Street (below), today's Bay Village, was made firm by Fort Hill's gravel and the old buildings were raised to take advantage of the good grounding in 1868–1869. The hotel so painstakingly moved was flattened for the Little Building. Though most of the 200 brick buildings raised near Church Street survive, those shown here fell.

Like miniatures in proportion to this mammoth enterprise, Boston workers stand at Park Street Station on the superstructure that went to bury the trolley to build America's first subway from 1895 to 1897. The wrecker's ball has destroyed most of the buildings so painstakingly preserved.

Urban Squares and Enclaves

Bulfinch's oasis of greenery defined his enclave at Franklin Place and set the standards for Boston squares and row houses forever after. Known as the Tontine Crescent from 1794 (above), it held the Boston Library and Massachusetts Historical societies above the arch that lingers only in the name Arch Street. Commercial buildings by Gridley James Fox Bryant (below) rose on the spot following the demolition of Franklin Place in 1858. Bryant, too, adhered to the curve of the street, which remained after the Great Fire of 1872 took the buildings lining it.

Fanciful subway entrances lent an air of carnival to two of Boston's better-known squares. The buildings of Scollay Square (above right) formed a focus for urban life. The less shapely nexus at Adams Square with its statue of Samuel Adams (below right) still left a breathing place and meeting space amidst a packed island of urban life. Hardly a trace of either square endures in the vast acreage of City Hall Plaza and the office buildings of Government Center.

"A street which had one uniform cornice seen against the sky would be a most important advance towards a noble architecture," Le Corbusier declared in the twentieth century. Bulfinch felt it two centuries earlier and as chairman of the board of selectmen wrote the town ordinance for a uniform height and style, which he followed for his Park Street design of 1804 (left) leading to the State House. The unit shows how "wonderfully all of a kind" he made his work. The eight row houses were obliterated, one by one, with no sense for the whole or part.

A tranquil oasis of park would help transform row houses into islands of repose in the brick-walled city. Pemberton Square (above), designed for developer Patrick Tracy Jackson, later became the Boston Society of Architects' first home. The placid pool and fountain of the South End's one-and-a-half-acre Chester Square (below) were the creation of Ezra Lincoln, Jr., in 1850. The Suffolk County Court House obliterated a good portion of the Pemberton Square row houses in the 1880s and Massachusetts Avenue cut a ruthless swath through Chester Square in the early 1950s.

Boston's noblest high Victorian buildings ruled Post Office Square with pomp and circumstance. The square began when the fire of 1872 cleared a swath before architect Alfred B. Mullett's half-finished but gargantuan federal post office on Devonshire Street (left). In 1874 the splendid double edifice of the Mutual Life of New York, by Peabody and Stearns (left half of building), and the New England Mutual Life Insurance Company, by Nathaniel J. Bradlee, joined the post office on the Milk Street side of the square (above). Farther up Milk Street, the Equitable Building by Arthur Gilman (below), reflecting the post office in its windows, opened by the end of the year. Gilman's handsome Franco-Italianate structure was the first to fall in the early 1920s for a new First National Bank, which itself lasted less than half a century. The glorious post office gave way to an updated version a decade later and a parking garage replaced the insurance companies after their 1945 demolition.

The Seemly Row

The bowfront buildings (circa 1830) on Essex Street looking to Chauncy show how variety might enrich uniformity in the old South End that became one of the finest residential sections of the city. The bowfronts fell before advancing commerce.

Typical of "the sunny street that holds the sifted few," the handsome Beebe and Brewer houses at 29 and 30 Beacon Street rose on the lawn of the razed John Hancock House on Beacon Hill in 1864. The sumptuous Eastlake interior at number 30 belonged to the Beebes. Despite their well-defined French Second Empire exterior, splendid furnishings, and prominent inhabitants, the brownstone row houses were pulled down for the extension of the State House grounds in 1917.

Not an inch inside the brownstone was immune to the Victorian urge to adorn in the most ornate era in Boston architecture. Thomas Gold Appleton, painter, writer, aesthete, and wit, inhabited this elaborate house at 10 Commonwealth Avenue. From ceiling to soffit, cupboard to tablecloth, the same profusion of decoration covered the hall and dining room in the Back Bay mansion designed by Edwin A. P. Newcomb on the corner of Boylston and Dartmouth streets (right). The 10 Commonwealth Avenue residence fell and the site remained a vacant lot for seventeen years awaiting the sleek annex to the Ritz-Carlton Hotel. Newcomb's creation was flattened in the late 1950s for a soulless office building.

Two joined brownstones held the treasures of Boston's prime patron of the arts Isabella Stewart Gardner at 150 and 152 Beacon Street. The palm-filled chamber held the Vermeer, Van Dyke, and other treasures destined to go to her palace on the Fens. The windows of the entrance showed changing floral displays. The row houses gave way to a new white stone mansion in 1904 shortly after her move.

121

The graceful conformity of these Beacon Street houses scarcely suggests the life of elegance created by the wealthy merchant princes within, nor the curious and eccentric fireplace tucked behind the old facade of number 37½, a turn-of-the-century design by architect Richard King Longfellow. This building and its neighbor went in 1940 for an apartment house, leaving only about half of the post–Civil War view of Beacon Street shown here still standing.

Every decade pasted its own stamp on the face of the row houses parading west from Beacon Hill through the Back Bay. In the 1870s and 1880s, you could see the textured inches on the row houses at 47–48 Beacon Street by Richard Morris Hunt (above) or the panel brick details at 261 Clarendon Street where architects Cummings and Sears projected their chimneys like a parade of flags. At 270 and 274 Beacon Street (below), H. H. Richardson and McKim, Mead, and White brought a new look to the row-house world. Designed to blend together in a "gracious gesture of architectural correspondence," their brick and stone structures housed Boston Symphony Orchestra founder Henry Lee Higginson (the left-hand entryway) and his neighbor, C. A. Whittier. Hunt's Beacon Street compositions came down for the Eben Jordan mansion and a turn-of-the-century high-rise; the rest went in the 1920s.

Given the ironic label Crystal Palace, this
brickworkers' housing with its ten wooden
bays stood on Lincoln Street near the manufacturing district (left). In the 1870s,
Henry Ingersoll Bowdich and the Boston
Cooperative Building Company undertook
"efforts at humanizing the tenants" by
ventilating and repairing the structure. In
the mid-1880s, it fell for a business block.
The three-deckers on Dale Street, Roxbury
(above), a Boston innovation, opened up the
long rows of the city house to make airier
living places for streetcar suburbs like Dorchester and Roxbury. Though long scorned,
and here demolished, the three-decker filled
one third of the city with well-lit, nicely de-
tailed dwellings.

–CHAPTER 6–

Granite in Athens, 1820–1850

Boston commands special attention as the town which was appointed by the destiny of nations to lead the civilization of North America.
— RALPH WALDO EMERSON

It was as if man in America, around 1820, had rediscovered his five senses; had suddenly, like one breaking through from the forest to sun-drenched, sea-bordered towns, all at once become conscious of bright sun and distance and freedom . . . Never before or since, I believe, has there been a period when the general level of excellence was so high in American architecture, when the ideal was so constant and its various expressions so harmonious, when the towns and villages, large and small, had in them so much of unostentation, unity and loveliness as during the 40 years from 1820 to the Civil War.
— TALBOT HAMLIN, *Greek Revival Architecture*

THE CITY OF Boston, it was said, fit Plato's ideal of urban life: It was small enough to hear the voice of a single orator and, they might have added, harmonious enough to let a single architect stamp his style upon it. But the town named a city in 1822 would not retain this homogeneity. In the second quarter of the nineteenth century, Boston was no Elysium of the likeminded. Daniel Webster, Ralph Waldo Emerson, Horace Mann, Henry Wadsworth Longfellow, and Samuel Gridley Howe all lived among this growing population of 60,000. It was the age of Jackson and Longfellow, of Lowell and Thoreau, of Hawthorne and Agassiz. A mixed populace — from Irish immigrants too wretched to push on to city-builders knotted to the soil by choice. Boston would become known as Athens or the Hub from this time forth. In transit, is another way to describe Boston's flux from cityhood to the Civil War.

Not even a Bulfinch could have sculpted a single outlook in the 1830s and 1840s. Returning to Boston from Washington, the architect might as well have wandered upon the Peloponnesian peninsula; his Federalist work was old-fashioned in a time when would-be Athenians began to plant Parthenons across the land. For whatever reason, Bulfinch would design no more in the coming age of golden pens and granite temples.

The age of sail and steam, of industry and invention, of immigrant arrival and pluralist hegemony was at hand, bringing with it new sounds; the thrum of the loom, the creak of canal, the clatter of railway would soon be heard.

First came canal fever. The Middlesex Canal had rolled smoothly, silently into the waters of Boston Harbor in 1803. Twenty locks, dropping 107 feet, carried the waters of the Merrimac across the rolling countryside for twenty-eight miles. A single horse could drag the seventy-five-foot flat-bottomed boats at three miles an hour in nine to twelve hours on the course laid out by Loammi Baldwin. Though the powerful engineer who created and superintended the canal is better known for the apple he found, the waterworks Baldwin built were the finest in America until the Erie. This waterway had borne the granite from Chelmsford quarries to build Bulfinch's buildings.

The revolution in water transport was matched by the revolution in production. With the first complete factory system opened in Waltham in 1815, Boston financiers pooled their capital and harnessed the Merrimac at Lowell and Lawrence to weave cotton faster than Uriah Cotting could envision for his tidal mills. By 1830, water power ran 130 Massachusetts factories. The making of clocks, carriages, textiles, iron, glass, and hats began to attract the capital away from commerce to industry, from ocean trade to cotton production.

Overleaf:
A monument to the age of granite and the Greek Revival style, the 1836 Suffolk County Court House, designed by Solomon Willard, was pulled down in 1912 for another neoclassical building on Court Street — City Hall annex.

The old stone mill of the Walter Baker Company, Dorchester Lower Mills, 1849.

The century of Victoria truly began with this second generation. The children of the Revolution had grown to lead a new order and everywhere they felt the "fresh and more vigorous spirit" of the New England renaissance described by Van Wyck Brooks:

On the granite ledges of New Hampshire, along the Merrimac River, in Essex and Middlesex counties, where the spindles whirred on westward, in the lovely Housatonic, life was filled with a kind of electric excitement. The air resounded with the saw and hammer, the blows of the forge, the bells in the factory towers. In all directions, the people were building turnpikes, hundreds of miles of straight lines that cut athwart the old winding roads . . . Dwellings were going up in clearings and meadows, or, being up, were carted boldly off to better sites. Churches grew like snowdrops in early March. Villages, towns, sprang from the field. A current of ambition had galvanized New England.

Henry Adams put it more catastrophically in his *Education:* "The old universe was thrown into the ash-heap and a new one created." The eighteenth and nineteenth centuries were suddenly "cut apart, separated forever," he wrote, "in deed if not in sentiment," with the opening of the Boston and Albany Railroad, the appearance of the first Cunard steamers in the bay, and the telegraphic messages that carried from Baltimore to Washington the news that Henry Clay and James K. Polk were nominated for president.

For a clear sighting of the new scale of the age in transportation, communication, and mobility, a Bostonian needed to look no further than neighboring Bunker Hill in Charlestown. On the landmark crest, Bostonians were building the era's most conspicuous signpost. Like Bulfinch's column for Beacon Hill, the Bunker Hill Monument attested to the new era while memorializing the fiftieth anniversary of the old. It was a sky-high show of Boston's strengths and weaknesses. Exuberance was written in the public will to spend eighteen years dragging 6600 tons of stone "quarried and hewn to size and shape in the wild craggies" of John Adams's Quincy, to cart it first by rail then by boat to the battle site and hoist it 221 feet high.

Few noted that all this awesome gravity-defying labor went into an odd aesthetic image — a likeness of the autocratic Pharaohs in the age of the Republic. "As substantial as the great pyramids of Egypt," Edward Everett exulted. Only the Egyptian edifices were higher, observed a guidebook of the time. The Bunker Hill Monument was not only antique; it was prophetic. In its engineering, the obelisk joined science and design with the parent of today's railroad, fashioned to carry its stones. This blend of down-to-earth inventiveness and peacock pride made the Bunker Hill Monument an emblem of the Victorian century.

Even the monument's creators were fit symbols of the age. In the days following the Revolution, the aristocratic Governor John Hancock brought about the Middlesex Canal. Now it was a self-taught country boy named Gridley Bryant who launched the extravagant enterprise. Bryant, the mason, conceived the rails for the sliding incline and coaxed five businessmen — who "thought the project visionary, and chimerical" — to fund them for $50,000. He devised its switch, swiveling cars, portable derrick, turntable, and other "contrivances." In 1826, the Granite Railway began to trundle the eight-ton blocks from the Quincy quarries down the steep incline to the Neponset River for the trip from Milton to the Charlestown work. Nine years later, the railroad as we know it was born. Soon, train routes went to Lowell, Providence, and Worcester. Proceeding at 12 miles a year, 111 miles of track were opened by 1835. In less than a decade, seven more lines came to Boston. The age of railroads was at hand.

So, too, Bunker Hill's designer, Solomon Willard — farmboy, carver, artisan — bore little kinship to the aristocratic Bulfinch who had designed the monument for Beacon Hill. "Omit the esquire from my name," Willard demurred, "I have no claim to such distinction." Though stout and slow with a lethargic walk that never broke into a run, Willard was restlessly inventive. A skilled carpenter, he apprenticed to Peter Banner, architect of the Park Street Church, carved figureheads and progressed to designing a hot-air furnace for Washington's White House and capitol. His interior for Asher Benjamin's 1808 Exchange Coffeehouse, a seven-story structure with a 110-foot dome and glazed skylight, multilevel rooms, dining area, and grand spiral staircase of Piranesi dimensions, gave him insights into the complex geometries needed for Bunker Hill.

"Boston would be changed from Brick to Stone as it was from Wood to Brick," financier Thomas Handasyd Perkins had hoped. So it was. Quitting the design profession to take charge of his quarrymen at the Bunker Hill Quarry in Quincy, Willard experimented and devised the machinery to handle his beloved granite; he cut costs by three-fourths and increased the size of the granite block. By doing so, the daring architect made monolithic blocks of granite the standard for public building in Boston — monumental, severe, and permanent. Bunker Hill's showpiece of granite inspired monuments in Concord, Charlestown, and Boston's Old Granary Burying Ground. The thirty or forty new blocks of stores and buildings that ran along Washington, Milk, Pearl and Franklin streets, and the wharves

The Boston Granite Style on Commercial Street opposite Quincy Market. This building by Bryant was leveled in 1970.

Mayor Josiah Quincy, in a portrait by Gilbert Stuart, in front of the Faneuil Hall marketplace, which he developed.

and warehouses that rose in the two generations of its vogue were bold, cheap, and serviceable: a fit testimony to Willard's art and industry.

They also attest to the city's vigor. Boston was booming in the decade after cityhood, greedy for good architecture and inventive in building types — hotels, warehouses, wharves, factories, railroads, charitable institutions, schools, and drydocks. The structures built by Loammi Baldwin's son at the Charlestown navy yard won this second generation engineer the label "father of civil engineering."

Bostonians entered a new time in engineering and architecture. Better able to cut, hoist and haul stones; in need of bigger spaces, and more adept at spanning them, they broached the early technological age. A contemporary labeled the post and lintel constructions "the Boston style." It was "the first idiomatic expression of American commerce," scholars contend.

What better than granite for the biggest development in Boston after Bulfinch, then? In 1825, Mayor Josiah Quincy ordered architect Alexander Parris to design a building of European polish to replace the worn and crowded wharves. The city's and perhaps America's most striking urban development, the project lapped over the waterfront at Faneuil Hall's edge, covering seven acres with three markets — Quincy Market to the center, North and South markets to either side. The central structure was a granite megabuilding; its two flanking buildings faced with granite blocks.

The new stone fit or bred a new style, too. While the Quincy quarries supplied the material, Parris, Bulfinch's heir, provided the style to make it "art." With Saint Paul's Church on Tremont Street, Parris had imposed the architecture of classical Greece on the colonial and Federal landscape. Popularized by the poet Byron and the Greek Revolution, the Greek Revival style stemmed from a region not unlike New England's own — "iron bound, sterile and free," Edward Everett would orate. Its architecture was translated into English fashion through the archaeological researches on Greece's ancient soil. Brought here in the book *Antiquities of Athens,* the fashion let many a Boston builder, housewright, mason, or carpenter adopt the title architect, and copy the bookish style to match.

The stately crown of the Greek Revival pediment, the repeatable grace of its colonnade, and the symmetry behind the noble portico appealed to designers. Parris, Benjamin, Isaiah Rogers, Ammi Young, and other professional architects created churches, markets, and houses in the mode. And if Parris's market was more Grecian *tube* than temple, it had its Attic dome and pedimented porticoes on either end. The Greek Revival style added the weight of the ancients to

131

the decrees of the judges housed within Solomon Willard's handsome Suffolk County Court House or gave a ponderous blessing to the clink of coins in his U.S. Bank on State Street. It stamped an aristocratic look on the interior of Moses Kimball's Boston Museum on Tremont Street by Hammatt Billings; gave substance to Isaiah Rogers' luxury hotel, the Tremont House, and bestowed an antique lineage on everything from the reservoir atop Beacon Hill to the brick houses on Summer Street. When alterations were made to the Old State House, they too were in the Grecian mode — "like plastering and painting a matron very far in years," a contemporary groused.

By, or even before, 1850 the style became a bit passé. Sandstone, brownstone, and Roxbury puddingstone joined granite. Gothic outflanked Greek in many new churches and when Ammi Young finished his enormous Custom House, winging wide at the water side at State and India near Long Wharf, it was the last gasp of grandiloquence in granite. The Custom House was begun in 1837 at the height of the granite age; its final completion ten years later came in a period when critics sniffed at the old style. Its columns were "shadowy obstructions," one observer declared. "Correct delineation" had become a bore and Young moved on to other forms in other towns as architect for the federal government. Nonetheless, in its time, Greek Revival granite was the proper mode for commerce and urban grandeur in an aspiring city.

The Custom House without its tower.

Of all the city's grand edifices, Bunker Hill Monument still stirred most civic pride. Patriotic in intent, lofty in outlook and arduous to execute, it drew the most celebration. Again, the city staged a mammoth gathering for the monument's dedication in 1843. "Such crowds of people as lined the streets and filled the city have rarely been seen in Boston," a visitor exclaimed. Flags fluttered above the thousands who crowded up to the crest of the hill. Wagons and carriages and private and public stages rattled onlookers in from all New England. Less than two decades earlier, New Yorkers would have had to sail or travel on land for five days to see Lafayette lay the monument's cornerstone. Now the trip on iron horse took just one day. "Hurry on!" Manhattan newspapers had urged out-of-towners to visit the shrine made famous round the world. Patriotism and happy prospects allied to launch this brave age of technology and growth. President Tyler and his cabinet filed on to the grounds and Daniel Webster commanded the rostrum. Bostonians basked in the "thrilling eloquence" of Webster's oration, exulted in the rippling, rising, cascading words; the phrases so in tune with the times that they "fell in Doric beauty from the speaker's lips."

When honored and decrepid age shall lean against the base of this Monument and troops of ingenuous youth shall be gathered round it, and when one shall speak to the other of its objects, the purposes of its construction, and the great and glorious events with which it is connected — there shall rise, from every youthful breast, the ejaculation — "thank God, I — I also — AM AN AMERICAN."

"There was the monument, and there was Webster," Ralph Waldo Emerson declared. To Emerson, the architectural landmark and the human one had equal weight. For the landscape displayed more than looming shafts; it boasted intellects more elevated than any obelisk. While planners spoke of the "distinct chapter in Boston architecture," the literature of Emerson, Thoreau, and their Concord peers, of the Boston writers and the Cambridge thinkers were chapters of another sort.

The familiar pantheon of Boston writers emerged in this Athenian hour: Hawthorne, melancholic recluse, clocking his hours at the old Custom House, tromping along "the steaming docks amid the coal dust"; Henry Wadsworth Longfellow strolling across the bridge from Cambridge to sup at the Parker House; James Russell Lowell in from the village off Harvard Square to edit the young *Atlantic Monthly;* Harriet Beecher Stowe writing the book ready to rival the Bible in popularity; Louisa May Alcott with her *Little Women,* and William Hinckling Prescott, the American Thucydides, both housed on Beacon Hill; Oliver Wendell Holmes; James Greenleaf Whittier; and William Dean Howells, so many pens flowing in time or out of sync with the creative energies of the ante-bellum town.

A galaxy of reformers paced Boston's streets. Literary Parnassus it might be, but Boston was no cloudless olive grove. In his dim and tiny room off today's Post Office Square, William Lloyd Garrison, elbow-deep in printer's ink, was the conscience of the abolitionists. And he was not alone. In the 1830s, Boston was a crusader's den, the reformist spirit joining with the literary one to condemn social injustice. The jaundiced eye of Whittier looked beyond Boston's booming landscape:

> Behind the squaw's light birch canoe,
> The steamer rocks and raves
> And city lots are staked for sale
> Above old Indian graves.

Henry David Thoreau deplored the mercantile bustle. What need for spilling and filling across the whole huge city, the naturalist declared, only to lose the earthly roots of life in narrow materialism.

"I intend to build me a house which will surpass any on the main street in Concord in grandeur and luxury, as soon as it pleases me as much and will cost no more than my present one." For $8.03, the author of *Walden* did just that.

Grandeur? Urban luxury? Thoreau's idea of luxury, a skeptic wrote, was to stand up to his chin in a retired swamp and be saturated with its summer juices. In Thoreau's and other Transcendentalists' views, city life was a "menacing artifact." The intellectual waged war against the city, twentieth-century historians would insist, and the antiurban attitude of Boston's literary elite bears this out. Edgar Allan Poe, born on Carver Street in 1809 in the modest quarters of today's Bay Village, scoffed at his native Boston. "Frogpondium" was his expression. Emerson suffered the city, but not gladly, in these words:

Solitude and the country, books and openness, will feed you, but go into the city — I am afraid there is no morning in Chestnut Street, it is full of rememberers, they shun each other's eyes, they are all wrinkled with memory of the tricks they have played, or mean to play, each other.

The seers of the New England Renaissance hankered for the untainted, pastoral life yet they voiced an environmental awareness too; for they had, as humanist Lewis Mumford observed, a deep sense of landscape and its influence upon the human race. Tinker with the environment and you could create a new race, they believed. Their notion of the impact of the environment created a "New England formula" of another sort.

"Each town should have a park, or rather a primitive forest of five hundred or a thousand acres, where a stick should never be cut for fuel, a common possession forever, for instruction and recreation," Thoreau wrote. He was not alone in preaching on the power of surroundings. Other bookish visionaries sought to perfect the human landscape in model communities. At Brook Farm, the Transcendentalists attempted to frame a workaday Utopia. A scant ten miles from Boston in today's West Roxbury, ink-stained hands became earth-caked in the building of a Promised Land. Here, Nathaniel Hawthorne, feminist Margaret Fuller, and preacher and philosopher Bronson Alcott, Louisa May Alcott's father, thought it their duty "to play chambermaid to a cow," walking to town to drink in the symphonies and returning the long miles home at night. "Elated and unconscious of fatigue," as one Brook Farmer recollected, "carrying home with them a new genius, beautiful and strong to help them with their labors." Gallant attacks on manure and stimulating visits

Brook Farm's remains.

from Emerson notwithstanding, the idealists lasted a mere eight years on the fringes of Boston. "Our Labor is the curse of the world," a disillusioned Hawthorne wrote. But Brook Farm survived — survives today — nonetheless, in Hawthorne's *Blithedale Romance* and in the influence of its ideals.

Likewise, Bronson Alcott founded an experimental environment in a dilapidated farmhouse with "a few cankered apple trees and a bit of woodland" forty miles out of town. In Harvard, Massachusetts, not too far from where the Shakers had made clean-sweeping brooms and functional furniture part of their code, he launched Fruitlands in 1843. Here, for a too brief year, Alcott shed city clothes and city beef, eggs, and milk. "To purloin milk from the udder was to injure the maternal instincts of the cow," he said. He pledged to practice farming and vegetarianism and wear no goods save those made by free men.

If all such visionary enclaves seemed short-lived, silly, and too spartan for the denizens of red-brick Boston, their belief in environmental wholeness has aged well. The intimacy of life and labor, mind and body, had a completeness not unlike existence in the walking city where work and life still went on relatedly.

In Boston, a citizen could walk the clichéd Athens and see that fit; could stop at 13 West Street, just off the Common, where Elizabeth Peabody, once disciple to Alcott's Masonic Temple school, began the *Dial* in her small bookshop, or hear Margaret Fuller give her Conversations. "Hospital for Incurables," a cynic sniffed. That was a minority report. A midcentury Bostonian could also visit West Street, the realm of the literary establishment, and pass by the head of Park Street to see its throne. There, in Bulfinch's Amory-Ticknor House, with the largest private library in America and a view of Boston Common through his western window, publisher George Ticknor presided from his parlor. The engraved plate of Ticknor and Fields on his volumes of *Boston Authors* heralded Bulfinch's row house across the world.

It was a close world, but a cosmopolitan one whose axis stretched from Cambridge, where book lovers might chat with John Bartlett compiling his *Familiar Quotations* at his bookstore, to Boston and the Old Corner Book Store where Ticknor's younger partner James T. Fields reigned. Literary impresario and tastemaker, Fields sat in his green-curtained corner, courting writers and readers, then walking home to Charles Street where his wife Annie Fields's soirées attracted the luminaries of nineteenth-century intellectual life: "The exchange of wit, the Rialto of current good things, the hub of the Hub," George William Curtis called it in *Harper's* "Easy Chair." "All I claim for

James Fields's library, "the votive temple to memory," fell in an early-twentieth-century widening of Charles Street.

Boston is that it is the thinking centre of the continent, and there-
fore, of the planet," Oliver Wendell Holmes blithely opined. Thackeray visited here and so did Dickens.

Dickens was first greeted by the citizenry on his tour in 1842.
Lodged in the Tremont House, escorted through the North End,
conducted to the social reform institutions of the day, and driven from
the glorious new cemetery at Mt. Auburn to "the Manchester of
America" in the factories at Lowell, Dickens was dazzled by the
young city in the New World and wrote of it in his *American Notes:*

*The air was so clear, the houses so bright and gay . . . the bricks
were so very red, the stone was so very white, the blinds and area
railings were so very green, the knobs and plates upon the street
doors so marvelously bright and twinkling . . . The city is a beautiful one, and cannot fail, I should imagine, to impress all strangers
very favorably. The private dwelling-houses are, for the most part,
large and elegant; the shops are extremely good; the public buildings
handsome.*

Once the saying went that young Bostonians manned half the
American merchant marine, now the literary generation bred by
the Boston that greeted Dickens so uproariously would staff half
the schools across the continent. "My father used to point to his
veins and say, 'There is nothing in these veins but the blood of ships-
masters and schoolteachers,' " the New England–bred twentieth-
century novelist John Cheever would one day recall. Transplanted
New England schoolteachers, zealots, and missionaries of many sects
founded colleges and religious and reform institutions across America. From the Hub went the preachers, the schoolteachers, and the
humanitarians, bearing with them the visual image of the New
England house and common and its Greek Revival architecture.

At the Hub itself, novel buildings arose to serve the causes of the
hour. The Suffolk County Jail and Deer Island House of Correction
manifested the reform spirit. The Boston schools showed the impact
of Horace Mann, father of universal education, while the labors
of Samuel Gridley Howe, a reformer of conditions for the blind,
were embodied in the creation of the Perkins Institution and Massachusetts Asylum for the Blind. "Circulation, motion and boiling
agitation," a critic labeled the intellectual environment where movement gave birth to movement — Unitarianism, Transcendentalism,
abolitionism, feminism; overlapping, contradicting, cannibalizing, all
at once, until, exhausted from the onslaught, another witness breathed
deep and labeled it all "the Newness." Bronson Alcott summed the
moral superiority felt by many in these words:

There is a city in our world upon which the light of the sun of righteousness has risen. It is Boston. The inhabitant of Boston is more pure than that of any other city in America.

Buildings rose to serve cultural as well as charitable needs. The Boston Athenaeum, the city's private library and art gallery, quartered here and there for years, held an architectural competition; Edward Clarke Cabot won the right to design the venturesome building still in use near the State House at 10½ Beacon Street. The Boston Public Library, once lodged in rooms on secluded Mason Street, occupied a new Italian Renaissance building on the south side of the Common before the Civil War. The Boston Art Club, begun in Washington Allston's day, now drew twenty-six artists from scattered dwellings around Washington Street and Tremont Row to its own studio; architects and artists like William Morris Hunt and sculptor William Rimmer shared the light-strewn space designed by George F. Snell on Tremont Street. Nearby, old and new structures held the burgeoning publishing business; William S. Pendleton founded the first lithographic press in Boston in 1825 and tooled it into a solid enterprise. All told, some twelve periodicals rolled out of the presses in the Milk Street neighborhood.

From time to time the pages of these ante-bellum periodicals discussed the environment they inhabited. Polemicists and popularizers criticized both the architecture and its surroundings, first in Bowen's *Boston Newsletter,* later in *Gleason's Pictorial.* Boston magazines like the *Dial* or *North American Review* advanced the latest ideas on architecture, finally debunking the Greek Revival and giving a foretaste of the Gothic. Architect Arthur Gilman wrote important critical articles on the coming eclecticism and Victorian design won its initial applause in Boston with his words. Gilman's Lowell Institute lectures on architecture stressed integrating buildings with their surroundings: How to site the Italian Renaissance palazzo in the streetscape mattered as much as its "pure design."

The phrase "form follows function" was first uttered in Boston by a brilliant sculptor-critic in the city's midst. The sculptor Horatio Greenough put it poetically:

The mechanics of the United States have already out-stripped the artist and have, by their bold and unflinching adaptation, entered the true track and hold up the light for all who operate for American wants, be what they will. By Beauty, I mean the promise of function. By action, I mean the presence of function. By character, I mean the record of function.

The son of a builder of Colonnade Row and a sometime student of
both Solomon Willard and Washington Allston, Greenough favored
a romantic functionalism. With Emerson, he hungered to see the life
of the mind joined with the work of the hand; like Jefferson, he
welcomed science and "the great multitude" of democracy. Often his
architectural criticism surpassed his art. Seeking originality,
Greenough found it in the clipper ship — a swift-lined manifestation of the maritime art that was itself perfected here now by a
Boston genius of another sort: Donald McKay.

In his East Boston shipyard, McKay drafted and sculpted the
decade's embodiments of Greenough's dream. Hall and Jackson,
Curtis, Uwell, Kelly shared in McKay's creation of the clipper ships,
the greyhounds of the age of sail. In shipyards across Boston their
names were synonymous with the magnificent ships brought to their
practical and aesthetic peak for the China-California trade.

Boston shared in practical commerce and invention too. Who can
say when or where or with whom Yankee invention began. With
the early toolmaker, the creator of the patent for the lightning rod,
the unknown inventor of the leather-splitting machine, or those who
pioneered in manufacturing gas or steam heat in the 1840s? The
water closets and running water bathrooms of Isaiah Rogers's
Tremont House were the wonder of the age; the layout of its corridors
and ample public rooms made it "the father of the modern hotel"
in the most traveling nation in the world. Ether was first used as an
anesthetic at the Massachusetts General Hospital in 1846 (later, a
monument was raised on the Public Garden to honor the occasion).
Asa Gray, the botanist who acquired the plant knowledge to serve
the Arnold Arboretum, and Louis Agassiz, who taught the geology
and zoology essential for the coming generations of landscape architects, taught at Harvard during this time. The very word *technology*
came from a Harvard man.

Steamboats, clocks, lamps, machines that could card wool or cut
nails began to emerge across the continent and the dynamic city laid
claim to countless manufacturing firsts: Mason and Hamlin reed
organs and pianos by Jonas Chickering; sewing machines invented
by Elias Howe, Jr., and produced by I. M. Singer; watches in
Waltham; the first tin cans. Unsung Bostonians crafted circular saws
and pegging machines needed for industry; well-known capitalists
financed and launched the factory system that brought the industrial
revolution to the surrounding landscape in Waltham, then harnessed
the waters of the Merrimac to turn raw cotton into textiles in the vast
mills at Lowell. The mill complex at Lowell, where "factory girls"
wove cloth and fabricated many a poem, delighted reformers round

Donald McKay.

View of Water Celebration on Boston
Common in 1848.

138

the world and looked likely to change the old order of factory life.

Some still credit the age of urban enlightenment to just one man. That man was Josiah Quincy, the charismatic and voluble second mayor who led the town of Bulfinch into its city framework. If Boston was to survive as the seat of the arts and literature, the center of capital, the terminus for railroads, the maritime and manufacturing center, it needed a Mayor Quincy to oversee the makings of an urban nexus served by better public works.

Even before his days as the city's chief, Quincy had headed the committee to build the House of Industry and House of Correction in South Boston. Now he would follow Bulfinch and Cotting to help Boston change "from a straggling provincial town into a metropolis," as city historian Samuel Drake recorded. Besides the market project bearing his name, the civic-minded mayor organized the first real fire department, improved and planted the Charles and Park Street malls, bought the land that would hold the Public Garden, and cultivated the park space on Fort Hill. While the Transcendentalists communed with their deity, the zealous mayor faced a host of earthy questions: Who would sweep the streets of the New England Renaissance? Josiah Quincy asked, noting later how the issue bothered him:

What was house dirt and what was street dirt and whether yard dirt belonged to either and to which there began to be questions of solemn and dividing import. No subject has been pressed upon the mayor with more earnestness.

If the Faneuil Hall Marketplace was Josiah Quincy's most visible monument, internal improvements were equally portentous in city planning terms. In little more than the first ten years of cityhood, 50,000 feet of common sewers were laid and more than 100 lamps and fixtures lit by gas. The dynamic mayor planned a network to carry the waters of Lake Cochituate through a fifteen-mile brick aqueduct to the Brookline Reservoir where long lengths of pipe brought them the last five miles to Boston. By 1848, its clear waters flowed into a fountain in Boston Common. The administration of a second Josiah Quincy, a son as active as the father, celebrated the event with parades and rockets and a two-day school holiday. The population that almost doubled between their regimes could not have survived without this enterprise.

With the smallest land mass of any major city, Boston again responded to its mounting numbers by habit and necessity, building bridges to reach Charlestown or South Boston, cutting and transporting soil to marsh, hill to cove. In 1830, by Boston's second centennial, the old peninsula was a centipede of wharves and bridges. Boston's

East view of Faneuil Hall marketplace.

citizens had joined Commercial Street to the north and Rowe's Wharf to the south with India and Broad, creeping to the sea, filling in the irregularly fingered shore. In the decades that followed still more made land joined terra firma for yet another cause — for the railroads that began to squeeze for space.

In other cities across America, the iron horses had preempted the best land sites; in Boston, naturally enough, they overlapped the sea. Trains rolled-in more dirt from Brighton, and the old Cove became terminus and yard for the Boston and Worcester Railroad. South-bound trains sat in the South Cove (today's Chinatown); northbound trains lodged around Causeway Street and Haymarket Square near where John Winthrop had first put foot to shore.

Still short of soil, the land-grabbers made their most dramatic assault since slicing off the top of Beacon Hill: Pemberton Hill, the final peak of the Trimountain, was carted down to its salty northern grave. The bucolic grounds that had once held the house of Gardiner Greene fell in the service of fill for the railroads and Patrick Tracy Jackson's urge to develop Pemberton Square. Down came the handsome mansion. The city's most spectacular garden bloomed no more. Its ginkgo tree was transplanted to the Common; its sod — 100,000 cubic yards — was sold for gravel by the yard and carried on the very back (or so it seemed) of another imposing figure: the farmer Asa Sheldon. Asa G. Sheldon of Wilmington carried the gravel with his yoke of oxen and his drivers, with his measuring tool and work crews. Sheldon's New England cunning was the engine. But the muscle that powered Asa Sheldon's enterprise — and the very building of Boston — was the willing brawn of his Irish shovelers.

Coming now in their "coffin ships," driven first by hard times and then by the Great Hunger of 1846, the Irish came to Boston. In years past, some Irish laborers had dug the Parker Hill quarry for Cotting's Mill Dam; now the Gaelic labor force would come en masse to help the Yankees dig their canals and lay their rails; to halve their hills and build their city. The newcomers poured down Long Wharf to provide the human power that constructed Boston's landscape.

What native Bostonians called the "Celtic locust swarm" landed slowly at first, tenanting the old slopes and seaside neighborhoods near where they landed, crowding the old North End with more workers' housing, filling the South End from Broad Street to Fort Hill, settling the outskirts of the Neck and South Boston or finding homes near the East Boston shipyards. Here Patrick Kennedy, great-grandfather of a president, shared lodging with his compatriots in cheap boarding houses. The coming of the Kennedys and their countrymen compacted an already dense city.

With land now too precious for gardens, houses filled in Beacon Hill, and tucked into the splendid old South End near Summer, Pearl and High streets and atop Fort Hill. The speculative spirit and the immigrant slums further crowded out the old mansion-house way. Row house was slotted between mansion house. Vegetable patch was raked over, pear trees uprooted, and, soon, detached estates became attached row houses. A solid wall of masonry covered many streets. The lovely architectural pearls that Bulfinch had spilled onto the green lawns of Beacon Hill and the old West End were strung together now, pearl to pearl, a chain of housing. Knock down one house, put up three and a Boston row house was joined.

Not everyone greeted this growth of the 1830s and 1840s with glee. Bulfinch himself looked worriedly at the trampling on old sod. Instead of open-armed hospitality old-timers complained there was a cramping. Why, Thomas Perkins had to *pay* his very neighbors just to keep his view of Boston Common! The squeeze was on in Copley's peaceful upland pasture. Divide and sell. John Joy and John Nutting had employed as many as fifty artisans on Beacon Hill in Bulfinch's Boston, but who could tally up the number hammering houses into the spaces in between these days.

Now as before, the Common endured, encased in its own gothic iron fence of 1836. Other "squares" also began to sprout in mimicry

Otis Place row house.

of Bulfinch's designs. The land fronting City Hall was well-land-scaped and decorated; the space before West Church was fashioned and named Lowell Square in 1852. Modest plots dotted Maverick, Central, and Belmont squares in East Boston and Telegraph Hill and Independence Square in South Boston. Squares in the adjacent towns of Dorchester, Roxbury, and Charlestown added to the total. Concerned for both tomorrow and today, the city funded the Committee on Common and Public Squares for their upkeep.

In two instances, developers imitated Bulfinch exactly to frame open space into their housing designs from the start. Despite the "wild and speculative fevers," they adopted the Franklin Place model of buildings around a mini-park at Louisburg Square from 1826, and at Pemberton according to a design by Alexander Wadsworth in 1835. In these two splendid enclaves, the handsome upstairs-downstairs buildings of the wealthy faced little lawns. Shaded by arching elms and enclosed by iron fences, they created the ambience of cosmopolitan London or Georgian Bath on the last heights of the old Trimountain.

Beacon Street — Holmes's "sunny street that holds the sifted few" — now walled the Common in a long bank of red masonry. Looser, fuller, freer than the tight high-stooped structures of Philadelphia or New York, the Boston row house began to roll along other city hills. The designs of architects Parris, Benjamin, Edward Shaw, and Richard Bond; of architect-builders like Cornelius Coolidge, or countless housewrights melded into a single wall along the contour of its streets. The proportions of Bulfinch's neoclassicism, straightforward and flowing, and the sameness of scale and substance absorbed the shifting rhythms of doors, windows, and ornaments in an overall order.

One new note sounded in the row, however. For within the narrowing lots, Boston builders found a way to break out of the flat mass of stone and escape the pinched confines of the row. That way, a mere undulation, a slow curving outward of the facade, would have names like "swell" or "bow front" and appear in the altered guise of "bay" or "oriel window." Yet it would fulfill one single need: for with the bow, the most nipped and corseted row house could catch the warmth and brightness of the sun, draw in a whole day's worth of light and offer views along the street.

A style of humble origins, the bowfront had mixed ancestry. In part it came from Regency England, in part from the oval rooms that Bulfinch curved to suit his country clients' taste for odd-shaped chambers. No chronology has traced how the bowfront moved to town, how the tubular form for the house of David Sears (today's Somerset

Otis Street row house.

Club) became the mode seized by unknown carpenters and masons and established as the curving signature of Beacon Hill, a new South End, and Back Bay. Nonetheless, the bow became Boston. For one hundred years, its inspired wave swept across the incapacious town and gave drama to the look of the urban landscape. As its windows graced row-house interiors with the shifting light, so its curve enlivened their exteriors. Along relentless city walls, the bow cast shadows and created massed effects: a chiaroscuro, light to dark to light to dark, was painted by the sun that slid across the curved brick walls until the clouds dimmed their crimson from a ruddy red to evening's somber purple. Pedigreed or not, the bowfront endured. In the end, though called the "detested vitreous" by Henry James and produced in dreary versions by indifferent builders, many a rolling facade recalled its inspired origins.

Across the now gentled elevations of Beacon Hill, along the final graded sidewalks of Pinckney and the north side of Mt. Vernon Street, by the edges of the Common and lining the granite-paved roads of Summer, South, Lincoln, and Essex streets, the rolling row houses covered the last leftover sod of old Shawmut. In 1830, the Common where the young Emerson had walked his cows was made off limits to four-footed beasts, its easy curves manicured with 600 trees of varied size and later enclosed with Richard Upjohn's gothic fence. By the 1840s and 1850s, the "pretty country town" of Edward Everett Hale had become a city with gardens.

Boston held on to its greenery despite the urbanizing landscape. The trees that gave Myrtle, Chestnut, and Walnut streets their names still budded and shed their seasonal leaves with a Puritan sense of God's own order. Horse chestnut, tulip, honey locust, and even the weedy ailanthus brought comeliness to city life. Historians Parkman and Prescott or High Street aristocrats cultivated their peach and pear trees nearby the close-packed houses. And the girth of the great elms swelled.

The period of cityhood added to the greenery, too, with the first new public park since the Puritans' forty-five-acre Common. On the site of the ropewalks, where cordmakers had once paced their ellipses just west of Boston Common, Mayor Quincy had made the city's second investment in public open space. In 1824, the Public Garden began its landmark life. Though the someday garden remained a marsh for years, it resisted incursions and lost not one blade of grass, contemporaries said, to the "landsharks" who tried to divide it into plots.

Boston also stayed a city within easy reach of country life. On balmy days, a brief walk brought city folks to the Mill Dam. Horse carriages trotted them to bosky nooks or to take the view from the

143

South Boston Bridge. Others sought more pastoral retreats, picnicking in groves in neighboring towns or in the new cemeteries laid out for the living among the dead. In the woods of Sweet Auburn in Cambridge and at Forest Hills in Roxbury, the movement for "rural Gardens for the Dead" blended with the need for more open space and greenery to launch the public cemetery movement. Robert Copeland and Horace W. S. Cleveland, whom some call the first landscape architects, argued for the public cemetery; Jacob Bigelow, the Harvard physician, claimed that public health depended on it; and civic leader H. A. S. Dearborn insisted that the common weal demanded it. Transcendentalists who wanted to cultivate art in nature described the cemetery's cultivated green swath as "an open-air church where nature's hand alone would dominate." And so, the crusade for the graceful "grounds of hallowed purpose" was born.

Mount Auburn Cemetery, the seventy-two-acre cemetery designed by Alexander Wadsworth in tune with the literature imported by Dearborn, was bought and planted by the Horticultural Society as a model. The Père-Lachaise of America, some have said. Like its French namesake, Mount Auburn Cemetery was a miniature Victorian City of the Dead, an outdoor art museum with tombstones and picturesque gardens leafed over by verdant groves, contoured by sinuous paths and fronted by an Egyptian gate. A place "for the living to delight in," traveler Harriet Martineau wrote. Similarly, Forest Hills Cemetery, approached through a ponderous Victorian gate, gave Bostonians fine prospects with groomed avenues, lakes of graceful swans and snowy ducks, and picturesque boulders. The bucolic tradition of these superb retreats inspired the movement to create public parks across America.

Bostonians traveled even farther outward to adopt the country life. For years, the gentility had summered out of town. Now a whole colony of wealthy merchants began to fill in the Nahant surroundings of ice king Frederic Tudor. Sweltering Boston plutocrats boated to the North Shore and settled in and around the great columned hotels from Beverly Cove to Gloucester's Eastern Point, to form the summer "Gold Coast." Citizens of lesser means joined them, too, journeying by horse carriage and train to summer and year-round villages and suburbs. Cheap travel and cheap land supported the ideal of suburban life and helped launch an exodus to South and East Boston for year-round houses. The future suburbs Jamaica Plain, Watertown, Brookline, Milton, Roxbury, and Dorchester now held more Greek Revival houses; some even boasted temple-fronted versions of Chelsea's Captains' Row. Serene Greek temples by Asher Benjamin and others reached even the outermost reaches of western Massachusetts.

Ornate floral designs at Forest Hills Cemetery.

Gothic-style house on Parker Hill, Roxbury.

Yet the style that came to seem the only proper one for this emerging country life was something else again. Out of the quest for rural ways, out of the memories of country roots, out of the romanticism of England's Sir Walter Scott and the fashion of English gardening came the Gothic Revival, followed in short order by kindred eclectic styles. Pick your favorite bygone style to adorn the rural landscape: the architect or builder would oblige. Greek Revival or Gothic, never mind. The designer could flit from style to style, offering a Gothic cottage or Italianate villa or appliquéing a bit of "medieval" trim or jigsaw decoration to make a dated building à la mode.

Boston's ring of villages supplied fertile soil for these cottages, and some predicted that the tempting hills of South Boston would soon hold the city's aristocracy. On Roxbury highland or Jamaica Plain, architect or housebuilder could copy Greek temple or Gothic cottage or duplicate Pliny's villa at Ostia from A. J. Davis engravings first brought forth in Boston. Davis called himself an architectural composer, offering the builder the parts of his melody. The homeowner of the 1840s need only thumb his worn copy of a second book, this one by Andrew Jackson Downing, to learn the way to plant Davis's fashion on the land.

It is Downing — child of Emerson in his delight in the winding path, the dell, the glade — whom some call the first conscious artist of the natural environment. In his *Cottage Residences* and *Treatise on the Theory and Practice of Landscape Gardening,* Downing told how to curl and swirl the landscape "informally." He insisted that whoever builds an "unsightly house, insults the community, wrongs his neighbor." Downing's eloquent texts created a model for the coming of the American suburb, vast and open; his words predicted the shaded lawn, the weeping willow draped across a listless lake that would be de rigueur. The countryside became a room with a Downing view. His homey cottages melting into the land and his lonely trees circled by unfenced plots became the nation's enduring suburban dream.

Slowly, a colony of Bostonians moved by rail or foot toward this dream, closing the once rural landscape into a tight half-circle around seaside Shawmut. In less than a generation, the villages and towns they populated would attach themselves to the old peninsula more formally. Some by slow assimilation, some by more formal annexation, they would become part of today's Greater Boston. Even in the midnineteenth century, a town's worth of citizens, 20,000 by one count, came to the city by steam train, coach, or ferry every day, commuting back to the suburbs once more at night. The new horsecars plied their first suburban passengers on rail.

The railroad became an ever more visible presence on the landscape. Six railroad causeways and eight major terminals were now headquartered at the Hub. Some eighty-three train stations inflated the radial towns into "railroad villages." The power of the steam engine astounded everyone. The railroad's "terrible energy" fascinated Hawthorne, unfixing every corner of the country from its age-long rest, he wrote. Even Thoreau who felt dismay at hearing the "hills echo with its snort-like thunder" admitted that he felt "as if the earth had got a race now worthy to inhabit it." Incredulous Bostonians watched the old farms and graceful estates around the city begin to take on village airs while even remote spots like Lowell, Worcester, and Salem seemed "almost suburbs" to their inhabitants. "From the moment that railways were introduced, life took on extravagance," Henry Adams wrote.

A windmill still lingers on the future site of South Station in this 1833 view of Boston from City Point.

Land values multiplied in the railroad's trail. The path of the iron horse appeared to be the route to real estate development and commercial boom. No wonder Bostonians saw the railroad station at South Cove, not the harbor, as the gateway to the town. The city's very prosperity seemed to ride upon the rails. The capital from commerce and manufacturing went to fund the new locomotives. Boston banks and bankers bolstered the system as it spread across the continent. The link with the western routes from Boston to Canada foretold golden days to come. Progress was on every hand, symbolized in so many things — in the new steamers that docked from Liverpool, in the telegraph messages from across the sea, in the prosperous factories and flourishing land development.

This iron harbinger of good times was celebrated most raucously in the Railroad Jubilee of 1851 and "for three sunlit happy days the city surrendered to joy," as one chronicler recalled. Timed to mark the laying of the final rail to Canada, the pageantry of the Railroad Jubilee recalled the shows for Lafayette or Bunker Hill. Only now it was not just the celebration of a patriotic past or static monument but a race through time and space, toward a future where progress and industry would preside.

On opening day, September 17, 1851, President Millard Fillmore offered congratulations to the crowds and the good feelings swelled into a wave of celebration. On the second day, Bostonians and guests came out in numbers to greet Lord Elgin, the Canadian governor general, at the railroad station. Receptions, dinners, parades, and a brilliant "illumination of the skies" dazzled the beholders. By day three, Boston's enthusiasm was overwhelming in the scene described below:

Harvard students and mechanics both marched through streets alive with flags, bunting and printed sentiments. The dinner on the Common was served in a huge pavilion, 250 by 90 feet, decorated with flags, representing trains in motion, and maps of Boston's railroad system. It all seemed a magnificent fulfillment of the magisterial prophecy made two years earlier in the Mayor's Inaugural address: "The long winter of New England isolation is broken, she now warms and flourishes in friendly and thrifty intercourse with the luxuriant West; and it is not too much to anticipate that the day will come when there will be no greater or more prosperous city upon the American continent than the City of the Pilgrims."

City of Pilgrims, city of reformers, city of Athenians — in three decades, Boston had become a city crowned by prosperity.

City as Celebration

A city is the center for the myriad activities of working day and festive afterhour. Its byways and roads hold the throngs attracted to its joyous or somber moments, to theater and museum, small shop and store. Rarely did one find what Henry James called "the blankness of the American street-page" on Boston's teeming thoroughfares. On holidays, Bostonians dressed up the architecture of their streets with banners and filled their roadways with marching bands. No matter what drew the crowds — be it the lively theater and entertainment district or the streets and buildings scaled for people — the chief celebration was the joy of human congregation.

Deck the Halls, Walls, and Wayfares

Bostonians dressed up their buildings to celebrate special events. Whether the ragtag Credit House at 851 Washington Street (left) or the big downtown grocery store Batchelder and Snyder on Blackstone and North streets in the North End (above), businesses knew how to costume their exteriors for any occasion. So did a fan of John F. (Honey Fitz) Fitzgerald's, who decorated a North End facade at 201 Salem Street, near Christ Church, with banners, probably for the one hundredth anniversary of the launching of the *Constitution.* The art of draping architecture for celebration has vanished along with the architecture shown here.

No jubilee was greater than the International Peace Jubilee of 1872 and no grander exhibit hall ever rose in Boston than this one designed by William Gibbons Preston. The lithograph struck for the occasion depicts the throngs arriving. The interior shows the crowds who heard a chorus of ten thousand trained voices accompanied by one thousand instruments. The temporary structure sat near today's Copley Square.

The centennial celebration of June 17, 1875, called forth all manner of flag and bunting. In City Square, Charlestown, citizens swathed the old city hall and set up a triumphal arch on Charles River Avenue. Charlestown's city hall, designed by William Washburn, was torn down for a twentieth-century courthouse and police station. Most of the buildings behind the temporary arch on Charles River Avenue also disappeared.

Streets for People

In street and alley what strange tongues
  are these,
Accents of menace alien to our air,
Voices that once the Tower of Babel
  knew.

— Thomas Bailey Aldrich,
Atlantic Monthly

Wave after wave of immigration gave a
strong ethnic character to the city. Boston's
mixed neighborhoods are visible in the
Buddhist ceremony on Harrison Avenue
in Chinatown in the early twentieth century;
in the black community on Northampton
Street in the South End depicted by artist
Allan Rohan Crite in a 1936 painting,
School's Out; and in the observation of Presi-
dent McKinley's assassination spelled out in
Hebrew script on Salem Street in the North
End. The Everett School fell in 1965.
"They chopped out my childhood," artist
Crite said. The Harrison Avenue and Salem
Street facades were lost or altered through
the years.

153

Busy Newspaper Row became busier after such banner events as the victory of Boston's own fighter John L. Sullivan on July 8, 1889. The city's thriving newspapers, the *Globe, Journal, Advertiser,* and *Post* all took up residences in these quarters, moving from one building to the next along the upper end of Washington Street. Winter

Street, Boston's elegant shopping district, shows the same jam of vehicles and pedestrians in the World War I era. The papers moved out of downtown and most of their dwellings went down for parking lots thereafter. The vivid ensemble of commercial architecture now hides behind banal remodelings.

156

Author Arnold Bennett described the North End as "bewildering congeries of crowded streets where every corner was dangerous with vegetable barrows, tram-cars and perambulators, and the legend of Paul Revere seemed to float like a long wisp of vapor." Later, such scenes seemed picturesque and today one may even find charm in the "bewildering" new Americans standing in front of Paul Revere's house with the awnings (left), in the narrow alley of Webster Avenue off nearby Hanover Street, or in the small trades that pocketed the North (above) or West End (below). Much of the third floor of the Paul Revere House was dismantled in a 1907–1908 "restoration" in search of history. The destruction of the adjacent apartment house followed to provide a garden for the famous dwelling. Webster Avenue came down in the creation of the Prado, or Paul Revere Mall, in the 1930s; the North End shown here fell for the Central Artery; and the West End was obliterated by urban renewal in the late 1950s and early 1960s.

A staccato of ornate windows and carvings helped make Washington Street a zesty place in the 1890s. The majority of the stores leading to the distant Old South Meeting House vanished in favor of faceless heirs. Raymond's, a holdout, resisted until 1967 when it went for the present Woolworth's and the realignment of Franklin Street.

Pick an occasion, stage a parade. The Ancient and Honorable Artillery Company, America's oldest, parades up State Street to the Old State House in the early 1880s. Next to nothing remains of these State Street buildings that seem to share the verve of the passerby.

159

Arts and Entertainment

The word *museum* was thought to camouflage the suspect theater going on inside
the magnificent Boston Museum on Tremont
near Court (left and above). "My purple,
splendid hours," one playgoer described his
visit to the chamber where Edwin Booth, the
brother of assassin John Wilkes Booth, and
others transfixed Boston audiences. The
building, designed by Hammatt Billings in
1846, held portraits by Copley, West, and
Stuart, as well as P. T. Barnum's crowd-
pulling "feejee mermaid." It yielded to a
business block in 1903.

Little did architect Isaiah Rogers guess that
his 1846 Howard Athenaeum for serious
theater would become the Old Howard of
twentieth-century burlesque fame. The first
Italian opera in America was performed
here, but the 1917 view comes later.
"Howard Street was the small time actor's
Broadway," Fred Allen wrote. Still later
were the raucous days of "Tillie the Tassle
Tosser" and Ann Corio. A fire ruined
plans to restore the building in 1961 and
nothing remains of the landmark or the
boisterous life of Scollay Square around it.

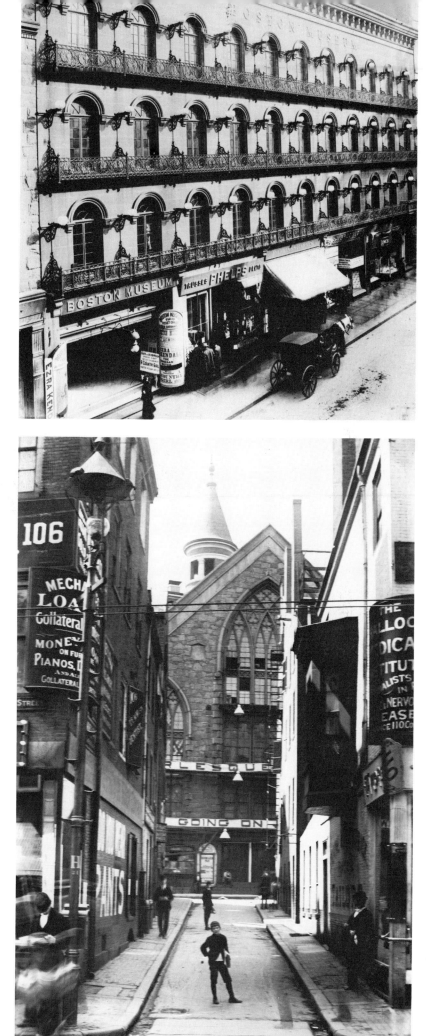

161

"I have heard that architecture is a kind of frozen music. If so I should call the Art Museum frozen Yankee Doodle." So Thomas Gold Appleton mocked the vivid polychrome building at Copley Square when it was new. Constructed in two stages, in 1876 and 1890, Sturgis and Brigham's handsome Museum of Fine Arts was Ruskinian gothic of an extravagance rarely seen. Terra-cotta ornament, the first used on this scale in America, depicted the "Genius of Art" and "Art and Industry" on the exterior and casts of the ancients populated the interior. The museum, which had fought to preserve the amenities of its low-scale neighborhood in a major court fight, moved out to the Fenway, and its old building became the site of the Copley Plaza Hotel in 1912.

Gilded inside and out, Boston theaters also greeted their audiences in high style. Even the 1880 box office of the Globe (Selwyn's) Theatre by Benjamin F. Dwight was a charming affair. Tier upon tier of operagoers packed the horseshoe-shaped Boston Opera House near Symphony Hall. It was designed by Parkman B. Haven with a ponderous neo-

classical exterior, and opened in 1909. Keith's
Theatre by J. B. McElfatick on the Tremont
Street site of Bulfinch's Colonnade Row applied a wedding cake exterior to its late-
1890s facade. The Globe Theatre is gone. The
Opera House, the city's favorite domicile for
opera and ballet, was wantonly destroyed
in 1958 and idled as a parking lot for
years before Northeastern University put
up its mundane successor. The Keith
Theatre's facade was butchered in the
twentieth century.

165

Bedecked with the borrowed trappings of the Egyptians, the color of holiday bunting, or electric illumination, Boston theaters had an architecture as make-believe as the performances set within. The interior of the Music Hall, later the Orpheum (above), designed by George Snell in 1852, held Ralph Waldo Emerson, Booker T. Washington, William James, and others on its stage. The bright lights of the Scollay Square Theatre designed by Clarence H. Blackall (right) showed the zest of the new electricity. The Egyptian Theatre in Boston's Brighton section (below), an extravaganza by an unknown architect, fit the style of the movie palace resurgence in the 1920s. The "delightful ghosts" of the Music Hall were driven out by an early-twentieth-century remodeling. The Scollay Square picture palace's site now holds the vast spaces of twentieth-century bureaucratic buildings. The Egyptian disappeared after World War II.

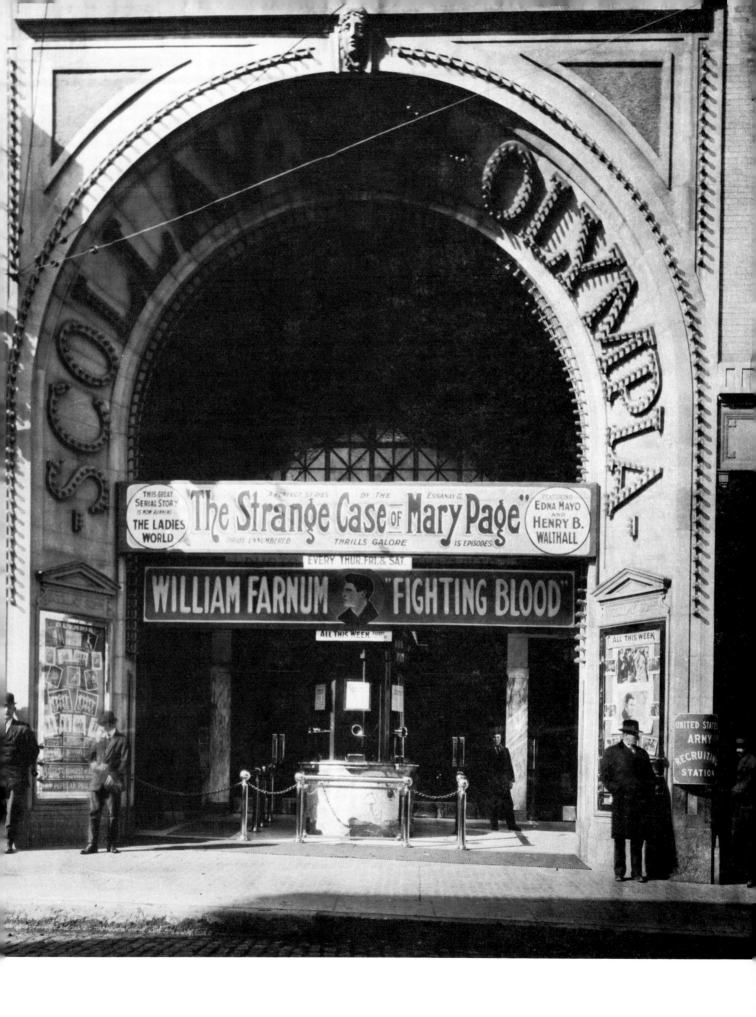

–CHAPTER 7–

New Land, 1850-1870

Wherever land can be made economically, on the circumference of
the city, without destroying commercial advantage, there it is bound
to appear.
— Boston Almanac, 1855

In the United States a man builds a house in which to spend his old
age, and he sells it before the roof is on [in the] bootless chase of the
complete felicity which forever escapes him.
— ALEXIS DE TOCQUEVILLE, Democracy in America

IMPATIENT WITH boundaries, Bostonians felt new times press upon their ancient hub. The age of energy — of machine energy — was racing toward them and yet their old peninsula idled within a preindustrial frame. Its crooked and narrow streets were held by foot power, its four-mile circuit cramped for space by a swelling population and a restless commerce. Neither the artisan hinged to a shop nor the luxury-loving merchant tied to trade could budge. Shawmut's dimensions were no longer than the shadow of a man walking.

Now as business crowded out old houses and new houses crowded out the last free sites, a new horde of immigrants appeared. The children of Erin fell in vast numbers upon the docks. Almost 35,000 refugees of the potato famine flocked to Boston in the five years before 1850. Within the decade, they numbered 60,000, more than one third of Boston's population of 177,000. Colonizing the beachheads, the Irish swarmed inland to power industry with their cheap labor. Boston was no longer a fist but a funnel, and a funnel that was overflowing. Clearly, the scores of hard-won acres of the last half-century would no longer suffice. Which way to go? To the east, there was Boston Harbor, an arm of the Atlantic packed with oceangoing life. To the north, more of the harbor. To the west, the estuary and marsh penned off by Cotting's Dam had made a fettered Back Bay out of the Charles River flats. It was "odiferous," Bostonians complained, and formidably large. It was "too big for a river and too small for a bay," Henry James observed, "a brackish expanse of anonymous character." Finally to the south, the neck of the funnel — the old narrow isthmus to the mainland — was blocked by tidal marsh. Freed of its gallows but not its soggy turf, the neck along soggy Washington Street still merited its name, Clam Shell Drive. Though crossed by more roads and fill, the southern land could scarcely support some 1000 souls.

Still more newcomers were driving natives from the teeming center: "Thousands," the Joint Committee on Public Land declared in 1848, "are leaving our limits for adjoining towns." And still the ten arrivals every day had not yet peaked. The Irish transformed the New England city into "the American Dublin." The homogeneity of Athens was fractured by the foreign-born. The Alien Commissioners despaired of even counting their numbers.

In a place like Boston it is exceeding difficult to trace out the parentage and history of the foreign poor. There are so many John Sullivans, Jerry Daileys and William O'Briens, who are all made in the same mold.

Overleaf:
Some 1860 row houses by Richard Morris Hunt.

Not in the *native* mold was what they meant; for the Sullivans and Daileys of Boston's Land of Exile scarcely partook of Athenian elegances. How could these Irish peasants forced into foreign labors breathe Parnassian currents while jammed along the six-mile waterfront or isolated in their squalid slums? The flock of Bishop Fitzpatrick like the flock of John Winthrop had a monument on this landscape, but it was a sorry sight. Standing high above them, the ruins of the Ursuline Convent on Charlestown's Mount Benedict were a symbol of the era's intolerance. Burned by native bigots in 1834, the ruins loomed in memoriam — the Irish monument, point and counterpoint, their leaders said, of the Yankee Bunker Hill. No native Webster preached a civic sermon on this mount but the Catholic newspaper, the Boston *Pilot,* of 1846 delighted in July Fourth oratory of another sort:

> Foul midnight deed: I mark with pain
> Yon ruins tapering o'er the plain;
> Contrast them with your Bunker's height,
> And shame will sicken at the sight.

Boston's Irish Catholic immigrants were aliens in every sense, living outside the tidy environs of their Puritan predecessors. Even the black Bostonians who held fast to the northern slopes of Beacon Hill and the West End, and the German immigrants, who began their move toward today's Castle Square area at midcentury, did not inherit such uninhabitable quarters. A sordid tenement was home to the Irish laborer: "The mason who finishes the cornice of the palace returns at night perchance to a hut not so good as a wigwam," wrote Thoreau. Boarding houses, sheds, and emptied factories made wretched quarters. By the 1850s, one corner of the city recorded thirty-seven immigrants per dwelling. The crumbling mansions that edged the water in the low-rent North End, Fort Hill, and Broad Street became little more than hovels for the first and worst of Boston's huddled masses. The cheap labor of 30,000 workers fueled Boston's boom and made Massachusetts the fourth manufacturing state before the Civil War. The houses bought by their meager wages helped transform "a neat, well-mannered city into a slum-and-disease-ridden metropolis," Oscar Handlin writes in his classic of *Boston's Immigrants:*

Every vacant spot behind, beside or within an old structure yielded room for still another. And eventually, to correct the oversight of the first builders who had failed to exhaust the ultimate inch, their more perspicacious successors squeezed house within house, exploiting the

171

last iota of space. This resulted in so tangled a swarm that the compiler of the first Boston Atlas gave up the attempt to map such areas, simply dismissed them as "full of sheds and shanties."

Some officials feared for the future of the city. "Many streets formerly occupied by some of our wealthiest and most respectable citizens are now wholly surrendered to foreigners in the older parts of the city, rents are exorbitant, and it is with extreme difficulty that a comfortable tenement can be obtained," they noted. Many worried that old residents would leave the low and reclaimed land to foreigners. They would head to the suburbs, pay less for land, and "build tasteful houses with flower-plots and gardens; availing themselves of the frequent omnibuses or of special trains [that] run almost hourly."

This was an ominous exodus, the guardians of public virtue warned. Low morals lay ahead for the meandering middle class. The Boston Society for the Prevention of Pauperism cautioned sternly:

Deprived of the society of their families, dining at restaurants and gradually alienated from the domestic hearth, the moral exposure is greater than can be well calculated.

Calculate, too, the Committee on Public Lands observed, more cunningly, the taxes lost to neighboring cities and villages by their flight and "every proper inducement should be offered to incline our citizens to remain within our limits."

Every proper inducement. To Bostonians, the portentous phrase meant just one thing: new land. And new land, close and uncluttered, could again be found in one familiar place — the waterside.

Here, too, the plan was limned in Bulfinch's day. Many credit the Federalist father with the first sketch for what would become the new South End. True, no one carried out this design for houses on rectangular plots surrounding a shaded oval park and approached by broad avenues. The drawings designed by city engineers Ellis S. Chesbrough and William Parrott at midcentury rendered what we would call an *urban infrastructure* more than an *architecture.* Their project begun under Mayor Jacob Bigelow called for fill and grading, raising and draining to supply a solid footing for the 570 acres on the tidal flats to the south.

When the private capital that sired Boston proper would not pave the way, the city went ahead with the fill and street layout, auctioning the land to the highest bidder. To cajole city folk to the once-forbidding wastes, the city planners would not only have to sell cheap but plan well. Abandoning Bulfinch specifics, they nonetheless adopted Bulfinch-like amenities: trees, parks, and row houses.

A plan of Boston that shows the original 789-acre Shawmut and the fill that tripled its size.

Full blown in size, self-confidence, and wealth, Bostonians had the boisterous energy to undertake this South End operation. It was "the first large-scale layout since English urban planning in the late eighteenth century." It still is what urbanists have described as the largest, most lasting Victorian district in the nation. Americans everywhere had the same self-assurance, of course. Their urge to grow was fueling speculative fires everywhere. City by city across the continent, private developers followed the grid, right-angling the empty acres into saleable lots. In an industrial America, municipalities surrendered their once-blue skies to sooty railroads and factories, and their soil to profiteering empire builders. The mill towns blueprinted by the Boston Associates thirty miles outside the city at Lowell were no model for the next generation. The mills' organic beauty and their founders' humane ambitions gave way to big machines powered by coal and serviced by cheap immigrant labor. In the years after the Civil War, industrialists and speculators would transform, if not destroy, village America, spreading cruel and unlovely blots across the country.

Boston was otherwise. The city did not suffer to the same degree. The more noxious factories stayed largely on the fringes; railroads were concentrated in the wasteland between the South End and Back Bay. But most important, new land or not, the citizens of the Bay State capital appreciated the graceful "prospects" of the past and tried to plan them anew. Their skill in the building arts flourished: their foresight and sense of public purpose were renewed in the new age. Were they not still the children of Bulfinch, the heirs to an attitude of care for the environment? The town engineers and countless city officials considered the made land more than a commodity. So did the constituency that demanded a spacious and elegant neighborhood to match the one they had inherited. Bostonians were both heirs to the past and guardians of its amenities for the future.

Their planners did well for them on the new land. To avoid the monotony of the long north-south thoroughfares of Shawmut, Front (Harrison Avenue), Tremont, and Washington streets, they dotted the new South End with parks. To add more life, they punctuated it with small side streets. Cell by cell, they transformed the watery acres of the South End. Using green and open space as a calling card to old Bostonians, they positioned here a curving park, there a rectangular one. Then they framed the parks with house lots. Sometimes the park were formal, sometimes intimate; sometimes ample, sometimes the merest spot of lawn. They were a farflung family of parks on a tribe of streets.

The squares of the South End evolved over time as a collection of

173

city planning ideas: Blackstone and Franklin squares, in the late 1840s, were planted, fenced, and decorated with a splash of Cochituate waters in the center of the park; Chester Square, in 1850, the most lavish mini-park, had one and a half acres with a three-tier fountain and fishpond designed by Ezra Lincoln, Jr., at the western end of the district; and last, in 1851, Union Park was almost as grand, and Worcester Square, had gracefully curved outlines and the new City Hospital as terminus. The ample houses of the coming rich in publishing (M. M. Ballou) or groceries (S. S. Pierce) rose there. The residences of Mayor Alexander Hamilton Rice, who signed the Back Bay development into law, or Jonas Chickering, whose pianofortes spread throughout the world, lined the streets and rimmed the tree-shaded parks.

In the morning, the nursery maids descended the steep stairs, took out their dangling keys, and unhinged the locks of the little gardens to let their frolicking charges play upon the dewy beds of grass. Ahhh! how "the dear old gardener Calvin" beamed at the key wielders of Chester Square. Ohh! the ornamental fountain and fishpond, the borders of flowers and crimson rose, an old South Ender remembered. Even Concord and Rutland squares and Braddock Park, built on a smaller scale, and Montgomery and Leighton, so minute they seemed interior nooks, were breathing space and cozy green carpets within the mounting walls of masonry.

Seeing the appeal of their city's row-house world, South End planners had simply tried to transplant it on new land: The South End was Beacon Hill deployed in fuller ways; it was High or Franklin Street shaded over once again. Extend Beacon Street and you see the broad Columbus Avenue. Multiply Franklin, Louisburg, or Pemberton squares and you get the South End's fleet of green and gated parks. Then devise urban planning extras — the pragmatic (alleys behind to allow service wagons hidden access); the purposive (a horsecar trotting out from the city center along Washington Street); and the luxurious (the soft spray of fountains, the arch of trees, the wrought-iron fences). Grade it, drain it, build it, plant it, connect it. A brave new town sat upon the barren land toward Roxbury.

Fill and build, fill and build, the pattern was not new, nor was the architecture. Again in long and lovely rows, Greek Revival town houses fanned out first, succeeded by the Italianate mode with its florid lintels and substantial cornices. Other revival styles lapped over the face of the basic dwelling and more modest designs slotted along the cross streets in a lively mix of middle class and rich.

Always, though, above the ever higher stoops, the builders set the bow to billowing. Its splendid rhythms, first fixed on Beacon Hill, be-

Blackstone Square when the fountain flowed.

came the hallmark of the new land too, rolling, contouring, shaping its endless corridors. The curving facades of the South End now held the fuller windows allowed by a new glass technology, too. The new Philadelphia brick toned its streetscapes to a dimmer shade. Goodbye to the flaky pinkish clays of Federal Boston. The duller tougher stone of the Brown Decades was image and metaphor. Brownstone foundations substituted for the early granite ones and mortar darkened with lampblack accented the solemn oneness of the mass of wall, made it more plastic and cylindrical. Beneath the grave brow of the mansard roof, a bolder ambiance emerged.

Countless, largely anonymous, builders mastered its design. The South End held a vernacular architecture realized by everyday workers, accented by ordinary masons, and adorned by simple craftsmen who attached the ironwork extruded by the mile in the foundries of a burgeoning industry. The speculator or his prosperous butcher, baker, or candlestickmaker client might riffle through a catalogue of ornament to find the thick black railings that lined the stoops and apply the airy tracery of a fence, the design of a wayward petunia or geometric wheel for individual flair. An iron crown atop a roof was a touch of royalty from untutored hands. The forms and finials on the simple screens, the lively balconies or elaborate grillwork came by the foot, like ordinary cloth.

The more opulent Victorian housebuilder in the South End might even go so far as to pick an architect. The name of a Luther Briggs, Jr., a Nathaniel J. Bradlee, or Ammi Burnham Young marks the sheets of drawings for some blocks of houses. Knowledgeable owners — Ballou, the publisher of a pictorial magazine, or H. H. Hunnewell, the developer who was a horticulturist with an eye to the artful contours of his Wellesley estate — had visual astuteness beyond the routine. Still, the housewright did the bulk of work. The swirling imagery of Persia in iron or the new mansard roof of France in tile belied the fact that the South End's architecture came for the asking — a vernacular form crafted by artisans schooled in a superb environment.

If the South End row-house architecture was inherited, its scope was not. It belonged to the Victorian century, it expressed the period's expansive, heroic, and all-embracing attitude toward the land. The scale of the South End was of a magnitude and the plan had an integrity and totality not seen before. The city ruled the setback, width, height, and material. All came within the purview of the urban plan: no more would the next building simply ride roughshod on the one before, the city planners decreed. Not content with creating the style and dimensions of this orderly streetscape, the South End builders

The South End home of historian Justin Winsor.

175

plotted out new institutions: hospital, hotel, church, and school. Designed to serve an expanding population, these structures became the South End's social, physical, and visual point and terminus.

Boston City Hospital was one such institution, a modern facility that spread its large and lofty pavilions on a seven-acre tract at the end of Worcester Square. Spacious wards flanked a handsome domed administration building by Gridley James Fox Bryant. Hotels provided other splendid edifices — the marble-faced Commonwealth, the Hoffman House, or the brick St. James with its steam elevator and 400 rooms built by Ballou to quarter the likes of General Grant. The St. Cloud was an early adaptation of the French style of living in the horizontal mode that forecast the apartment house.

The spirit of do-good and do-for-God made itself manifest in the South End, too, and soon the spires that defined downtown began to peak over the new land. In Hammatt Billings' Tremont Street Methodist Church: in two successive edifices by the Shawmut Congregational Church, and in a church on Union Park Street designed by Bradlee for the congregation of the Reverend Edward Everett Hale, the house of God still sat side by side with the house of man.

The Roman Catholic Diocese of Boston joined the Protestant move out to the south land to plant the soaring gothic churches of its heroic age of building. Despite fervid opposition and the lack of a congregation there, the Jesuits began the Church of the Immaculate Conception in 1858; then, in 1863, they launched Boston College next door. Deserting Bulfinch's Holy Cross Cathedral downtown, the Catholic church created the majestic cathedral on Washington Street. The 3500-seat puddingstone structure designed by Brooklyn's prolific church architect P. C. Keeley was no smaller than Westminster Abbey. Symbolically, the bricks from the ruins of the Ursuline Convent made its vestibule arch.

Countless charities joined the churches. Charities for sick and destitute servant girls, for penitent females, for children, for Scots (the longest surviving charity of the lot), and for aged men (where Gridley J. F. Bryant, its architect, would die) settled in among the unfurling town house blocks. So, of course, did schools, schools, and more schools. To Bostonians, everyone should be schooled, and Girls' High School, Boston Latin and English High, and others rose to testify to the city of schoolteachers. Schools for newsboys, schools for bootblacks, schools for the deaf, schools during the day for industry and at night to carry on the lyceum spirit. Louis Sullivan, son of a Boston Irish dancing master, and one day to be called parent of the skyscraper school, learned new lessons of urban life and the more

ordinary three R's at the grammar school named for Mayor Rice, "the

Boston Latin and English High School by
George A. Clough.

lightness and brightness and cleanliness of which put him at once in
exceeding good humor," in the words of his *Autobiography of an
Idea.* No mean structures roofed these classrooms either. Boston Latin
and English High School by George A. Clough, the city architect, was
the world's largest free school, some 420 feet long. With a drill hall
holding 3000 seats, it was big enough to hold the school battalion
that tramped out to celebrate civic events on the streets of the South
End.

Factories also began to fill the shores bordering the area. Manufacturers of textiles, clothes, and stonework moved to the edges of what
looked likely to become the center of the city. Entrepreneurs saw the
South End's fringes as an ideal spot for facilities to transport coal.
World famous pianomakers constructed factories of somber but imposing heft, and secured them to the South Bay and sea travel with
their own docks. Four hundred workers manned the machines of
Jonas Chickering's Tremont Street factory alone. Some say the piano
alcoves built into countless South End parlors showed the place of
Boston's music industry.

On the eve of the Civil War, the settlement of the filled land marched apace. Ante-bellum Bostonians by the hundreds took the new horsecar out, riding the rails to the neighborhood of pleasant homes and oval-shaded squares. In a blink, the South End became a prosperous new town leaving the medieval city in its wake. School-houses in Boston's old residential center lost their pupils and sold at half their cost; empty Protestant churches went for small sums to the Catholic parishes in the West and North ends. "So rapid was the hegira at last," a guidebook on the old North End records, "that in one year, nine families who had their previous Thanksgiving in this neighborhood [Sheafe Street] partook of the next one in their new homes at the South End." Ballou's *Pictorial* described fashionable growth boastfully: "It is to the southern part of the city that we now must take a stranger if we would give him a favorable first impression of our Athenian capital."

Fashion, fickle fashion. Fashion is a god that never blinks once but twice. Even at the peak of its vogue the South End was about to swap its place as the seat of fashion with Henry James's "brackish expanse of anonymous character," the Back Bay. For, there, the tidal marsh was proving itself a foul nuisance, so foul that the city would have no choice but to end the stench and groom the unhealthy, unsightly western shores. A masterful plan would evolve and soon that plan, that zone would hold the greater appeal. With its greater nearness to downtown and Beacon Hill, with its Public Garden and, perhaps, with its greater distance from work and workers alike the Back Bay would reign.

Not yet though. First crossed by Uriah Cotting's Mill Dam (Beacon Street) in 1819, the bay had settled into a state of filth by this period; the laying of the railroad tracks toward the South End had turned it into a stagnant pool, "Lake Asphaltics," in the contemporary phrase. By 1856, the land was too valuable to stay in such a cesspool state, however. At long last, enemy camps of would-be owners joined under the Commonwealth of Massachusetts. They directed architect Arthur Gilman to lay out a plan to fill and build on still more new land.

Here, then, the generation of the Civil War would practice its favorite art afresh. With a gusto and self-confidence never seen before, Bostonians would change marsh to building site. Some 450 acres — a land mass more than half the size of the old Shawmut tadpole — would emerge. By the time the century turned, the Back Bay would be the place and "state of mind" made famous round the world.

No question, the infant Back Bay would adopt the airs, the art, and the self-conscious architecture to match its status as cultural center of

This classic 1850s view from the State House shows Back Bay beginning to stretch across the mudflats on Commonwealth Avenue.

America. Slowly, gloriously, Boston's latest new town edged across the water flats in a straight and determined line. The South End had diced itself in a cellular style, with curving parks and side streets clustered in the English mode. Too mincingly; it came to seem more like the crabbed silhouette of old times than the modish Back Bay. The new land made a *grand geste;* its commissioners dared to strike a majestic pose with an axial plan of great splendor. The twin drives of Commonwealth Avenue framed a long green mall with parallel planes. They made a 240-foot-wide boulevard lined with pomp and circumstance, heading west toward a brave infinity.

"In the simplicity of a long straight line, used without deviation, there lies a tremendous courage and self-assertiveness," the critic Siegfried Giedion has observed. The tree-lined drives designed by landscape architects Copeland and Cleveland and architect George Snell sprang from the same certainties as the baroque visions of France's Baron Haussmann. Boston's brownstone lots, plotted from end to end, matched the style and confidence of Napoleon III's Second Empire. Imperial visions for the city's cultural empire. And why not? How better could an age gaining dominion over the sea by steam, the hand by machine, and the land by rail express its unbounded optimism? Stretching toward a promising tomorrow, the Back Bay plan would fulfill the dream of a city with cosmopolitan ambitions.

Citizens of two continents, midcentury Bostonians turned their eyes across the sea. They began to move back and forth across the Atlantic on the Cunard Line from East Boston, to roam the cultural centers of the Old World and import their latest architectural fashion. "Your best people only talk about Europe," an aristocrat in one of William Dean Howells' novels noticed. Henry Wadsworth Longfellow also left the primitive landscape of *Evangeline,* steaming off to Rome to pose beneath the Arch of Titus. There, the popular Boston Irish artist George P. H. Healy, who painted John Q. Adams and Daniel Webster, tucked the white-bearded poet and his daughter Edith "with the golden hair" under the arch, provincial folk beneath the craggy ruins of ancient Rome.

More often, it was not Rome but France (or France via England) that appealed to Bostonians; France that launched the city's era of revival style. "All good Americans, when they die, go to Paris," Thomas G. Appleton declared. Long before that funereal event, they danced to the strains of "Gaîté Parisienne" and sipped French wine. The men sporting Napoleon III moustaches and the women with Second Empire hair styles piled high and Gallic bows and crinolines fluffing out could not do otherwise than promenade down a French boulevard, adopt the French roof of the Messieurs Mansart, admire the dignity of darker stone, and mimic the Louvre or Tuileries. Oh, the wearisome pertinacity of the swellfront, no less an architect than Charles Cummings observed. The advanced Bostonian disowned Georgian England with its organic planning and simple houses in favor of the spacious vistas of the Second Empire and the elaborate trim of its bell décor. Even the doughty Old State House now bore a mansard roof.

Jean Lemoulnier, a visiting French architect, forecast the Parisian style. In 1848, he designed the Deacon House, the city's first mansard roof mansion in the then-barren South End. Though Gridley J. F. Bryant shaped its exterior, Lemoulnier adorned the interior in the height of French fashion with a boudoir belonging to Marie Antoinette, murals by Fragonard and Boucher, mementoes taken from the vanquished rural estates of France, and tall footmen in livery to complete the scene. Less than a decade later, in 1857, the Hotel Pelham brought the novel French style of suites on a single floor to Boston's upstairs-downstairs world. It was the first apartment house in the east.

Deacon House, Washington Street.

Boston began to build mini-Louvres to hold city institutions, from architect Bryant and Gilman's City Hall to Alfred B. Mullett's enormous post office, a behemoth gift from the government of General Grant. The city's builders planted hundreds of French-inspired structures on the city landscape while the city itself, that hub of education and publishing, broadcast the Gallic style far beyond its shores.

Some Boston architects even began to boast a French education.

Interior of MIT's Rogers Building.

Henry Hobson Richardson, who would become Boston's most famous nineteenth-century architect, studied at Paris' École des Beaux-Arts before the Civil War. Other architects gained their French education at second hand in the New York studio of Beaux-Arts graduate Richard Morris Hunt. "The white light of knowledge had broken in upon the superstition of romance," Henry van Brunt, a Hunt student, proclaimed. William Ware, another disciple and partner to Van Brunt, brought Hunt's French methods back to the Bay State and founded the first architectural school in America at the Massachusetts Institute of Technology in the Back Bay in 1867. In tandem, then, the teacher Ware and the translator Van Brunt affirmed the beliefs of France's principal rationalist, Viollet-le-Duc. In Van Brunt's words: "We Americans occupy a new century having no inheritance of ruin and no embarrassment of tradition . . . all the past is ours." All the past is ours! This was the thesis of Victorian architecture and the Back Bay was the clean slate on which it was scored.

Foot by foot, the Back Bay commissioners supplied the sod, swapping fresh made land for more fill, then auctioning off the lots to eager buyers. The work advanced in an endless exchange of land for fill. The gravel crept across the western flats. Since Boston itself had exhausted its native sod, the turf now came from nine miles out. The gravel hills of Needham (one as high as fifty feet, and twelve acres round) fell in the city's greedy, and familiar, press for space. What matter how far away the source of gravel in this industrial age? The twin gods of power — steam and rail — eased transportation and excavation. Victorian technology served the era's grandiose appetites. How Asa Sheldon with his plodding oxen or Harry Otis with his dogged carts would have envied the modern Victorian pace! How they would have gawked at the 145 dirt cars powered by steam that traveled back and forth from Needham at forty-five-minute intervals to ready the new land.

"Going, going, gone," the auctioneer at Berkeley Street shouted to the waiting crowd. Bostonians snapped up the soil for house lots at the rate of two a day. Fashionable citizens left the old walking city at an ever faster pace. As rapidly as they dismissed their roustabout seagoing past, the elite opted for the dignified row houses of the emerging Back Bay, favoring the sunny half of Commonwealth or the water side of Beacon. Shunning the old streets named for natives like Otis, Pinckney, or Revere, the Bostonians opted for the English lords Berkeley, Clarendon, Dartmouth, or Exeter, and so on, in an alphabetical progression to the west.

"Cousinship," that curse and joy of old Boston, persisted. Kin followed kin from Beacon Hill and the last elegant resorts of Franklin

Street or Temple Place, from downtown's Pemberton Square or the old West End onto the western land. Old-line links even accounted for the manner of building in the matching facades of the Russell and Gibson houses. Together Appletons and Bigelows and cousins by the score filled in the lengthening blocks. Did Oliver Wendell Holmes mourn the old days when he could take his row on the watery Back Bay? No more so than Otis had grieved for his youthful swims in the old Mill Pond. *Improvement* was the word. Holmes boasted that his new house was on an island he had once spotted from the shore. So what if crotchety Henry Adams sighed for his youthful days skating on the bygone Back Bay: He was but a melancholy canker on the *corpus vivante* of the times. And the times? They belonged to the new wealth of new industrialists: to a Silas Lapham on the rise shuffling over from the less chic South End to the Back Bay; to John Gardner who brought his New York bride, Isabella Stewart, to the house at 152 Beacon Street; to the up-and-coming who shared space with the ancestrally endowed; to those who felt that "money is the romance, the poetry of our age"; or those like Henry Lee Higginson who felt that "trade was not satisfactory to the inner man as a life-occupation."

The materialistic times went against the more spiritual values of the heirs of the Bible Commonwealth. But culture seekers like Higginson himself began to seed a host of lofty institutions upon the made land; for the Back Bay, too, was designed as a complete environment. Half the Commonwealth's gain from its development went to a fund for schools and colleges; almost a tenth of the Back Bay holdings, nine acres, was allotted to public buildings while nearly half the total, forty-five acres, went to public grounds.

The idle patch between the Common and the booming Back Bay was one eyesore groomed into the Public Garden, a flowering approach. The winning plan of architect George S. Meacham called for a three-acre lake within the twenty-four-acre park, raising the lower portion of the Garden to the level of the surrounding streets, removing the greenhouse and enclosing the Garden with an iron fence. A statue of Venus given by a nearby resident launched the adornment. In little time, the sculpture of George Washington mounted its post before the garden, the mini-bridge spanned the lagoon, and fountains and flowers bordered and beautified the Back Bay's romantic "front yard."

The Back Bay's plan had shortcomings, of course. It gave too scant space for the commercial necessities — back alleys for grocery wagons were the only concessions to entry for the staff of life. It barely provided for the coming horsecars to collect passengers and creep around its streets. It largely disavowed the unsavory Charles River

A New York lithographer named John Bachman created this midcentury view of Boston from the Back Bay.

A Civil War view shows the partially groomed Public Garden with its short-lived greenhouse.

and largely disowned the South End by neglecting crosstown linkages. The South End had offered a mixed style of work and play for middle class and rich, but the Back Bay was aloof and specialized, homogeneous and largely residential — the isolation that was favored in this turbulent industrial age.

Nonetheless the Back Bay, too, had totality in its environment: the cultural, social, and educational buildings had primacy beside the residential ones. Twelve churches, four schools, and such structures as the Museum of Fine Arts would spring up on the made land from the Charles River to Art (now Copley) Square. When the old Federal Street congregation moved into a church designed by Arthur Gilman and took on the name of the Back Bay's first cross street (Arlington) in 1859, the exodus had begun. Five years later the Massachusetts Institute of Technology and the Museum of Natural History sat near Berkeley, the second cross street in the nexus of a total plan. The Back Bay thus must follow a preformed plan. Its cornice height and profile, like those of France or Beacon Hill, were regulated by law into a blank but firm profile awaiting the hand of the architect.

In a generation the number of these architects had grown sixfold. The Back Bay provided their canvas and their clientele. "Yes, sir," that well-heeled patron of architecture, Silas Lapham, boasted, "give an architect money enough and he'll give you a nice house everytime." Not only a nice house but a high-style one, one to flaunt the archaeological riches of the past in a profuse and eclectic display. The Back Bay was the text for nineteenth-century architecture, a tour of styles through time along its 1500 row houses, east to west, revival style succeeding revival style from the Greek Revival to neoclassicism before World War I.

Some call the Back Bay's shifting appliqué of academic formulas frivolous. They deplore the heated debate between the styles and dismiss the passion to attach the correct academic facade to each row house. "Medievalists saw no merit in classic art; devotees of Renaissance thought modern gothic beneath contempt; pre-Raphaelites believed in another," as one scholar summed the practice. Boston's most popular late-century architect Robert Swain Peabody recalled the extremes of his student days:

When we began, Victorian Gothic was at its best. You were expected to declare that you belonged to the English Gothic School or the classical school and it was exactly like saying you were a Baptist or a heathen.

Every object had its proper style — be it a cast-iron birdhouse by Luther Briggs, Jr., or a sewing machine. With competition cutthroat,

183

Boston's fifty or so pre–Civil War architects schooled themselves in the precise detail to beat out the mere design-monger or untutored speculator less taken with this fine art.

Louis Sullivan, in his *Autobiography of an Idea,* dismissed all "the misch masch of architectural theology" with scorn. Yet, it was here he saw his first vision of the novel species known as "archeetec." Strolling down Commonwealth Avenue, the young Sullivan glimpsed a large man of dignified bearing with beard, top hat, and frock coat come out of a nearby building, enter his carriage, and signal the coachman to drive on. The dignity was unmistakable, he wrote, but what was behind the stance, he asked a worker on the site:

"Why he's the archeetec of this building."
"Yes? and what is an archeetec, the owner?"
"Naw; he's the man what drawed the plans for this building."
"What! What's that you say: drawed the plans for this building?"
"Sure. He lays out the rooms on paper, then makes a picture of the front and we do the work under our own boss, but the archeetec's the boss of everybody."
Louis was amazed. So this was the way: the workmen stood behind their boss, their boss stood behind the architect — but the building stood in front of them all. He asked the man if there had been an "archeetec" for the Masonic Temple, and the man said:
"Sure, there's an archeetec for every building."
Louis was incredulous, but if it were true it was glorious news. How great, how wonderful a man must have been the "archeetec" of his beloved temple! So he asked the man how the architect made the outside of the temple and the man said:
"Why he made it out of his head; and he had books besides."
The "books besides" repelled Louis: anybody could do that; but "made it out of his head" fascinated him.
How could a man make so beautiful a building out of his head? What a great man he must be; what a wonderful man. Then and there Louis made up his mind to become an architect and make beautiful buildings "out of his head."

Whether Baptist or heathen, the Back Bay builders tallied up some of America's most beautiful buildings and successful residential enclaves. In seven decades, architects who doted on their labors painted in brownstone facades, sparked sepia tones with the rainbow colors of brick and stone. They dressed similar silhouettes with slate and multicolor tiles of terra-cotta ornament, with copper roofs and wrought-iron trim. A vast array of doors and bays and endless adornment re-

Home of Oliver Wendell Holmes at 296 Beacon Street.

lieved the severity of the upstairs-downstairs row. Gifted designers fit into the formula, so did humble builders. Even the genius of H. H. Richardson found parallels in the residential design of Sturgis and Brigham, Peabody and Stearns, Carl Fehmer, Snell and Gregerson, William G. Preston, Arthur Gilman, Shaw and Shaw, Hammatt Billings, Luther Briggs, Jr., E. C. Cabot, George M. Dexter, or the ubiquitous Bryant. Countless architects adapted to the demand, became adept at everything from the curving gables of the Queen Anne style to the incised line of Eastlake, all set within the idiom of the row. Bold or unobtrusive, inventive or slavishly derivative, plastic or severe, the blocks edged out splendidly, tailor-made to the city limits and the buyer's keen eye. Be it the "panel brick" patterned at the mason's whim, or some architect's formal geometry, Back Bay housemaking was an exacting art for exacting customers.

A student of the arts and no mere shopper, the Boston patron was a rare client. "Tomorrow night I appear before a Boston audience," Dickens wrote, "four thousand critics." Boston's visual acumen matched its vaunted literacy. In a world where intelligences of many sorts conversed, the educated citizen could skip back and forth at leisure between all the arts. In the Cambridge-Brookline-Quincy circle of which Boston was the hub, Holmes had studied painting; Henry James wrote art criticism and was even tutored by the glass designer John La Farge. The articulate Van Brunt was friend to Lowell and Longfellow. Henry Adams coded his perceptions in color while Charles Eliot Norton took his stance as "benevolent dictator" to Boston's cultural life from his post as Harvard professor of fine arts.

"Renaissance man" applied equally to the architect. Hammatt Billings, for one, knew far more than the narrow builder's art. The manifold designer illustrated Whittier's *Poems,* Hawthorne's *A Wonder-Book for Girls and Boys,* and Gleason and Ballou's *Pictorial* with its views of city buildings. He designed everything from the Boston Museum to fireworks for the Common's July Fourth fete, from the Great Organ of the Music Hall to florid business blocks. Billings symbolized the literate Boston artist as Henry James represented the art-conscious Boston author.

Fondness for the arts did not mean indulgence in their excesses. While Americans donned the costume of the Gilded Age, conservative Bostonians disdained mere glitter. Few Back Bay chambers would be muffled in cumbersome red velvet; only a handful of walls drooped under breathless swathings in the Back Bay. Nor would private clubs display the period's opulence. Homebody Bostonians didn't need a lavish palace to house a dance or entertainment. They simply sheathed the carpets with canvas and opened wide the parlor doors. Not for

Puritan Shawmut, the conspicuous avarice of New York or Chicago's crass rich. ("Vulgar and in bad taste," the Boston *Evening Traveler* had sniffed at the Deacon House at midcentury, "like a diminutive dandy loading his person with flashy clothes and ornaments for a dandified giant.") The very Back Bay plan — honoring the cornice line and hewing to setback and other neighborly concerns — testified to the cultural constraints. The Burrages' fancy palace on Commonwealth Avenue (later the Boston Evening Clinic) would cause snickers when it rose late in the century: All those carved animals, those winged cherubs, rams' heads, satyrs, not to mention stained-glass windows, mosaic floors, marble arch, and bronze cupid lamps. And still, the mansion stood on the wrong — the shady — side of the Avenue. Built for out-of-towners, wouldn't you know. A Bostonian knew better. Colonel T. B. Lawrence put his money into collecting armor for the overflowing Athenaeum and Thomas Gold Appleton bought art for the infant Museum of Fine Arts with a declaration of the spirit of the hour: "My money may fly away, my knowledge cannot. One belongs to the world, the other to myself." Material ambition must cloak itself in selfless ends and not the display of personal wealth. Old values held in this new land.

Behind the facades and boulevards that bespoke new times, the row house lifestyle also endured. An owner might display carved fireplaces or marble mantles but the narrow dimensions caused a lookalike interior as well as exterior: reception room downstairs, front parlor up; a large library for papa's work, a sewing room and wardrobe for mama; third- and fourth-floor rooms for children and staff; basement for the kitchen work. The stratified domestic life of Boston was embodied in the row house wherever it appeared — in the old downtown, the South End, or Back Bay. Forget the academic ornament, the rosettes, carvings, and murals of Little Miss Muffet. It was the twenty-five-foot lot that dictated the layout inside.

A way of life both formal and orderly, "necessitating an immodest number of servants, whose orbit within the house covered five flights of stairs from cellar kitchen to their small bedrooms under the roof," a critic wrote. "Little more than a string of stairs," an architect in *Century* magazine agreed. Its existence depended on a rigid hierarchy of country farm girls or immigrant Irish "perpetually toiling as on a treadmill" and careful wives to supervise the lot. The count of help recorded in Morison's *One Boy's Boston* was staggering: nurse, cook, lady's maid, parlor maid, waitress, chambermaid, laundress, once-a-week cleaning woman, and chore man. The run from basement to top floor could keep a staff afoot from dawn to dark.

With its isolated entrance halls, formal living rooms, and separate family quarters, the row house reflected the polite, almost ceremonial life of Boston's wealthier urban households, unchanging in time, patterned in stone. Comforts came with central heating or steam, but technology lagged until after the Civil War. Houses lacked today's support system of pipes and plumbing until the last half of the century. Catherine Beecher's *The American Woman's Home* needed no updating in the three decades between its two editions: the rituals of the Victorian house had withstood almost half a century of social and political change.

Though the architecture of the facade seemed more in flux — an architecture of the minute for the flower of society — it too had an unchanging stance, a static envelope. The era's individuality like its materialism was submerged within the monumental order of the broader boulevards and streets — and the broader social purposes that they symbolized. Plotting the spires and schools, the museums and libraries that crowned its architecture in the decades after the Civil War, a city ever more "swollen in population, prosperity and self-esteem" would transform its buildings of the Gilded Age into a truly golden zone.

Interior of 330 Beacon Street, now the site of a high-rise.

187

Magnificence for the Municipality

Public magnificence matched the private splendors of Boston's architecture. Be it city hall or reform institution, club or hotel, the city never settled for a squalid facade for its community or charitable life. "It has always been in Boston's creed to render life safer and happier for the coming generation." So Helen Keller described the attitude that made the city shelter even an orphanage in a "spacious edifice." From Perkins Institution and the Massachusetts Asylum for the Blind to the Beacon Hill Reservoir, from a prison designed for the meanest citizen to a hotel designed for the most affluent, Bostonians lavished "godless cathedrals" on their public environment. Edward Bellamy's *Looking Backward* projected his fantasy of an ideal community based on Boston. "We might, indeed, have much larger incomes, individually," an inhabitant of his novel's Utopia declares, "but we prefer to expend it upon public works and pleasures in which we all share, upon public halls and buildings, art galleries, bridges, statuary, museums or transit, and the convenience of our cities . . . At home we have comfort but the splendor of our life is on its social side, that which we share with our fellows."

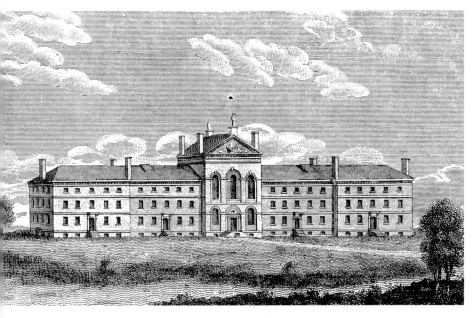

Landscape of Reform and Charity

"No great city like Boston is ever without want, misery, or crime," a late-nineteenth-century Bostonian stated. The Leverett Street Almshouse by Charles Bulfinch in 1801 (above) was demolished in 1825 after the granite House of Industry for the "virtuous poor" and the House of Correction for the "vicious poor" (below) opened in the early 1820s at City Point in South Boston. "Regarded with just pride by the inhabitants," they were a model for other cities. The late 1860s Charity Building and Temporary

Home on Chardon Street by Sturgis and Brigham (above) served the needs of the city's poor in the midst of ever more crowded West and North ends. The Marcella Street Home for Vagrant Boys in Roxbury by city architect George A. Clough (below) opened in 1880; later additions updated the ornate earlier style of Ruskinian turrets. The houses for the poor in South Boston moved out. The Chardon Street refuge was replaced in 1924, and the Roxbury home was abandoned when the city found other means to deal with "vagrant boys."

The Charlestown State Prison boasted imposing granite walls on the exterior and an airy schoolroom in the interior. Initially designed by Charles Bulfinch, it was successively enlarged by Boston's best architects, Alexander Parris, and Gridley J. F. Bryant with his co-architect Louis Dwight. Sacco and Vanzetti were executed in the prison in 1927, thirty years before it was torn down.

The immaculately groomed Boston Lunatic Hospital at City Point, South Boston (right), helped establish Boston's reputation as the hub of reform and experiment in the 1830s and 1840s. The hospital, which stood on Dickens's list of charitable institutions on his tour of America in 1842, fell in the late 1890s after the institution moved to Austin Farm in West Roxbury.

Master architect Gridley James Fox Bryant who contributed handsome designs for civic and charitable institutions designed the Discharged Soldiers' Home (left) as a hospital and died here in poverty when the structure served as the Home for Aged Men. The building was demolished in about 1957 and the architecturally undistinguished Hurley School and its playground now cover the site.

Boston City Hospital by Gridley J. F. Bryant (above) served a desperate need when it opened in 1864 and stood as a visual finale to Worcester Square on seven well-kept acres in the South End. The 1882 Harvard School of Veterinary Medicine (below) tended to a different kind of patient who entered through a suitably symbolic horse collar door on the structure on Village and Lucas streets. It boasted a shoeing forge in the basement and such spaces as a grooms' room, padded stalls, and kennels. The centralized pavilion plan of City Hospital was submerged behind other less carefully calculated twentieth-century additions and its domed administration building vanished altogether. The Harvard Veterinary School's successor, an animal hospital, was demolished in 1964.

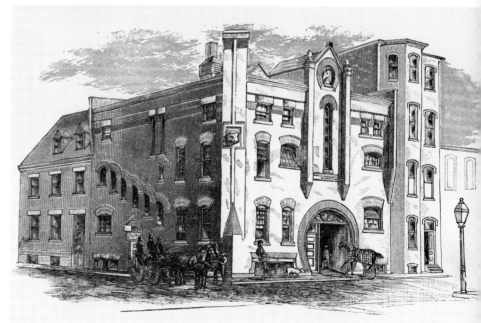

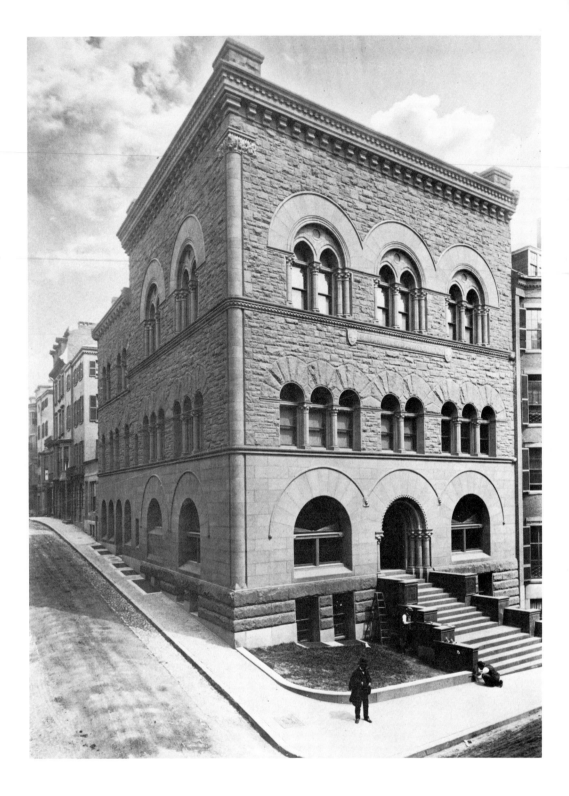

Boston's humane and church groups didn't want for an elegant architecture. The 1886 American Unitarian Association Building by the prolific firm of Peabody and Stearns stood on Beacon at Bowdoin Street, where the Bellevue Apartments now stand.

The bold portals of the Young Men's
Christian Association welcomed young citizens to the life of virtue and good health.
The 1883 Boston YMCA by Sturgis and
Brigham opened out with a generous staircase and looked out upon Boylston at
Berkeley Street with ample windows in a
style called Scotch Baronial, totally hidden
in twentieth-century alterations.

Houses of Hospitality

Julien's Restorator (above), a private dwelling of 1670, was renamed for its cook, a refugee from the French Revolution. It led a charmed life on Milk and Congress streets, resisting the fierce fire of 1760, but falling for Julien (later Congress) Hall in 1824. Fire took the Exchange Coffee House (below) on Congress and State streets after only a decade. Completed in 1808 from plans by Asher Benjamin, it stood seven stories high. Its marble pilasters, complex interior staircase, vast dome, and dining room for three hundred that once included President James Monroe made a "showy" structure that staggered Federal Boston. Still more luxurious, the Tremont House (right) bested them all for the company it kept. DeTocqueville, Dickens, Andrew Jackson, John Wilkes Booth, and William Makepeace Thackeray shared such modern accommodations as public rooms lit by gaslamps, and the unheard-of convenience of interior baths and water closets. "It has more galleries, colonnades, piazzas and passages than I can remember, or a reader would believe," Dickens observed. "Grandfather — a Puritan of the Puritans — fled from it in terror," wrote the daughter of Julia Ward Howe. Designed by Isaiah Rogers in 1828, its prompt success launched luxury hotels across America. A business block supplanted the glorious old hostelry after its 1895 demolition.

197

With a floor of marble tile and mirrors that
doubly "reflected the spaciousness and
beauty of the main entry," the Greek Revival Revere House of 1847 by William
Washburn was considered one of the finest
hotels in America. Presidents Fillmore,
Pierce, and Johnson; generals Sherman
and Grant; Jenny Lind; and the Prince of
Wales rested in its fashionable Bowdoin
Square quarters. The Revere House, an
enlargement of Bulfinch's Kirk Boott dwelling of 1804, was taken down in 1919 and
the fire station that replaced it ten years
later was removed in the early 1960s for
a government office building on the fast-
changing site.

The Hotel Vendome, built in two segments on Commonwealth Avenue at Dartmouth — first by architect William Gibbons Preston in 1871, then by J. F. Ober in 1881 — became Boston's first commercial institution with electric lighting in 1882. It had reception rooms like this one, bedecked for the visit of President Grover Cleveland. A slick addition replaced part of the hotel after fire gutted and collapsed nearly half the Vendome's Dartmouth Street facade in 1972.

Public Buildings

The jovial calls of countless Last Hurrahs and the stamping and sealing of endless documents echoed in Boston's storied town and city halls. Roxbury Town Hall (above left), attributed to Asher Benjamin and built in 1810, and Johnson Hall (City Hall), designed by Bulfinch the same year (below left), were distinguished works of public architecture. The Roxbury Town (later City) Hall, fell for a school in 1873. Some of the Chelmsford granite from Bulfinch's octagon-centered Johnson Hall went to erect its successor, the Second Empire-style City Hall by Bryant and Gilman, during the Civil War. In turn, this splendid heir (above) was gutted for offices little more than a century later. Although preservationists struggled and saved the shell, the interior with its woodwork of butternut and pine, its foyer of black and white marble flooring, its iron balustrade and oak newels and its city council chamber surrounded by pewlike galleries passed into legend.

"How it gleamed and glistened in the afternoon sunlight. How beautiful were its arches, how dainty its pinnacles; how graceful the tourelle on the corner rising as if by itself, higher and higher," architect Louis Sullivan would recall, "like a lily stem, to burst at last into a wondrous cluster of flowering pinnacles." The building (left), the Masonic Temple designed by Merrill G. Wheelock and dedicated in 1867, was demolished before the turn of the century.

Pomp and circumstance characterized the festive building put up by the Mechanics of Boston. Mechanics Hall on Huntington Avenue, designed by William Gibbons Preston in 1881, held displays of fireplaces, fairs, flower shows, and Paul Whiteman's Rhythm Boys (one of whom was Bing Crosby). Modern Bostonians disliked its Ruskinian gothic mode, however, and tore down the "ugly duckling" for a grimmer architectural goose, the Prudential Center, in 1959.

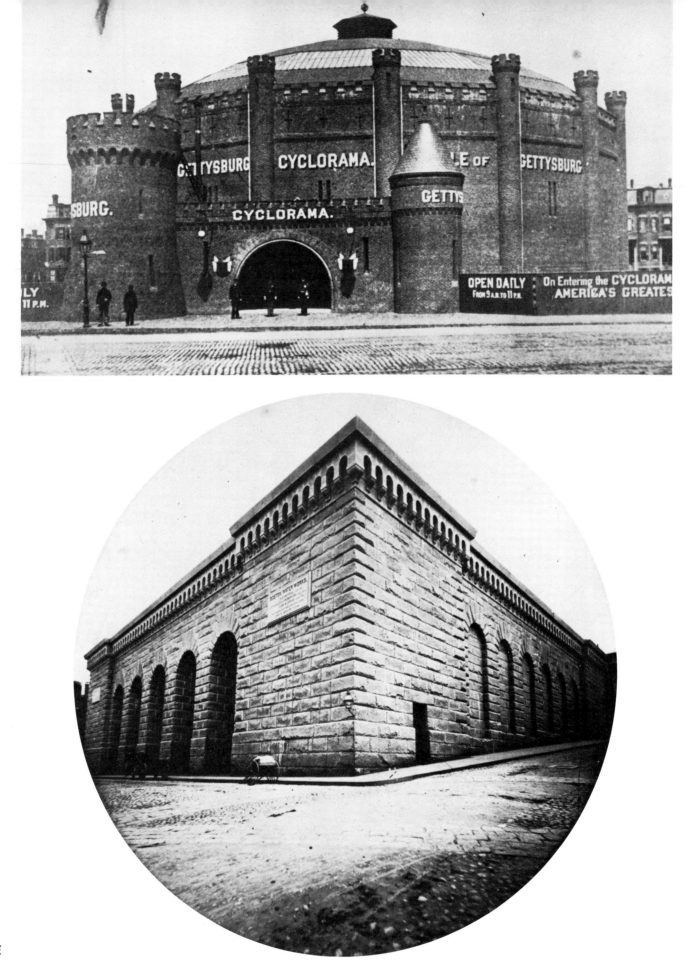

204

Boston's public landmarks were made more so by mammoth stone arches, turrets, battlements, and ornament. The Beacon Hill Reservoir (below left), designed in 1848 by William S. Whitewell, held the city's water supply behind impressive arches atop Beacon Hill. The circular brick Cyclorama (above left) opened in 1885 on Tremont Street in the South End. Designed by Cummings and Sears, it boasted a painting of the Battle of Gettysburg, which was 400 feet long and 50 feet high covering 20,000 square feet and attracting hordes of Bostonians from morning until almost midnight. Creatures of the sea cavorted in carvings on the exterior, and youngsters surveyed the fish in the cavelike interior of the Aquarium designed by architect William Downes Austin and opened in Marine Park, South Boston, in 1912. The reservoir came down in 1888. The Cyclorama long ago lost its view of the two great armies "seen in their momentous death-struggle" along with its moatlike castellated look. Neglect took its toll on the Aquarium, which was demolished in the 1950s.

CHAPTER 8

The City Afire, 1870–1880

Paris, the city of beautiful architecture, ever fresh and clean, can show no such costly marts of trade as these of Boston. Not on Rue Rivoli, with its massive colonnades, nor on the Boulevard Sebastopol, are there to be found structures so imposing as those that rear their majestic fronts, adorned with pillar, capital and cornice, in the heart of Boston. London, commercial capital of the world, sleeping to-night beneath its sooty pall, has no business centre so inviting as this granite quarter of the commercial capital of New England, and of the chief manufacturing industries on this side of the Atlantic.
—''CARLETON, an eyewitness to the Great Fire''

There is no section in America half so good to live in as splendid old New England — and there is no city on this continent so lovely and loveable as Boston.
— MARK TWAIN, 1871

I saw tall buildings catch in their roofs like huge matches, and blaze there.
— HENRY CABOT LODGE

How IMPOSING beneath the moonlight on November 9, 1872! How impressive the buildings looked in their garb of granite, marble, brick, and iron, a Boston witness to the fire recalled. Downtown was dressed for all eternity, it seemed, with stately buildings as immutable as time:

So solid, so firm, that they will not reel or totter in the wildest elements; so secure that fire can never sweep them away; so safe that the merchant owning silks and velvets, and laces to the value of uncounted millions, is sitting in his easy chair at home, confident that no calamity can come to him; that by no combination of circumstances will it be possible for his riches to take wings and fly away before the morrow's dawn.

Surely, the merchant had every right to his easy chair in prosperous Boston.

No Civil War guns could muffle the affluence with which the postbellum period began. Across Boston's new lands, the sound of hammers had accompanied the tramp of feet to war. Now the noise of unbounded building matched the anvil chorus heard when a joyous city staged its Peace Jubilee. In a coliseum bigger than anything P. T. Barnum ever raised, a throng of musicians (noisemakers to the classicists) rang out Verdi's "Anvil" chorus in 1869. One thousand musicians, ten thousand singers, a drum corps, church-bell ringers, and one hundred firemen armed with sledge hammers and anvils, played in unison and, for a finale, a cannon fired by electricity from the stage shattered the quiet air at today's Copley Square.

Why shouldn't they celebrate? Stillness at Appomattox meant union, and union meant business unabated. The Irish laborer and the Yankee merchant, in harmony for now, were making Boston the fourth largest industrial center in America, the producer of one quarter of its spindelage and the center of its leather trade.

Who but a Cassandra would note that the square-rigged clipper ships that graced the harbor were sailing into a setting sun? Who would predict that the age of coal and steel would one day bypass the town? Who would note that the wealth was tempered by the strain of urbanization, immigration, and industrialization — or that Boston's greatest fire would soon level sixty acres and render $60 million worth of property into ash?

The victorious North was busy beating its spears into the tools to build the Kingdom of Cotton and Wheat, the Principality of Oil and Pork, the Empire of Coal and Iron and Timber, it was said, and Boston was no exception. Clattering out of the city, backed by Boston capital, the symbol of the hour chugged to the west: the first through-

Fire station at 133 Salem Street, North End.

Overleaf:
The arched facade and chiseled letters of Macullar, Williams, and Parker frame the ruins of the Great Fire. The clothing factory, rebuilt behind its marble facade, was taken down for another commercial building.

train to California crossed the continent in 1869. It marked the stretch from sea to sea by stirring a jug of Boston brine into San Francisco Bay. At home, Boston was zesty and bustling, fulfilling America's need for ready-made clothes, boots, ironwork, and furniture. It was the chief wool market of the nation, the exporter of cotton from the ring of mills on southern New England's waters. Its central district housed these manufactured goods in splendid buildings each in its own zone.

The city was making such strides in street paving and gaslights, in sewage and in the large waterworks hooked to a new Chestnut Hill reservoir that the encircling towns sought tax relief by linking to the public works of the vigorous municipality: the town of Roxbury was annexed in 1868; Dorchester two years later; and within four years Charlestown, Brighton, and West Roxbury, including the districts of Roslindale and Jamaica Plain, joined to complete a total of twenty-five square miles of new land. The lengthening horsecar lines and the extending utilities would move settlement out to these so-called streetcar suburbs at a rapid pace.

The core had registered prosperity and progressiveness even before the Civil War. "A citizen of Boston, returning after an absence of two or three years would hardly recognize the place, were he set down in some portion of it," Ballou's *Pictorial* had declared:

Within a few months what changes have taken place in Franklin Street and its vicinity; the private residences all demolished and a double curve of commercial palaces, piles of granite reared in their stead.

The architect who fixed the Victorian curves of Franklin Street atop the rubble of Bulfinch's Tontine Crescent also fitted out countless other streets with the "commercial palaces" of the hour. Gridley James Fox Bryant (1816 to 1899), as much a merchant as the financiers, dry-goods lords, or princes of the boot who came as clients, produced a vast and diverse architecture. His City Hall, that Parisian wedding cake of a building done with Arthur Gilman, dropped the most sophisticated showpiece into the city. It brought countless projects to his 8 Court Street office. There the architect designed a host of dignified Second Empire buildings. Residences, businesses, jail, school, railroad station, hospital, and courthouse issued from his office, often co-designed by Gilman, Louis Dwight or talented students like Charles Cummings. "With [Isaiah] Rogers to do the designing and drawing and you the letter-writing, wire-pulling and 'bunkum'; I should say you'd make a very prominent firm," a fellow architect wrote. Notwithstanding such manipulations, Bryant's severe granite

Winthrop Square.

State Street block and Horticultural Hall show a self-assurance and
vitality that were his own. The son of the enterprising railroad man
of the Bunker Hill Monument days, Bryant was a product of the
civic and commercial era for which he designed. His "tradition" was
the evolving tradition of mass production, for he masterminded more
than "coutured" or customed his design. If a Bryant-built city
emerged, it was through powers of persuasion and organization that
matched his design skill.

Post–Civil War Boston boasted a fleet of designers and builders
secure with the name *architect*. Seventy-three listed themselves by the
brave label in the city directory. Imbued with a sense of professional
stature, nine of them formed the Boston Society of Architects on
May 15, 1867. A mixed breed, not one schooled formally, the
architects of this body dined in the Parker House and sat in the office
of Nathaniel J. Bradlee in Pemberton Square, discussing plumbing
or historic precedent according to the mood; setting up lectures;
sending out a monthly publication and traveling about the city to
critique one another's work. There was Bradlee himself, a business-
man on many boards, and William Ware, patient "Billy Buddy"
mumbling to a generation of students at MIT where he helped found
the first school of architecture since Asher Benjamin. Edwin Clarke
Cabot, once a convalescent on a sheep farm, now architect of the
Athenaeum was aesthetician and wise man to the group. S. J. F.
Thayer, "man-of-all-work," a designer whose scientific bent helped
him lead the way to the modern office aids of blueprint, phone, and
typewriter balanced William R. Emerson, the homespun synthesizer
who populated the suburb with his woodsy shingled homes.

A distinguished architecture arose to serve domestic and business
needs. Everywhere expanding retail stores housed themselves in
elegant emporia with the latest trim. An elevator of the best and
newest pattern soared up the interior of the Sears Building in 1868,
a stunning sight to Bostonians. Italianate structures celebrated the
solid strength of their inhabitants. Cast iron, first produced in
America by Daniel Badger, was brought to Boston in 1842. It
allowed large shop windows, light interiors, and ornate trim; by
the end of the Civil War, Badger listed more than 300 feet of iron
storefronts.

The central business district dazzled out-of-towners. It was "sixty
acres of such warehouses and stores as no other city on the continent
could show," the *Nation* waxed on:

The merchants of Boston have long been men of a breed aspiring to
the title of merchant princes and earning it by their public spirit,

The Equitable Building by Arthur Gilman.

The 342 Washington Street home of the first phone company.

munificence, administrative ability and the honors which have followed them. Governors and ambassadors have been taken from among their ranks; they have founded and endowed colleges and encouraged learning everywhere to the ends of the earth, have been known for their energy, ability and integrity. In their warehouses, they have of late years been accustomed to hold a pride and many a line of solid and handsome buildings attest to the dignity of the solid men of Boston.

Not only business castles but cultural and educational palaces enhanced the city. The first outfitted Boston's industry; but the second — built for Harvard, Tufts, Wellesley, Boston College, the Massachusetts Institute of Technology, and Boston University — reflected the intellectual ardor. Universities and their bold, proud new buildings, attracted keen minds; so did the abundant artisans, craftsmen, machinists, and engineers. "The technological elite of the nation" made Boston a crucible of scientific and electrical invention. The creative atmosphere held the restless Thomas Alva Edison for a while and inspired Alexander Graham Bell. Bell was drawn to the Boston Athenaeum, the brick and sandstone public library, and "standing out boldly on the flat half-vacant new-made land of the Back Bay, the Massachusetts Institute of Technology an edifice with a Corinthian countenance but a thoroughly modern brain," his biographer wrote. Bell, who was teaching at Boston University and the Horace Mann School for the Deaf, would invent his phone of the future in 1876.

More melancholy changes accompanied the boom years. Some buildings, like Bulfinch's church on Hanover Street or the innovative Hotel Pelham, were saved by heroics; crews raised them on their haunches and slid them back to allow for widened streets. Others were simply flattened in the name of "utility." Fifty tenants now squeezed inside the Old State House and a flock of billboards sat on its antique facade. The Ames Plow sign took possession of the proud portico of Quincy Market. To some, it seemed that the picturesque landmarks of antique Boston would fall before the "march of improvement." Expressions of regret stirred "within the breasts of those who had been accustomed to regard antiquities with a feeling almost bordering upon veneration," as one contemporary wrote. The anguished cries over the tearing down of the venerable John Hancock House in 1863 were the first soundings of a preservation movement in the city. The sounds echoed louder still when the Old South Meeting House, abandoned by its congregation for a Back Bay locale, looked likely to share its fate.

Old Bostonians joined the mournful lament of historian Samuel Drake as the green town shed its leaves:

Time was when the trees were everywhere, now they are indeed rare and the places that once knew them now know them no more. Formerly there were few, if any, situations in the town in which trees were not seen, but they are now fast following the old Bostonians who planted them or dwelt beneath their graceful shade . . . Occasionally, during our pilgrimage, we had discovered some solitary tree in an unexpected place but it only stands because its time has not yet come.

By now the boisterous merchants had uprooted the old elegant mansions that made Pearl Street and Fort Hill "a princely quarter." Not ones to stamp out squalor by halves, they looked at these once lovely areas, saw tenements and slums standing in the way of trade, and determined to "remove many of the noted places of filth and sickness." The city that boasted the nation's first board of health had a conscience of convenience to reinforce its economic will. In 1865, the city council voted to dig up Fort Hill, homeless inhabitants notwithstanding, and appropriated $1,250,000 to do the "work of reduction," leveling the hill to grade over twenty new acres.

Stubbornly, pitifully, some hill-dwellers clung to their houses "until the roofs were taken off, and their rooms laid open to the city," an official document testified. To no avail. Down went the last untouched drumlin of old Shawmut. The peak that once held Widow Tuthill's windmill fell in favor of more thriving shops and stores. Some of its gravel filled in a new Atlantic Avenue, dumping 7570 cubic yards on the old and tired wharves. The rest of Fort Hill raised the moist soil on the Suffolk and Church Street neighborhoods. As for the hill's inhabitants, they were packed off to South Boston, there to carve up tiny plots around West Broadway — carrying "the disease of congestion" later social workers observed, and transporting the granite of old St. Vincent de Paul's church to cover two sides of a second church by that name.

Not every pocket of Boston was elevated by the boom, then, nor had equal share in this prosperity. A state board described some dwellings of the period as "hovels rotting with damp and mold, foul and unhealthy." If some found that the jumble of Beacon Hill's north side or the North End now resembled "Dr. Johnson's haunts for quaintness," their residents might find them less picturesque. Scan the pages of William Dean Howells, a critic suggests, and you find more than the Boston of philosophical isms. You see Bostonians other than

Digging on High Street.

the fashionable socialites who found black walnut woodwork a bore. Here lived the immigrants in their "melancholy warrens," and the underground town of pickpockets and tramps lodged in "misfit parlours." Boston paid for its affluence. Industrialism exploited the old landscape, Lewis Mumford notes: "Warehouses, offices, shops, dingy over-crowded tenements to house the new proletariat to say nothing of railroad tracks and yards, venting noise and smoke were the price of Boston's lusty economic growth." A report of city physicians noted "a nest of miserable tenements." To Mumford, "the obvious increase in pecuniary wealth was offset by the disorder and human poverty that accompanied it."

To social critics at the time, however, the seemly city overcame such disorders. Dickens, whose pen lashed England's "great haunts of desperate misery," praised the Hub. He was happy with the Boston that he found on his return to America in 1867:

The city has increased enormously in five and twenty years. It has grown more mercantile — is like Leeds mixed with Preston and flavored with New Brighton; but for smoke and fog you substitute an exquisite bright light.

The English novelist basked in Boston's air. Its citizens returned the compliment, flocking again to his lively readings in Tremont Temple. Charles H. Taylor, the journalist who would one day build the Boston *Globe,* recorded the eagerness — and excellence — of Dickens's audience in this report:

The vast crowd had simmered down to a state of comparative quiescence. And it was indeed a vast audience, such a crowd is seldom gathered in a single hall to meet any one man. The line of carriages ran down all manner of streets and lost itself in the suburbs . . . Inside the house the scene was striking enough. Few cities anywhere could show such an audience of such character . . . There sat Longfellow, looking like the very spirit of Christmas with his ruddy cheeks and bright soft eyes looking out from the . . . snow-white hair and snow-white beard. There was Holmes looking crisp and fine like a tight little grapeskin full of wit instead of wine. There was Lowell, here, too, the older Dana, Charles Eliot Norton, Edwin Whipple. Yonder is Fields to whom we all owe this pleasure.

Lodged in the Parker House in a corner room overlooking the new City Hall, taking his four- or five-mile walk with publisher and friend James T. Fields, Dickens barely recognized the leisurely city or the open country of a quarter century before. Acting out parts of *Copperfield* or *Nickleby,* the two men strode down the Mill Dam (Beacon

213

Street) past the developing Back Bay, out by Brookline's growing Longwood area to the village of Newton Center around the train station; then back again, at the same vigorous pace, "puffing like two steam engines," into the marble lobby of Parker's elegant hotel. So it went every morning at 11 A.M. throughout his stay, taking in Boston's masonry and greenery in a single morning's walk — the gracious suburbs, the intimate walking city alive with fresh buildings, with handsome buildings, with buildings "so solid, so firm, so secure." It seemed . . .

The Parker House.

No noise punctured the serene city that night. All was still on November 9, 1872, the special stillness of afterhours when the corridors of business, purged of life, refresh themselves with sleep. Working Boston had drifted off long before sunset when the first sparks ignited within the cellar of a four-story dry-goods store and hoop-skirt factory on the southeast corner of Summer and Kingston streets. Lit, some would surmise, by the steam boiler of an elevator, the embers snapped into a blaze; fed by raw goods, they began a dance of death.

Though no one is quite sure of the details of its prologue, the drama of the Great Fire would become clear soon enough. Within twenty-four hours after a passerby had turned in the first alarm on Summer Street at 7:24 P.M., 776 buildings and 60 acres of goods would be consumed. Acre for acre, historians would call it the most costly blaze America had ever seen. One historian reckons that its $60 million damage would be more than $400 million a century later.

Boston could not have come to its great fire less prepared. Although its fire department ranked high among the nation's cities, the ninety-three horses that powered it had fallen prey to a disabling disease. For several weeks, fire department vehicles had been inoperative, and vigorous men took to pulling handcarts, drays, express wagons or hacks (to the tune of brass bands playing "Oh dear! What can the matter be"). The matter was that on November 9, the city lacked human and horse power. It had emptied out down to the last reporter lulled by the annual postelection dinner at the Revere House in Bowdoin Square.

All the chariots of Phaeton wouldn't have helped Boston anyhow. By the time the first alarm rang and the first engines arrived, the burning building had become an inferno beyond containment. The fire was ignited and the flames set on their deadly mission as they

Summer and Kingston streets, where the fire began.

leaped across Summer Street to Otis Street, bursting the windows,
sealing off the stone, and sending their little shoots of fire into every

crevice, nook and corner, and with white-heat driving the firemen
from the street, and charring long lines of hose.

Here, within footsteps of firebox 52, the pattern of the ravaging
fire was set: For when the flames had engulfed the impermeable
granite of this first four-story building and inhaled its mansard roof,
they did not die for want of fuel but jumped to the next timbered
mansard roof nearby, and from this combustible post, hopped south-
ward to a nearby building's roof, quickstepping across the business
district north and east until, in Oliver Wendell Holmes's words, "the
great high buildings seemed to melt away." Driven to ever greater
intensity by the goods under the roofs, the heat created a fire storm
that would help the blaze consume vast blocks before a second sunset.

What had happened to Chicago a year before could never happen
to the Hub, Bostonians had thought. The new blocks of buildings,
faced with granite, "gave the area an aspect of almost impregnable
security," an architect recalled. But the height of the so-called impregnable buildings and the combustible skeleton beneath their
mansard roofs devastated this dream. Before the "snapping, rattling,
bellowing, crashing" fire-fiend, mere granite could do nothing but
crack and topple, and panes of window glass simply snap and blow
out from the madly searing flames.

To be sure, fire was an ancient and implacable enemy. Yet even in
an age possessed of power to combat it, Boston lacked defenses. To
add to the distemper of the horses, the fateful height of the close-
packed buildings, and their tinderbox construction, the city's water
supply was inadequate. Plans for a comprehensive water system were
under way but the downtown mains were rusty and the pipes too
narrow on that November night, a fact to which fire department chief
John S. Damrell would later testify:

During the past three years, at large fires, much difficulty had been
experienced for the want of an adequate supply of water for our
steam fire engines.

Such water as there was merely "surged and hissed against the
melting walls!" It was no match for the fire that made a waste of
thirty streets of buildings worth $18 million and turned vast store-
rooms of goods — housewares and carriages, crockery and steel,
patent machines and saws, groceries and cutlery, clothing and furniture — into an odd-shaped rectangle of ash from Washington Street
to the harbor.

Not even that sea could stop the flames. Seven wharves and several
vessels waiting to unload were consumed beside the bay. Through

the long fiery night, the sky above the water took on its rosy glow.
The eerie sunset silhouetted buildings and caused witnesses to mistake
a flock of flying ducks for meteors, so black were they against the
orange night. Across the harbor's reddened waters, South Boston
residents watched the scene from their housetops, sopping wet
blankets on their roofs to prevent the flying flakes of granite,
firebrands, and fragments of slate from starting a second blaze. All
the way to South Abington, twenty-one miles south, a resident picked
up a scorched $50 bill. Citizens north to Portland, Maine, could see
the light from Boston against the horizon.

Early on, many Boston businessmen realized that salvage was
hopeless and invited citizens to save what they could from the flames.
Here and there, then, a scavenger clutching a hard-won coat or pot
added his ghoulish outline to the scene. Poorer residents from Harrison Avenue, fearing the worst, packed their valuables and fled their
homes. They were saved when the fire went against the wind and
hurried northward. Hillocks of crockery, mini crests of furniture,
and, here and there on the Common, a sleeping baby curled next to
the goods, made strange silhouettes beneath the light of the grim
fireworks.

By Sunday, the inferno that engulfed downtown had not yet abated
and word traveled out to adjacent towns. Vast crowds came to survey
"all the aspects of a bombardment" with soldiers in long blue over-
coats standing guard and firemen still battling to control the flames.
Nothing seemed to help as the fire edged ever northward, threatening
to take down the vaulted wealth of State Street and the historic
treasure of the Old South Meeting House. A host of worldly buildings
on Congress, Franklin, and Devonshire streets had succumbed and
the otherworldly architecture of gothic Trinity Church was collapsing
into a heap of stone. There was small hope, they said, of saving any
portion of the North End.

With streams of water so useless, firemen had adopted the device
of setting explosives, but the gunpowder blasts had little effect,
except to send more buildings sailing to the sky, shattering windows
and fueling fires afresh. Nonetheless, on Sunday morning, when the
flames crept northward, some clamored that the only recourse was
to blow up all the buildings on Milk Street. The Bostonians clustered
round the Old South Meeting House awaited its demise while firemen, darkened with fatigue, took a last and perhaps futile stand near
the post office. All waited for the end. Before that dire fate, however,
an event famous in the annals of American fire lore occurred. At a
critical moment, the engine *Kearsage* steamed in from Portsmouth,
New Hampshire, and, to the cheers of hundreds, dowsed and saved

the historic house of worship. For the second time in the century a blaze had threatened — and missed — the Old South Meeting House.

Early Sunday afternoon, the fire seemed to slacken finally; for reasons no one knows, the tireless flames began to die. Chronicler Colonel Russell Conwell vividly describes the mysterious final act of Boston's greatest fire:

For there was then a perceptible lull and a hesitancy, which gave the exhausted firemen new courage. Little cared the monster for the revered localities where Benjamin Franklin was born, where Edward Everett once lived, or where Daniel Webster's family gathered about his fireplace; and, with more than usual fury, it lashed about Governor Winthrop's homestead and the site of Widow Tuthill's windmill. But when the massive walls of the new post-office, with their nicely-carved towers, colonnades, and arches, arose in its path, it shook its lurid locks in rage, but respected and avoided the huge barriers of solid iron and granite which they held in its way.

So it was that at the mammoth, still unfinished post office on Devonshire Street at Milk, the course of the Great Fire reached a dramatic turning point. In the rear of the Merchants' Exchange on State Street, the might of Boston's greatest fire ceased.

With the fire thus under control by dusk, firemen began to frolic, pulling their steam engines here and there. Their mirth created no responsive echo in the crowd, for the fire had thrown "a gloom into the hearts of all Boston such as has never been seen before," a con-

A view of digging out from Devonshire Street.

temporary wrote. Leathermen ransacked the smouldering ruins for
their account books and clothmakers peered at the glum piles to pick
out the traces of their shops. The damage was endless. Guards, from
police to the young MIT student Louis Sullivan, were posted everywhere. DEVASTATION, headlined the Boston *Globe*. The *Pilot* and
Transcript were totally burned out. They could not print their anguish, but *Harper's Weekly* illustrated it and the *Nation* recorded the
grim loss:

*Now, from Summer Street north nearly to State Street and from
Washington Street east to the water's edge with two or three small
exceptions, there is nothing but rubbish remaining of the many
hundreds of granite and iron structures in which drygoods merchants,
wool merchants, and leather merchants of Winthrop Square, Summer
Street, Pearl Street, Milk Street, Federal Street, Broad Street, Kingston Street, Water Street, Devonshire Street and Congress Street
carried on trade.*

To add further to the gloom, gas exploded at Summer Street. It ruined
the opulent Shreve, Crump & Low and caused the gas company to
turn off the city's lights, plunging Boston into a darkness to match
the blackened mood.

Under the moonlight, the central business district was a bizarre
sight. Much of the center of the Hub was black rubble, "a deserted
waste of trembling walls, tottering chimneys and the ashes of millions
of dollars worth of merchandise." Eerie heaps of granite, skeletal
monuments, and huge boulders like relics from an avalanche of
doom hunkered across the landscape. It remains a spooky sight to see
the full-groomed merchants posed for photographs or to read the
macabre humor in their signs ("How do you like yours, hot or cold?")
stuck into the lifeless streets. Tuesday night the First Corps cadets
were released from duty and marched from their headquarters in the
Union Boat House up Beacon Street singing an old hymn remembered long afterward for its dramatic effect:

*The lurid light of the fire in many spots and the red streaks of dawn
were blended together in the east as the hymn brought the corps into
measured tread, and the effect of strong men's voices and their heavy
foot-falls breaking the quiet of a crisp November morning was grand
as they sang:*

> *The morning light is breaking,*
> *the darkness disappears*
> *a wicked world is waking*
> *to penitential tears.*

Certainly fire did not quell Boston's spirits — notwithstanding the latter-day Cotton Mathers who preached on the town's avarice and the good Lord's punishment. Diligent churchgoers overflowed the Music Hall to hear sermons with titles like "Knowing That Tribulation Worketh Patience" and other homiletic refrains from the past. "We must not be altogether absorbed in our brave plans for rebuilding the city and re-constitutioning our lost wealth," said the pastor of Old South Chapel. The pragmatic minister at the Somerset Street Baptist Church better fit the mood, however: he took the Great Fire as a warning from God on the folly of narrow streets and large warehouses with combustible roofs. Taking its own page from the Lord's book, the Emigrant Savings Bank opened its doors with a placard to boast why it had saved its valuables: "God has watched over the savings of the poor. In him we trust forever." Alas, His watchful eye did not look quite so favorably on the more than 20,000 workers thrown onto the streets.

In dire need from its own fire the year before, Chicago recalled Boston's charity and the mayor pleaded the case for the Athens of America before a cheering crowd:

What place is it that has been stricken? Boston, the historic city of America; I think, the greatest of all our cities; not, perhaps in bulk, or in area, nor in population, but in character, in education, in religion, in asylums, in hospitals, in charities, in everything (— cheers —) in everything that a consummate and perfect civilization can do towards developing the abilities of the active, and ministering to the wants of the helpless.

No time was lost waiting for charitable outsiders, however. Within twelve hours, hundreds of dry-goods merchants were en route to New York. By Monday, the post office was reopened in Faneuil Hall, and soon thereafter land was leased from the city to hold temporary stores. At the end of a year, the wool merchants had imported 39,691,990 pounds of goods, the city had raised $320,000 and Boston builders were carrying the rubble of this latest fire to fill the South Boston flats along Fort Point Channel. With typical resourcefulness, the insurance money from a ruined horde of armor bought tapestries for the new Museum of Fine Arts.

Most of all, the fire gave Boston a chance to do what it had done after fires for 200 years — to straighten out its crooked streets. "The best form in which we can commemorate the great disaster which has overtaken us is by establishing wider streets in the district covered by fire and in improved methods of construction of buildings throughout the city," Mayor Henry Pierce declared in his 1873 inaugural speech. (When a brief fire broke out a few days later, another citizen was heard to mutter that "the Lord was going to take it into His own hands.") The pursuit of straightened streets in the fire district cost the city more than $4 million. The money went to widen Water, Summer, Congress, Federal, Milk, Hawley, and Arch streets; to extend Pearl, Franklin and Oliver streets; and, most dramatically, to clear the land around the mammoth new post office for the grand Post Office Square.

The Chicago fire had taught such landscape architects as Frederick Law Olmsted, Horace W. S. Cleveland and his partner Robert Morris Copeland to opt for "rational planning," for generous space and boulevards. Perhaps the Boston blaze confirmed this need, for planning efforts of a visionary nature got under way. Copeland's scheme for Boston — a circus around the State House, parks, lagoons, and the like — earned him the label "spiritual father of modern planning." If such grandiose designs faltered, individual buildings inched ahead. The flattened Fort Hill would hold the leather district; Winthrop Square was rebuilt with granite structures capped anew with handsome roofs and abundant ornament; and Gridley James Fox Bryant, productive as ever, redesigned 111 of his 152 downtown structures near their burned foundations.

All was not mere copy or repeat in postfire Boston. Quite the contrary. For this was the period for fancy: Individualism reigned and a picturesque and personalized architecture was its hallmark. Iron fronts, tile floors, and brick insulation met the more stringent building codes while the tenets of Ruskin or Viollet-le-Duc served the flourishing imaginations of their architects. The gutted and savaged stores of Summer and Hawley streets rose anew with a high Victorian decor. A. T. Stewart's department store displayed a Venetian polychrome exterior by Emerson and Fehmer to match the lively baubles sold within. Macullar, Williams, and Parker saved the marble facade of its Washington Street store, still miraculously standing, and in a stroke of Yankee ingenuity extended and expanded it behind. As if to celebrate the glittering effect, Bulfinch's State House dome was covered with gold leaf in 1874.

Despite money problems, Boston buildings blossomed with terracotta and stone ornament; a foliage of ironwork adorned them. Lidded by mansards; serrated by gables; grooved by geometric lines; and textured by glazed tile, brick, stone, terra cotta or copper, nothing restrained postfire architecture. The jobs in the central business district and the work of the Back Bay busied Boston architects. They rose to the task with all the picturesque drama manifest in medieval turrets and conical corners. Their asymmetry and massing seemed as medi-

Only Liberty Tree Block remains in this view of Boston at the corner of Washington and Essex streets. The rest has gone the way of the rails and wagons.

eval as the seventeenth century's Old Feather Store, but sprang from sophisticated sources across the seas. The eclectic styles would culminate in romantic monuments in every corner of the Hub, of course — in the Back Bay's vivid conglomeration; in Harvard University's robust effulgence by Ware and Van Brunt at Memorial Hall, and in the suburbs' vivid Queen Anne concoctions. But it shone brightest by contrast in the wastelands of the fire and climaxed atop its ashes with an insurance company by N. J. Bradlee or the walloping post office by Alfred Mullett sent from Washington.

The Depression of 1873 that hit a year after the fire dampened the early zeal. Money was scarce and interest rates high. Dismal years of bankruptcy and real estate collapse, of idle factories and mills registered on the landscape once again. The slack half-decade took its toll especially in the South End but did not halt growth in the burnt district. A surge of prosperity enabled business to build ahead. In the end, a guidebook writer six years after the disastrous November days could scarcely see the remnants of the catastrophe:

There are probably fewer vacant lots on the territory swept over by the fire than there were on the morning before it occurred; and the buildings in this part of the city are as a whole incomparably more convenient, commodious, beautiful and artistic than those which preceded them. Let any one, for profit of this, stand at the head of Franklin Street and compare its present appearance with the faithful representation of its aspect before the fire . . . the dull uniformity of material and of architecture has given place to variety of form and color, to grace and beautiful and tasteful ornamentation.

Carving on Jordan Marsh building, destroyed in 1976.

The Flaming Landscape

For two and a half centuries, fire ravaged the Boston landscape. The seventeenth century had called its first fire the Great Fire as early as 1653, then lost North Church and forty-five dwellings to a still greater one in 1676 and suffered the loss of still more houses and warehouses near the Town Dock in 1679. So it went into the next century, reckoning with disastrous fires in 1711 and 1761. For two hundred years, wood made the town a tinderbox, compelling a nineteenth-century bard to write on the inflammatory nature of the town in 1803:

A pyre of shapeless structures crowds the spot,
Where taste, and all but cheapness is forgot.
One little spark the funeral pile may fire
And Boston, blazing, see itself expire.

If all these fires were disastrous, none approximated the Great Fire of 1872 that laid waste the city's glorious period of commercial building. More costly to the city than Chicago's better-known blaze in 1871, the Great Fire on November 9 and 10 made all the city's fires of the past seem slight. Turning block after block of stone buildings into lurid skeletons and rubble, it transformed a bustling city into a hideous graveyard of wasted architecture. "The desolation is bewildering," said the Reverend Phillips Brooks.

Fire engines fruitlessly sprayed water at the Boston *Pilot* on Franklin and Hawley streets (left). The rubble piled into hillocks and skeleton stones made poignant markers for the downcast Bostonians who posed near the directory of a once-bustling building at 60 Pearl Street.

Fire engines proved futile in stopping the flames but the gigantic half-finished Post Office Building, seen in the distance in this view from Devonshire near Franklin Street, still endured. Charles Francis Adams, a Bostonian of a commemorative cast, said the wall of the post office should be saved as a monument. It was completed but later replaced.

The Chelsea Veterans Company posed before some wasted columns. The eerie Giacometti-like forms of charred buildings made much of Boston's downtown unidentifiable.

A panorama in *Harper's Weekly* shows the
burnt district bordered by the harbor with
the State Street financial district still intact,
but the rest of downtown a ravaged heap of
stone and ash lined by once-flourishing
streets.

—CHAPTER 9—

The Greening of Boston, 1880–1900

By making nature urban, we naturalize the city.

— LEWIS MUMFORD

. . . schools, libraries, music and the fine arts. People of the greatest wealth can hardly command as much of these in the country as the poorest working girl is offered here in Boston at the mere cost of a walk for a short distance over a good, firm, clean pathway, lighted at night and made interesting to her by shopfronts and the variety of people passing.

— FREDERICK LAW OLMSTED

THE NINETEENTH century could have cast no odder couple
to play principals in Boston's final act of building than Henry
Hobson Richardson and Frederick Law Olmsted. Richardson,
the architect — Falstaffian in his physique, with Elizabethan appetites
in food and drink to match — was surrounded by clients who could
well afford his Romanesque monuments and shingled mansions.
Olmsted, the landscape architect, was "a charming simple quiet little
man," by some accounts. Limping a bit, he paced Boston's wasted
fringes to coax natural beauty from its grim outskirts and cajole its
citizens to create the first city park system in America. For all their
differences, this unlikely pair staggered under burdens of national
scope; similarly, they had few years to live in their adopted city, yet
possessed genius to more than compensate. Richardson and Olmsted
set standards for the built environment; they had heroic roles in
Boston's final turn from seaport to metropolis, from walking city to
suburban hub.

Richardson's buoyance fit the spirit of the day; his exuberance, his
robust designs, like the swelling arches that were his signature across
America, matched the temper of expansive times. His architecture —
libraries and houses, schools and churches — fit into Boston's context.
His clients displayed a Boston spirit unlike the attitudes that
shaped parvenu chateaux and palaces in New York in the Gilded
Age.

Henry Hobson Richardson was born to plantation aristocracy in
1838. A stutter deflected him from West Point to Harvard where he
made the professional connections and absorbed the built environment helpful in his mature work. On the eve of the Civil War,
Richardson left America for France's École des Beaux-Arts. Short
of funds, the nascent architect went to work for Theodore Labrouste,
where he learned about the pragmatic planning of libraries and absorbed the efflorescent style of Second Empire France. That knowledge
would serve him well.

Richardson was slow to settle in the city. Not until the Brattle
Square Church had revealed his individual style and a competition
earned him the commission for Trinity Church did Richardson take
up residence near Boston in 1874. Surely, though, Boston ways had
taken residence within his soul. Like Bulfinch almost a century
before, the ambitious student with his dreams of an engineering
career must have paced the wharves of a growing city. Those imposing wharves so bold and monolithic in the granite style foretold
the massive simplicity of Richardson's later work. Scholars have
sought the European source of Richardson's designs in the Renaissance palazzo, the Roman aqueduct, the Spanish cathedral. Students

Overleaf:
Horticultural Hall by Bryant rose
on Tremont Street during the Civil War
and fell for a business block.

of Boston will find it near to home in the stone reservoir, the mills, the solid business blocks transformed into the walls and arches labeled Richardsonian.

It was Trinity Church facing Art (Copley) Square that first projected the Richardsonian image in the booming Back Bay. There on the dusty trapezoid of land adjoining the new terra-cotta art museum, Richardson's landmark building rose. Sheathed with a tough mantle of colored granite and massed in a splendid composition, Trinity was a monument to God and architect — and to the most powerful pastor of the day. Its church and parish hall stood on 4500 wooden piles rising out of the soggy Back Bay. Atop its glacial boulders, a tower modeled on Salamanca was transformed into a free and daring display.

Inside, Trinity was a "colour church," blazing with the vivid life of its popular minister Phillips Brooks, who beckoned Bostonians by the hundreds to his Sunday services dedicated to the arts and sciences so evident in the architecture within. Rarely had the union of the arts been sought with such constancy. Never in America had such a skilled architect's ally shared in so luxuriant a work as did John La Farge, creator of the stained glass and murals of the dramatic interior. Richardson's call to La Farge foretold his invitation to the finest decorative artists of his day. It showed his broader capacity to secure the best in all the arts and trades throughout his career: Norcross Brothers, the masterful builders; Charles Follen McKim, Stanford

Henry Hobson Richardson.

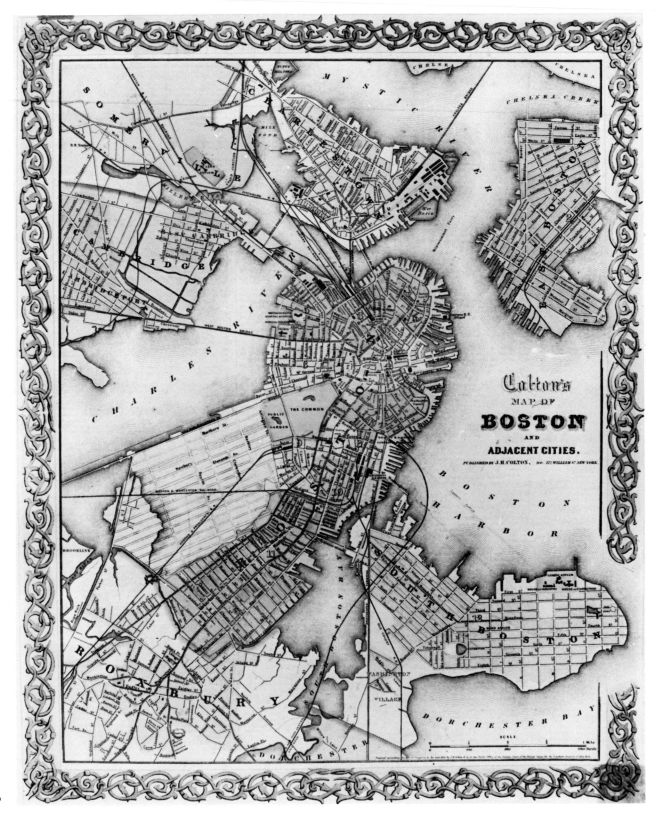

White, Charles Allerton Coolidge, and a host of gifted architect-associates at his Brookline atelier ("the abode of the Great Moguls," White would joke); Saint-Gaudens, the most talented nineteenth-century American sculptor; and, above all, many feel, Frederick Law Olmsted. Olmsted, master of the landscape, would be Richardson's companion and chief theorist. Richardson conducted the chorus of voices, as historian James O'Gorman observes, "but the absence of any member of the choir would have produced far different music."

Architects everywhere re-created the cavernous arches, the soaring towers, the coarse stone, the picturesque asymmetry and monumentalism shown in Trinity. They lent dignity to a roster of utilitarian buildings across America. Richardson was "the first architect of distinction in America who was ready to face the totality of modern life," says Lewis Mumford. Warehouse or store, train stop or train interior: "I'd plan anything a man likes from a cathedral to a chicken coop," said Richardson. The simplicity and wholeness of Richardson's commercial architecture led to the steel-frame construction of the sky-scraper mode. His Hayden, Ames, and John D. Pray buildings near Boston's burnt district, like the seminal Marshall Field wholesale store in Chicago, were "monuments to trade, to that organized commercial spirit, to the power and progress of the age," said Sullivan, who acknowledged the legacy. "The outpourings of a copious, direct, large and simple mind." By the time of Richardson's tragic early death from nephritis in 1886, a poll of his fellow architects ranked Trinity number one and listed five other Richardson buildings among the top ten of their day.

Richardson was all things to all architects, historians now concur: "The modernists see the vigorous man of affairs, the mighty user of the arch, the man who wanted to design a grain elevator and the interior of a large river steamboat. The Eclectics saw the lover of fine materials, the trainer of craftsmen, the man who would advise a bogged down designer to 'spend an hour with the photograph.'" Richardson bridged nineteenth- and twentieth-century architecture. He took to the building types of the times as if he had invented them, designing those platformed stations whose ample brows and sweeping driveways ennobled the middle class in their exodus to the suburbs. And the libraries! Those libraries were his special gift. In the growing towns and villages of Quincy, Woburn, and North Easton, they served as museums, community centers, and monuments in an age of the expanding suburb.

Out along the tracks — first on train and horsecar, then on streetcar and trolley — Bostonians began to move toward the perimeter. Down the old country roads by ones or twos, commuters settled upland

Colton's mid-nineteenth-century map shows the origins of the streetcar suburbs that flourished in the last quarter of the century.

pastures and broke up farmland. The prolific designer supplied icons
for the full household of late-nineteenth-century life. That household
was ever more private and domestic and its domain was Boston's
suburbs. Here, Nova Scotia carpenters or amateur developers might
hammer up solid houses for the middle classes but the wealthier
patrons with their Richardsonian churches and city halls had still one
more Richardson design in mind — the Richardsonian suburban
homestead.

In the 1880s and 1890s, Bostonians were sighing for the vanished
arcadias of their youth. They pined for Brookline where Audubon
had sighted rare species of birds just a generation ago, for a sleepier
Dorchester that viewed a proposed railroad station as "so great a
calamity," for the Cambridge of young Eliot Norton. "Everywhere
the new supplants the old," the professor mourned, "and the present
supplants the past." Equally wistful clients would summon Richardson to create this last insignia of the pseudorural life: the house type
that bore the label shingle style.

The shingle style bespoke both colonial days and the more ample
ideals of upper-class Victorian America. With its textured, horizontal
exterior and open interior, the new style spread across the Boston
suburbs, earned a major place in the architecture of the American
house, and swayed the twentieth-century genius Frank Lloyd Wright,
a small boy growing up in a town outside Boston.

If its name derived from the common shingle, the wood siding
that covered the early house, its earthy garb was made more so by
the base; puddingstone or granite boulders were mounded for its
foundation and wedded to the soil. William Ralph Emerson, a distant relative to the philosopher, is credited with the first examples
of the shingle style on the New England landscape. Tucked into
the craggy loneliness of seaside sites or stationed on romantic suburban lots, the shingle style was a rich organic mode that Richardson
evolved and the clients for country estates made their own.

Not only did the exterior of the suburban Boston house blend
antiquity and novelty, grandeur and "homeyness," the interior took
on a fuller look: Its modernity was horizontality. In contrast to the
uptight, upright row house, the suburban house of the 1880s and
1890s, be it labeled shingle style or Queen Anne, spread forth spa-
ciously. Stairs cascaded, windows let in light from four sides and the
cramped insides unbuckled into an airy space that could be custom-
made. It was an open plan warmed by far better central heat. It was
an inner flexibility in contrast with the stiff, narrow parlor that
hemmed in the downtown dwelling.

234   Enlarged from a constricted chamber to a flowing continuous

The home of feminist Lucy Stone and her
husband, reformer Henry B. Blackwell, on
Boutwell Street in the streetcar suburb of
Dorchester.

space, the suburban house was as welcome as the suburban lot. Bostonians in the streetcar suburbs fashioned it into a panoply of styles to match the effulgence of the high Victorian city, from the Italianate, mansard roof styles of post–Civil War days to shingle style or Queen Anne's asymmetry. No inch of surface was saved from picturesque detail. Shingles shaped in many geometries splashed down to clapboard walls; lively bays and voids and irregular forms were embroidered by an architectural petitpoint. Even the most modest copy of the shingle style took on a quilted appliqué, an ornamented turret or gable. The country carpenter paralleled the city mason with scalloped wood, jigsawed timber, and a random geometry of forms topped by a massive roof. To historian J. B. Jackson, it is that roof above all that remains the central image. It symbolizes the search for shelter in late century design and emphasizes the retreat into the safety of family life far, far from the chaos of the urban industrial world.

Certainly the rapid pace of Boston's suburban exodus suggests a flight. Nineteenth-century suburban inhabitants fit the pattern of today's bedroom communities: city by day, town by night. Even then, they fit the mold. No longer planned new towns held in check by topography, the streetcar suburbs followed the city-built utilities. With the lure of miles of waterworks, better schools, roads, and sewerage, the old hub tried to hold a fleeing populace once more: one reason Boston's public services led America. "Its citizens view things which are elsewhere considered municipal luxuries as municipal necessities," Mayor Frederick O. Prince observed.

Amateur builders followed the path of the advancing city services, skirting shore and highland, bridge and marsh; they planted houses on the old Dorchester farms or Roxbury Highlands estates beyond the three-, four-, or six-mile circle and multiplying Boston's land mass. Dorchester alone became a city second in size to the Hub while the hills of Brighton, packed with Catholic institutions, earned the label Little Rome. Again an influx of foreigners speeded the exodus from the Hub to these spots: the "second colonization of New England" was at hand.

It was now the two hundred and fiftieth anniversary of Winthrop's landing, and old Bostonians took stock of their history in ways their ancestors would have understood. The four volumes of Justin Winsor's *Memorial History* of Boston placed the bygone city in unwieldy but proper perspective. Sam Adams' statue by Anne Whitney was mounted in Adams Square and John Winthrop, charter in hand, sculpted by Richard Greenough, was set in Scollay Square to mark the historic date, September 17, 1880. Yet no retreat into antiquity in art, literature, architecture, or nostalgia could salve the

The Steadman Estate stable, Savin Hill, Dorchester.

city's consciousness or ease the growing pains from the population's swell.

Old Shawmut, central Boston, had long held immigrants; one third of its citizens were foreign-born Irish by the last quarter of the century. But this new wave of immigrants were from Italy and Eastern Europe, and, to fearful natives, seemed an alien race. "You go 100 yards south of Boston Common, and behold; you are in a polyglot slum!" one witness wrote. "If the gulf between Yankee and Irish had always been deep, the latest newcomers caused a rift that Boston could not bear."

"But where do the tenants and the workmen live," Matthew Arnold questioned on a Yankee trip to pristine Boston. They lived in the North, West, or South ends now, and native Bostonians despaired of their ragged quarters. The North End had become what missionary Robert A. Woods called "Boston's classic land of poverty." Its hard-pressed immigrants were herded together on thirty-five acres. The West End, Ward 8, slipped further into bad times, little eased by the good deeds and political ruses of the city's most famous ward leader, Martin ("the Mahatma") Lomasney, the first and best of Boston's special breed of city boss. The South End was but a small step better. It could be "portrayed by a series of red dots, each the symbol of a saloon," a troubled Woods wrote in 1892.

Boston's bosses — Patrick J. Kennedy in East Boston, a liquor dealer and paternal grandfather to John F. Kennedy; "Smiling Jim" Donovan in the South End; John F. "Honey Fitz" Fitzgerald in the North End, maternal grandfather to Kennedy; and lesser lights — staked out claims to the constituencies in the lofts, sweatshops, factories, and stores. "Human driftwood with its humanity gone," was one charity worker's phrase to describe their followers. "This South End, which once rose out of the water to become a refuge for the older American families, has now become a common resort for all nationalities," Woods wrote.

Some barroom pundits of Boston's vivid politics have divided the Hub into Irish counties. In truth, though, the Irish were now undermined. Italians soon inhabited the North End, Poles and Lithuanians filled South Boston, and Chinese took over the South Cove. Even the old beachheads were not secure from the foreign wave that pushed the more prosperous or working-class Irish outside Shawmut. Italian brawn rivaled Irish muscle. Jewish tailors labored in sweatshops from dawn to dark while state inspectors looked the other way. Everywhere Yankee officials had eyes that saw not as whole families stitched their lives away on piece goods in dim rooms or jammed in crowded tenements. A young priest who would become the powerful

Webster Avenue, site of Paul Revere Mall.

Cardinal William O'Connell remembered the sights and sounds of Boston's old West End:

I lived in the room on the second floor back. The outlook was upon a back yard, hung with clothes lines, and just across the way was a maternity hospital. Summer nights with open windows, were often made hideous by the cries and shrieks of the poor patients.

The Jewish preacher, Zvi Hirsh Masliansky, thought he was on the old continent:

I could hardly believe that I was in America. The streets of Boston reminded me of those in Vilna. Large synagogues with truly Orthodox rabbis. Talmudic study groups . . . almost all the stores are closed on Saturdays . . . Hebrew schools in the old style.

The children of John Winthrop and the children of Erin alike had reason to detest the airless, treeless tenements, to feel the foul hallways and streets were pits of crime and misery. "The streets and alleys reeked with the effluvia of a slave ship's between-decks," Edward Bellamy wrote in 1887. His novel *Looking Backward* launched a national move for reform.

"The United States as a dream of human goodness seemed to have lost its way," Van Wyck Brooks said. "Escape was the answer. Civilized withdrawal from a brutalized society encouraged interminable summer vacations [the real decadence of New England here?] to Nantucket, Martha's Vineyard, and the coasts of Massachusetts and Maine, where the old houses weathered silver, floating like dreams of forever in the cool bogs of the sea."

If some responded to the evils of industrialism by recoil, others tried reform. Wendell Phillips, Edward Everett Hale, Julia Ward Howe, Colonel Higginson, and countless others still had aspirations for their city. Edward Atkinson, reformer and economist, enlisted them in his search to relieve the urban slum: "The necessity or convenience of living near their work has caused an unwholesome concentration of the working people in the narrow streets of the older parts of the city," Atkinson pointed out in the *Memorial History*. "Within the municipal limits, however, are still great areas of almost unoccupied territory in which the mink may be trapped and musk-rats are the most numerous inhabitants."

To Atkinson, the answer lay in moving more workers into the suburbs. To others, it lay in cheap transit and the cheap three-decker house. The nickel fare and the three-family suburban dwelling became a moral crusade. Even traction magnate Henry Whitney called

the dispersion of the population a do-good deed and promoted the
nickel ride of his West End railway as if charity and his swashbuck-
ling real estate were soul mates.

To still others the way to solve Boston's dilemma lay in another
kind of greening and, in this too, reform followed an urban planning
approach: "Boston is a crooked, confused territory," a park-lover had
written to Frederick Law Olmsted after Olmsted's lecture in 1870.
"If we ever get straightened out it must be in the next or succeeding
generations; if we ever have parks, now is the time to secure the
lands for the purpose." Boston was about to harbor its second design
genius of the era.

The landscape designer finally called to Boston to consult with the
park commissioners in 1875 was not the picturesque figure with the
cape and floppy hat who had trod Mount Auburn Cemetery years
before, not the uncertain young man who had tried farming and
taken trips to England in a tortured search for his life work. By the
time Frederick Law Olmsted came to Boston his career had coursed
from journalist to head of the Red Cross to creator of Central Park.
He was America's leading landscape architect and a public admin-
istrator of national renown. Olmsted, in fact, founded the profession
and his work with Calvert Vaux, which transformed Central Park
from a wasteland into a pastoral oasis, had led him into countless
acts of urban beautification. The sickly son left to run wild in his
youth had become the nation's most tireless student of trees, fields,
and wildlife and its prime apostle of the need to use them as civilizing
backdrops in an urbanizing America. In wild spots at Yosemite and
Niagara Falls, Olmsted founded conservation efforts. With tamer
urban areas from Chicago to Montreal, Washington to California he
sought to relieve the "demoralization" of the tenements. His sculp-
tured city parks softened the harsh industrial landscape, and his graceful contoured suburbs broke up the grid of rapacious developers.

A friend of cultural impresario Charles Eliot Norton and colleague
and confidant to H. H. Richardson, Olmsted was a natural choice
as consultant to the expanding park system. Once consulting, Olmsted's choice as chief was inevitable. The story goes that Richardson
asked his talented friend to make the city his permanent base. Olmsted obligingly passed a stormy night at his house in adjacent
Brookline. Upon awakening, the landscape architect discovered that
the snow-covered streets of the town were freshly plowed. This act
of municipal efficiency so impressed the refugee from New York's
bureaucratic tumult that he took up pen and residence in the town.

No city in America was readier to greet him or to use the skills
that would make him what some call the first regional planner in

Frederick Law Olmsted.

The Boylston Street Bridge designed by
Olmsted and H. H. Richardson.

America. Bostonians had a love of landscape and a long history of
horticulture. For decades, the Massachusetts Horticultural Society had
annually festooned its large hall with sumptuous greenery and laden
its tables with vast displays of the produce of its Brighton fields and
vines. Mount Auburn Cemetery was its child. Horatio Hollis Hunnewell's rhododendron show drew 40,000 Bostonians to the Common.
Other members like historian Parkman developed the lily that bore
his name, and the great Webster, a keen squash grower, spoke for
all when he declared:

*The botany we cultivate, the products of the business of horticulture,
the plants of the garden, are cultivated with us by hands as delicate
as their own tendrils, viewed by countenances as spotless and pure as
their own petals, and watched by eyes as brilliant and full of lustre
as their own beautiful exhibitions of splendor.*

Private country estates set a pattern and isolated developers (like
Hunnewell with his eight-foot-high fuchsias) showed the way, but
the whole community had ennobled these private acts to a *public* art.
The New England commons had created a tradition of the "country
park" and Boston's flowering Public Garden, its malls and squares,
showed the heritage of civic concern " 'Boston doesn't need a park,' a
visitor to Boston may say," Horace W. S. Cleveland wrote. "The
whole place is a park."

Nonetheless, Bostonians of all kinds, fearing speculators, had
pleaded for more public grounds since 1869. They set up a commission in 1875. By 1877, the city had bought 106 public acres to supplement the "noble forests" of Boston Common, the ornamental graces
of the Public Garden, the shade trees in great abundance, and the
open green carpet of Commonwealth Avenue Mall. If such existing
parks were precedents and public opinion an incentive, it was the
festering nuisance of the Back Bay that made the westward extension
inevitable. Bostonians had to resolve an urgent ecological issue: the
stench and sewage of the Muddy River and Stony Brook were so
unsanitary that even clams and eels could not survive.

Olmsted was not optimistic. America's political corruption and his
own New York embroilments had dulled his activist impulses. Yet
the sorry plans submitted by applicants for the job made the weary
landscape architect set aside his misgivings and take on the work
himself, little knowing that help would come from the enthusiastic
alderman who was elected Boston's first Irish mayor in 1885. Bulky,
bearded Alderman Hugh O'Brien had promoted parks for the workers
eight years earlier.

*The parks would be the vineyards of the laboring man, and would
also give his family now crowded in narrow streets and tenement
houses a place for health and recreation.*

Olmsted had only the vaguest sense that the park system would
harness Yankee reformers and Irish leaders to charge the best
energies of a dynamic time and place. Of all the era's transformations,
Boston's greening held the most promise: release for the oppressed
worker and refreshment for all those bound within the city's walls.
The urban park was a shared cause for Boston's planners and its
whole populace.

The parkmaker par excellence still had his work cut out for him as
he sought to transform the brackish landscape into an "Emerald
Necklace." The project would turn an often uninviting topography into a six-mile chain of greenery from the Public Garden to a
500-acre country park in West Roxbury. It was one of the most
complex and vast undertakings of Olmsted's career and a landmark in urban planning in America. The Boylston Street bridge
designed with Richardson provided the gateway for the country's
first greenbelt. Over twenty-two years, Olmsted's corridor of continuous parkland grew in bits and pieces from the salt marshes of the
Fens to the sheep meadows of Franklin Park. In time, it linked the
five erratic open spaces of the Back Bay Fens, Muddy River, Jamaica
Pond, Arnold Arboretum, and Franklin Park. By culverting the
noxious Stony Brook, contouring the marshy Fens, and shaping the
Muddy River artfully into a storage basin and marsh-meadow, Olmsted formed the first of his Boston "breathing spaces." Enlisting city
and town, speculators and engineers, specialists in vegetation and
specialists in legislation, he proceeded to hook these open spaces to
connecting boulevards along the Fenway, Riverway, Jamaicaway and
Arborway throughout the 1880s and 1890s.

While other cities succumbed to sprawl on their bleak and wasted
outskirts, Olmsted joined a naturalistic girdle of greenery to the
emerging Back Bay. A stretch of water for canoeing, banks for picnicking, and paths for horseback riding were tucked between the
city's close-packed row-house world and its advancing suburbs. The
landscape architect used nature to visual and ecological advantage:
"blooming islets" screened passing trains; a receiving basin held
swollen flood waters; native ocean-loving species insured long life on
the salty banks; and foot and wheeled traffic were screened from one
another everywhere. "Formal and relatively flat as it passes the Fens,
intimate and sylvan as it skirts the Muddy River and Jamaica Pond,
and majestically ample in width as it approaches the Arborway, the

Hugh O'Brien, mayor of Boston, 1885–
1888.

Ward's Pond in Brookline.

240

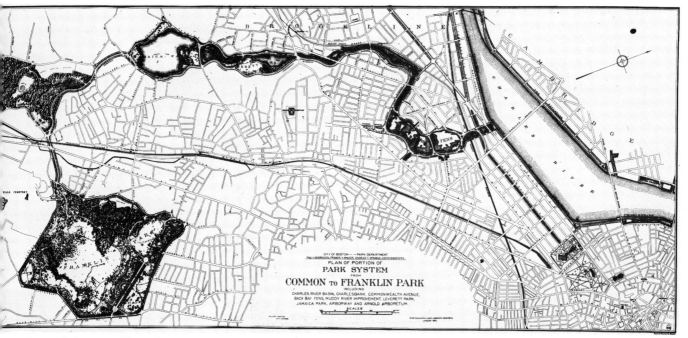

Map of the Emerald Necklace.

Boston parkway is one of Olmsted's grandest conceptions," historian Cynthia Zaitzevsky has written. "I do not think that at so early a stage any other park work has come so near to being recognized and treated as a work of art!" Olmsted assessed the progress early on. With mere scraps of no man's land, Olmsted created a linked landscape. In two instances — Arnold Arboretum and Franklin Park — he did something more: he inserted open spaces of monumental scope.

"A tree museum," founder Charles Sprague Sargent would call one of Olmsted's masterpieces, the Arnold Arboretum on the Arborway. There, Harvard University had held "a worn-out farm partly covered with native wood ruined by pasturage and neglect." Horticultural deficiencies were nothing compared to political ones. The 265 acres belonged to the Kingdom on the Charles and "asking President Charles W. Eliot to allow the city to operate the Arboretum as a park, restricted or not, was almost like asking Congress to let Imperial Russia administer Alaska as a playground," said Sargent. Boston politicians returned the chill. "A school for the study of the culture of trees," a leader of the opposition sniffed. "To my mind it must be either a phantasy of the Park Commissioners or a scheme of individuals for personal glorification or public notoriety." Five years of "exceedingly disagreeable semi-political work" finally reconciled squabbling leaders. In 1882, the city got a thousand-year lease on the land in return for road building and maintenance. The art of Olmsted and the science of Sargent secured an urban Eden.

"Cool as a rock," conservationist John Muir had called the garden-maker whose labors planted this amazing collection of greenery on Olmsted's artful contours. "There you stand in the face of all Heaven come down to earth, like a critic of the universe, as if to say 'Come Nature, bring on the best you have. I'm from Boston!' "

Well might Boston boast. Despite slowdowns and obstacles, the greening was under way: park corridors channeled out; plantings were designed; pick and shovel crews carved excavations; the office in Brookline was expanding. "Nothing else compares in importance to us with the Boston work," Olmsted wrote his young partners, stepson John C. Olmsted and Charles Eliot, the son of the reforming president of Harvard, in 1893. "I would have you decline any business that would stand in the way of doing the best for Boston all the time."

His parks of varying size — Wood Island in East Boston, the harbor and Charles River front improvements, his boulevards, and especially the other "masterwork" — the country park in West Roxbury, today's Franklin Park — were nearing completion. From the Public Garden through its many chains, the Emerald Necklace was leading to its final gem. The most unlimited, most magnificent spread of all was unfolding at Franklin Park. Only Central Park and Prospect Park, in New York's great metropolis, compared to the space planned for the park in Boston's outermost streetcar suburb. From 1887 to 1900 Olmsted divided the West Roxbury park's scenic acres

Wood Island Park, East Boston.

Franklin Park grotto.

into smaller zones, turning rolling, rock-strewn fields into a mix of rural landscapes: the "country park," the "wilderness," the grand mall or "greeting," and the "Playstead." If the core of Franklin Park was rural, Olmsted responded to the urban recreational urge with tennis courts and a child's lot. His playground and sports field bred city parks and America's first outdoor gym at Charlesbank along the Charles River where immigrant groups had their "breathing space" near at hand.

Some call Franklin Park design by subtraction, design to accent the natural turf: Boulders of Roxury puddingstone scattered about Franklin Park became shelters, arches, walls, gates, and fountains; rocky outcroppings loomed over undulating fields; depressed ground became manmade Scarborough Pond. Olmsted plotted fine touches and allotted shares of the work to those most skilled in their execution. "It is impossible to apportion credit," Olmsted insisted. "So much to one, so much to another." Harmony had top priority, not only human harmony but harmony with the forces of nature — floods, droughts, erosion — and with the site. Harmony in the architecture and harmony in the engineering. Blending architecture and landscape architecture with the dictates of the locale, Olmsted was an organic designer in the deepest sense. He was an ecologist before the word was used. His sense of the complexity and duration of the park work led to his willingness to bring not only Richardson heirs Shepley, Rutan, and Coolidge and stepson John into his work, but to expand beyond even Marine Park and the roads that stretched to South Boston's shore. "In your probable lifetime," Olmsted wrote his young associates, "Muddy River, Blue Hills, the Fells, Waverly Oaks, Charles River, the beaches *will be* points to date from in the history of American Landscape Architecture, as much as Central Park. They will be the openings of new chapters of the art."

As Olmsted's powers declined and the century neared its end, Charles Eliot began to write the vital chapters outlined by Olmsted. He took up Olmsted's pen in Boston's behalf: "Boston and her surging sister city grow continually," Eliot wrote. Farm after farm and garden after garden were invaded by streets, sewers, and water pipes. This eloquent protege worried:

As our towns grow, the spots of remarkable natural beauty, which were once as the gems embodied upon the fair robe of Nature, are one by one destroyed to make room for railroads, streets, factories, and the rest. The time is coming when it will be hard to find within a day's journey of our large cities a single spot capable of stirring the soul of man to speak in poetry.

The slim long-legged seeker of poetry who paced the country estates and vanishing open land of Boston in the 1890s became the galvanic writer, creator of the landmark Trustees of Reservations, and advocate for the Metropolitan Park Commission founded in 1893. With Eliot as landscape architect and the persuasive journalist Sylvester Baxter as secretary, the park commission took a landmark step toward regional planning. Eliot had argued for the state to hold land "just as the public library holds books and the Art Museum pictures." Now he chose and mapped Greater Boston's open space. Through his labors the Metropolitan District Commission came to hold 10,000 acres of parks and reservations, thirty miles of river banks, eight miles of seashore and twenty-seven miles of boulevards and parkways. Franklin Park would be nearly the last lavishly created country park in America, but Eliot and the "epoch-making" Trustees of Reservations and Metropolitan Park Commission bought up and conserved vast natural acres from the brutal carvings of developers. Like Olmsted and his office, Eliot bridged both inner city and countrified suburb. Before his death at thirty-seven, the crusading landscape architect did the work of a whole firm. In turn, the expanding park system bred broader efforts to design and organize water and other services along a more holistic metropolitan line.

Distant groves with babbling brooks did not suffice to earn Boston's place at "the cutting edge of urban reform in America," however. Olmsted himself knew that the green spaces on the periphery needed an inner-city counterpart. Close to the West End's breathless tenements Olmsted had planted Boston's first riverside park at Charlesbank in 1894. Now, the city's third Mayor Quincy capped the decade of advance with more urban improvements. Well-groomed and silent Josiah Quincy issued forth from his father's house on Charles Street to help the teeming wards of the city. The Dover and L Street bathhouse, indoor showers for the North End, twenty-two playgrounds, twenty schools, and the first indoor gym in East Boston were inner-city supplements to the larger ring of parks. On a large scale (at Revere Beach, twenty minutes away on the trolley, or Nantasket, Middlesex Fells, Stony Brook Reservation) and on a small (in the ballfields of North and South ends, Dorchester, Charlestown, and Roxbury) Boston's late-nineteenth-century planners had come to grips with the social, topographical, ecological, and political forces of their day. Their work was ample evidence for the *Review of Reviews* statement that Boston had "furnished the country with the best example of modern knowledge and ability applied to the corporate life of a metropolitan city." Whether prompted by Yankee Mayor Josiah Quincy, who believed that the more for athletics, "the

Charlesbank playground.

less . . . for punishment of crime," or Honey Fitz with his immigrant constituency, the parks were a popular and prominent undertaking.

Notwithstanding all this planned parkmaking, the most famous of the city's open spaces had come almost as an afterthought. If Copley Square didn't "just grow," the parceling of the plots around produced it in a random way. Almost by happenstance, the 1870s saw not only Trinity Church but a host of mature institutions frame the sides along two adjacent plots in the heart of the Back Bay: to the south, the Museum of Fine Arts by architects Sturgis and Brigham; to the north, brick row houses, Second Church, and Cummings and Sears' towering New Old South; and angled to the west, S. Edwin Tobey's picturesque grocery store for S. S. Pierce.

Only one side was left free and clear, and, by 1880, when the democratic policy "which almost thrusts a book into the hands of every inhabitant, and insists upon reading it" had jammed the old library, the empty space could have but one occupant, a larger shrine for books. Unable to sell the open space, the city gave space and site for a new Boston Public Library. In 1883, Art Square took on the name of John Singleton Copley. "This palace is the people's own!" Oliver Wendell Holmes exclaimed poetically at the 1888 laying of the Boston Public Library cornerstone. Across the reach of Copley Square, a castle to literacy would arise. Unlike the jaunty, colored pattern of its architectural neighbors, the building by McKim, Mead, and White was cast in a new mold — discreet, serene, and imperial. Though both McKim and White had apprenticed to Richardson, this work heralded a coming mode of architecture. As Trinity had advanced Richardson's Romanesque Revival from the 1870s through the 1880s, so the library brought the era of the classical revival to the late 1890s.

The Boston Public Library was a Renaissance palace in every sense. Borrowed more literally from the textbooks, its facade brought a cool pinkish gray copy of Rome via Paris to Boston. Its thirteen arched windows graced Copley Square creating a model of Beaux-Arts academicism for Back Bay residences and institutions to emulate. The 1888 budget of $400,000 tallied in at $2.5 million by its finish in 1895. The funds secured by the persistent architect and "impresario of the American Renaissance" were spent to buy embellishments of the richest sort.

They also bought what in later years would be called a "machine for living" containing, by one contemporary reckoning, "a heating, lighting, ventilating and electric plant with three one hundred horse power boilers and two tandem compound engines of 150 horsepower each; also two dynamos with capacity for 3600 sixteen candlepower, 110 volt electric lamps." Chugging away unseen were eight pumps for ventilating fans, eight electric motors, two passenger elevators, ten electric booklifts, and a vacuum cleaning apparatus with piping arranged to clean all the books on any floor.

It was not the pneumatic tube for book slips or even the million books themselves that dazzled turn-of-the-century Bostonians, however, but the treasures within. The finest collective art of the period was created for its interior with murals by Puvis de Chavannes, John Singer Sargent, James McNeill Whistler, and Edwin A. Abbey; carvings by Saint-Gaudens; sculpture by Daniel Chester French; and adornments of fine marble and materials from McKim himself. A people's palace indeed! for there wandered Mary Antin, whose *Promised Land* is the odyssey of the aspiring immigrant, "very slowly up the low, broad steps to the palace entrance." There, Antin "spent rapt hours studying the Abbey pictures [and] felt the grand spaces under the soaring arches as a personal attribute of my being. The court yard was my sky-roofed chamber of dreams," she wrote.

The harmony of art and the monumentality of expression achieved by McKim found a parallel in the historic World Columbian Exhibition held in Chicago in 1893. Its architectural inspiration, many say, was the Boston Public Library. Chicago's White City, which McKim and Olmsted helped lay out on grandiose lines, proclaimed a new civic style and aesthetic consciousness across America; it upstaged the vivid eclecticism of the Victorian period with its showy classicism. Rome had all the answers for this period. Reminders of its classical vision would bob in the public imagination for more than a half century.

The library that a contemporary critic had called "cold, uninteresting, severe, unsympathetic, monotonous and conventional" also spawned a domestic style. In search of their colonial roots, McKim and White had journeyed to Boston's North Shore in the late 1870s; afire with zeal for the centennial, they sought to find a truly "American" architecture. Out of their quest came the Georgian Revival. "Colonial" design became a major paste-on style. By century's end, the passion for antiquity and archaeological correctness ruled, for reasons obvious to architect Robert Swain Peabody:

It is because we want to live amid wainscotting, nestle in elliptical arched nooks, warm ourselves beneath the high mantles at blazing wood fires, and go up to bed over boxed stairs with ramped rails and twisted balusters, and see our old chairs and pictures thus environed . . . that we seek for an excuse to do it all again.

Bacchante with an Infant Faun by Frederic W. MacMonnies, in the courtyard of the Boston Public Library.

246

The search for bygone design also prompted rescue acts for the genuine article. The Old State House was restored to its "antique" origins in 1882, and the Old South Meeting House saved from a sad end. Salvation joined hands with re-creation to evoke the visual forms of preindustrial America. Was it that late-nineteenth-century Bostonians thought old trappings could camouflage the haunting bigness of Boston's burgeoning institutions? Could tradition intimidate and inculcate foreigners in the American way?

Certainly, the Boston Public Library inspired proper awe. More than that, it was what McKim's biographer has called "a visible manifestation of the civic consciousness of Boston." On every side similar institutions began to build. Bostonians brought forth the cultural and educational establishments of its second Athenian Age. To the west, McKim's Symphony Hall in 1900 and Wheelwright and Haven's Horticultural Hall in 1901 created "palaces of the people," too. Schools of every stripe from Wellesley College to the Boston Normal Art School, from Northeastern University to Tufts demonstrated the climate of higher education in the final decades of the century. Public schools and business schools, hospitals and libraries paralleled them on the municipal scale.

The city had always been the center where Godkin's "seasoned wealth allied with seasoned consciences" to produce the institutions that rippled out across America. Frederick Tudor, the Nahant ice king who sold his frozen cubes on six continents, was typical when he turned his profits to found the *North American Magazine* in 1815. Sea-rich Colonel Perkins benefacted the Athenaeum, and the wealthy Irishman Andrew Carney paralleled the generosity. So did countless humbler givers. The Yankee tradition of charitable endowment, the brighter side of noblesse oblige, flourished now across the land. "Boston is not a plutocratic city, something continues to count here beside mere money," as a character in *The Chippendales* put it. The spiritual points of the compass for a New York lady might swing no wider than the path from dressmaker to silversmith, but in Boston it was otherwise. The novelist wrote:

A cultivated woman was bounded on the north by Harvard College, on the east by the dome of the State House and by Boston Common, on the south by the Boston Art Museum, and on the west by Mount Auburn Cemetery.

The cultural life of the Medicean donna of Boston was broader. Isabella Stewart Gardner ranged the world to collect the finest arts and ornaments for her palace on the Fens. The house that "Mrs. Jack" built was constricted by few temporal or financial concerns.

This lady, who entranced and affronted old Boston by taking her two pet lions to stroll down Beacon Street, dangling voluptuous pearls around her waist for a Sargent portrait and, sporting two diamond antennae in her hair, closed the nineteenth century with plans for a lavish palace. Out upon the desolate Fens, as tranquil as a private garden, her latest dwelling had an integrity of art and architecture: and the engaging autocrat willed it to last forever. Sharing credit with her architect Willard T. Sears, she joined her laborers as mason, plasterer, and carpenter and drafted that North End boy-turned-connoisseur Bernard Berenson to help. The lady with the pearls produced a Venetian palace poised above Olmsted's landscape of marsh and upland scenery. Her Fenway Court, like Richardson's bridge, formed a gateway to what looked to become the "court end" of the town. The developing Fenway seemed destined to hold the lofty institutions, the cream of cultural and residential Boston.

Was it all museums and connoisseurship, collecting and not creating, as some witnesses of Boston's literary and economic decline have catcalled since? "I am just like a Cabot, so are we all — nothing but Cabots, and run Art Museums and change our wills walking down State Street," Henry Adams wrote, lamenting the loss of Yankee patrimony. Sad omens did abound. Somber citizens mourned the abandonment of Bulfinch's State House chambers for a new annex. On March 7, 1895, the sergeant-at-arms took down the Sacred Cod-fish, wrapped the salty old symbol of Boston in an American flag and walked with fifteen legislators to the new (and much loathed) State House yellow brick annex by Sturgis and Brigham. "Not a tradition of art but has been outraged," said *Leslie's Weekly*. To some it seemed the best of Boston was passing. The Immigrant Restriction League, which rose to keep out "Slavic, Latin, and Asiatic races" attested to the uglier passions of the hour. The private clubs and club buildings sprinkled downtown suggested their founders' escapism. Henry James looked at the Boston Public Library and sighed for the hidden recesses — the "penetralia" — of its old self. James too was dubious about the youngsters scampering up its sculpted lions and the whole multitudinous bustle, "the coming and going as in a railway station of persons with carpet bags and other luggage."

Yet in all their very multitudinousness, Bostonians would show themselves impassioned once again in the art of citymaking. More than that, they would defend that art dramatically in the face of an alien invader. For now, on the eve of the twentieth century, the city was about to be attacked by a noisy and destructive intruder. Henry Whitney had proposed to fell trees along the Common and mount an elevated railway high above Tremont Street along the Common,

Crowds collect along the Tremont Street trolley line.

casting its blight and noise on the shopping street. He cared not one whit for the urban consequences.

Reformers likened the Battle of the El that closed the flowering era to a classic morality play. Traction king Whitney, the incarnation of plutocratic evil, employed two dozen lobbyists, paid off rival syndicates, retained eight attorneys including former mayor Patrick Collins, and spent a quarter of a million dollars wining and dining in the Algonquin Club, by one report, while Harvard "dude" Josiah Quincy, the "people's attorney," Chief Justice-to-be Louis Brandeis, and "Save the Common" crusaders personified the good.

The angels of civic salvation had their work cut out for them, for the trolley had seized the city's imagination; its electrification in 1889 doubled the speed along the line. The lengthening streetcar tracks carried commuters and all Bostonians out to picnic places — to new Revere Beach, to Franklin Park, Grove Hall, Forest Hills, or Oakland Gardens. In turn, amusement centers such as Norumbega Park in Newton fed the idle trolley lines on weekends and made transit profitable. Scant wonder the streetcar and the streetcar suburbs seemed a panacea for all of America's ills. "Make transit to the suburbs easy, swift, and cheap," Governor Billy Russell had said, "and the squalid tenement houses of the city cannot compete, as experience shows, with the attractions of a country home."

By 1889 Whitney had bought and consolidated most of these city rails and the elevated clamoring through the downtown would cap and combine the rest. Noise be hanged! Dirt be damned! Far better than 6 different horsecars pulling 303 cars per hour past staid Park Street, the transit czar argued.

Even Whitney's enemies would concede that city transit was in a crisis state. Downtown Boston's one-third square mile held 16 miles of track, 55 miles of trolleys, cross and guard wire, 714 posts, 195 crossings, 257 switches, and 149 junctions. Congestion was so bad on Tremont Street that the hour and a half from 5 to 6:30 P.M. saw an uninterrupted line of streetcars stretched from Scollay Square to Boylston Street; so closely packed, it was said, that a pedestrian could walk the entire distance on the streetcar roofs. The clamor rose to open Tremont Street, dig into the Old Granary Burial Ground, raise high the tracks, and, of course, widen, widen, widen the tortured streets.

What matter Mayor Nathan Matthews' reminder that the city had spent almost $40 million in two generations to widen thus. Would the benefits of cheap urban travel cost the city its first, most precious open space? Unconcernedly, Whitney applied to the legislature to allow his El to arc where the old elms stood. Twice again, however, Bostonians voted it down. "An entering wedge in a scheme to parcel out the Common," reformers declared. After a sordid and complex scandal, the public vetoed the fearful elevated in a referendum in 1893. A year later, they followed up by enacting a more positive urban measure. In 1894 the fighting Bostonians found their solution: a commission proposed America's first subway tunnel.

The notion of digging underground had great appeal. Boston's Mayor Matthews endorsed it. Enlightened merchants applauded it. The big department stores, R. H. Stearns, Houghton Dutton, and Jordan Marsh, plumped for it and, in the end, the citizenry voted for it. By the narrowest of margins the Subway Bill was passed.

The tunnel excavation was not an altogether happy event, however. It undermined and disrupted central Boston, the Common and Garden. Trees were balled and raised, and old graves turned upside down. Yet all this was paltry compared to the havoc of the proposed elevated rail. In deciding that the inexorable wheels of progress would not ride roughshod on the old landscape, Boston had said no to progress at any price and a resounding yes to its last century of civic splendor. Three years later, the city became the first municipality to complete the burial of its transit in town.

At 6:02 on the morning of September 1, 1897, the subway beneath the Common opened for its first public ride. Some 175 enthusiasts packed into a trolley built for fifty and traveled the one-and-two-thirds-mile underground route. People clung three deep on the running board, jumbled in a solid bunch on the platform, and trailed behind the fenders, according to accounts. Two excited passengers were waving American flags and the rest were cheering mightily as the trolley swung out of Boylston Street and into the Public Garden on its way to the entrance. Crowds eight and ten deep lined the rails to either side. Between six and midnight, 100,000 excited Bostonians took the trip. More than five thousand an hour were jammed "like sardines and . . . yelling like a jungle of wild animals," the Boston *Globe* reported. By the end of the first year, 50 million passengers had made the trip.

Reformer Sylvester Baxter raved about the results:

The completed subway is a marvel of convenience and public comfort, with its white enameled walls, its brilliant electric illumination, its sweet and wholesome air, its commodious stations where people await their cars sheltered from wind and rain, from summer heat and winter cold — everything as cleanly as the traditional Dutch housewives' kitchen.

There was no end to the subway's marvels. "The tunnel gives certainty of prompt transit in place of vexatious, halting progress," Bax-

Boston Museum and other long-gone structures on Tremont Street braced for subway
construction.

ter wrote. It ended congestion in the streets and paid a rent to the city,
too. "Our park system, our union stations and now our subway have
opened the eyes of the country to the fact that this city is more than
a centre of literary and historic associations," the Boston *Journal*
concurred, "and that it has an eye on the future as well as to the
past."

So the old century ended on a note victorious: in the Back Bay,
new institutions for the arts, triumphant and elevating; on the outskirts, airy residences and suburbs to gladden every heart; downtown, commerce well endowed; and, lacing all, a ring of parks with
roots in Boston's earth and Boston's past. For all the tumultuous and
ugly growth in urban America — and Boston's temptations to do
likewise — its citizens had expanded in high style. Bostonians had as-
similated a splendid new environment while holding firmly to old
ideals.

251

Planting the City

"The mind needs to come into tender relations with the earth and treat that most intimate of all spots with something akin to piety." The words of reformer Bronson Alcott expressed Boston's sympathetic eye to the natural environment. The city softened its masonry surroundings with trees and greenery and spaced handsome statuary of human dimension in its parks. Frederick Law Olmsted, the father of its most fertile period of greening, bridged the two Bostons — the brick row-house city and the wood-cottage suburb — with his superb Emerald Necklace. The great Victorian transit network from the bike to the omnibus, from electric trolley to train, strengthened the link. Boston reinforced it still further by building amusement parks and beach resorts served by rambling public buildings

at the end of the line. City dwellers partook
of the refreshments of country life with one
rail ride. In turn, noble train and trolley
stations welcomed suburban residents to
city splendors.

The stately mansions that circled the city
also displayed Alcott's "tender relations"
toward the earth. Builders followed the
contours of the land with artfully sited
mansions, tied again to city life by rail.
The Victorian's integration of city and
country, unlike the roughshod and rapacious
development of their successors, enhanced
the best of each.

A Delight of Gardens

Bostonians created fine parks and boulevards with overarching elms along the Common on Tremont near West Street (left)
and down Boylston Street near the Public
Garden. The graceful elms on the Common
were chopped down in the mid-1890s
during digging for the nation's first subway.
Their counterparts on Boylston Street lasted
until a street widening in 1914. The last
three 1840s bowfront row houses left standing at 269 Boylston Street and occupied by
the Women's Educational and Industrial
Union were toppled in 1977 for a proposed
high-rise.

Gazebos, small bandstands, and public statuary refined the cultivated grounds of the city. This charming cast-iron gazebo (below) stood briefly on the Public Garden before it vanished. The more robust Cogswell Fountain on the Common near West Street (above) was donated by Henry Cogswell, a millionaire dentist who launched a crusade of fountain-giving in the name of temperance in the 1870s. Moses King's *Handbook of Boston* found Cogswell's pseudobronze dolphins "astonishingly ugly," however, and the city could tolerate the Victorian exuberance for only a decade before sending it off to points unknown.

Designed with the land, the manmade elements of Franklin Park, Frederick Law Olmsted's expanse of country for the city, offered active recreation in its tennis courts and passive respite in this shelter on Schoolmaster Hill. Designed by Olmsted's son John Olmsted and roofed by city architect Edmund March Wheelwright in 1892, the rustic structure harmonized with the landscape. Both courts and hut are long gone.

At the bucolic end of the trolley line where the Charles widened, Norumbega Park in suburban Newton (left) provided one of the finest amusement parks in America. By 1897, a collection of fantastic buildings by architect Samuel J. Brown and twenty-one acres of manicured grounds by landscape architect Franklin Brett came with the twenty-five-cent trolley ride out of town. Picnic and boating areas, rides and games, spaces for 1025 bikes, electric fountains, a casino, zoo, dozens of double wooden swings in the Grand Swing Court, and the open-air theater that became the Totem Pole Dance Hall greeted Sunday visitors. In the 1960s, the city of Newton refused to buy out the owners. They sold Norumbega to the Marriott Hotel whose building and parking lots occupy the once splendid public grounds.

Once a scruffy waterway, the Charles River was groomed in the late nineteenth and early twentieth century. Edwardian ladies and gentlemen promenaded on the section of the Esplanade near Massachusetts Avenue later enlarged by Mrs. James Jackson Storrow. It is now under the paving of Storrow Drive.

257

By the turn of the century, Marine Park stood at City Point, South Boston. First laid out by Olmsted in the 1880s, it held thirty-two acres of land, a Head House modeled after a German pavilion by city architect E. M. Wheelwright at the Chicago World's Columbian Exposition of 1893, and curving and landscaped beach frontage for sweltering summer days. The beach long ago lost such nineteenth-century amenities. The Head House vanished in a 1942 fire; the caretaking of the grounds fell prey to the poverty of twentieth-century urban life.

From the first statue of Venus planted on the Public Garden to the last lingering projects of the Public Works Administration, public art gave a humanizing touch to the environment. A fountain bathed the statuary supplied by philanthropic citizens for the Public Garden's *Venus* (or the *Maid of the Mist*). The federal government provided the funds for George Aarons to sculpt a symbolic group consisting of a longshoreman, a fisherman, and a foundry worker for the Old Harbor Village Housing Project, South Boston, in 1938. Both projects were ill fated. The nude Venus deteriorated; Aarons's cast-stone statue suffered vandalism and was removed and lost.

Riding the Rails

Trains and trolleys shot out on countless city rails for more than a century. The mighty transportation network would eventually grow to include the elevated commuter rail on Washington Street in Roxbury (left); the terminal of the Beacon Street line at Cleveland Circle in Brighton (below); and a North Station backyard of turntables and rails (right). The row houses on Washington Street, the three-deckers on the Brighton/Brookline line, and the old North Station backyard, now a parking lot, are a part of the past.

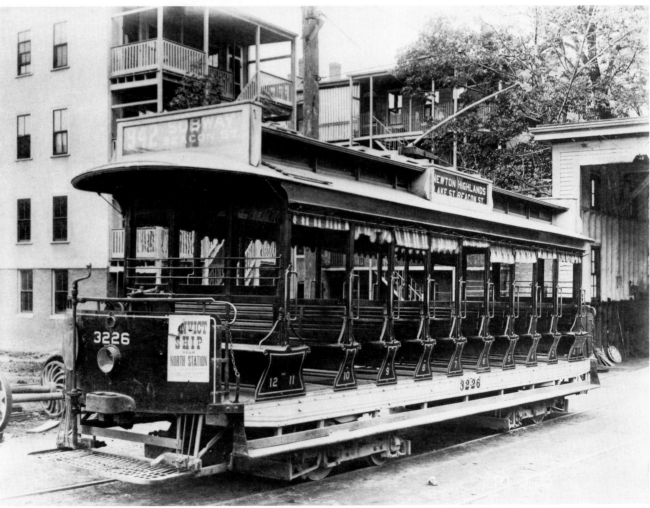

Gateway to the city, the complex of depots at North Station created an imposing structure for turn-of-the-century travelers. Shepley, Rutan, and Coolidge's arched imperial Union Station (left) in 1893 added a Roman presence to the daily trips of Bostonians. The grandiloquent civic entourage lasted only a generation. North Station and the Boston Garden took over the site in 1927.

Thoreau sat at the Fitchburg Depot (above) and Jenny Lind sang there. "The only room in Boston I visit with alacrity is the Gentlemen's room at the Fitchburg Depot, where I wait sometimes for two hours, in order to get out of town," the author of *Walden* wrote. The feudal granite building cornered with medieval turrets in an 1847 design by George M. Dexter, sat on Causeway Street "with an air of imperishable permanence." Removed after the turn of the century, one of its towers went to North Truro on Cape Cod as a memorial to Jenny Lind.

Peabody and Stearns's Boston and Providence Railroad Station at Park Square (below) earned praise as "the most convenient and comfortable, as well as most beautiful, architecturally speaking, in the United States." At the time of its construction in 1872, it was also the world's longest, 850 feet with billiard, reading, smoking, and dining rooms. The Boston and Providence Station lasted little more than a quarter of a century when the railroad departed to the new South Station.

Casual as the corner bus stop, the depots for train and trolley lines displayed an architecture of a wide and handsome range, whether the Romanesque New Haven Railroad Station at Highland Street, West Roxbury (above), the Beaux-Arts monumentalism of the Hyde Park Station built in 1914 (below), or the complex of rails at Haymarket Square (right). None of these waiting posts remains.

More Stately Mansions

Seeking quiet retreats and ample sites for their Greek Revival houses, Bostonians retreated to the adjacent towns of Roxbury and Dorchester, which would one day become parts of Boston proper. The Alvah Kittredge (above) and Frederick Gleason houses with their broad expanses of lawn and garden, curving carriageways and trees, and colonnaded verandahs reflected the urge to imitate the English estate. The Kittredge House, seen in an 1880s photograph of growing Roxbury, was further impacted by approaching row houses and turned 45 degrees to face Linwood Street where it lost its wings, observatory, and two of its columns. Frederick Gleason's Belvidere Hall, built by the owner of Gleason's *Pictorial* on Blue Hill Avenue, Dorchester, disappeared without a trace.

Not every suburban dwelling was an estate. Bostonians of the mid-nineteenth century made the most of smaller sites and less lavish budgets. They fashioned the delightful duplex on Walnut Street (right) in the Neponset section of Dorchester or the Huse House at 119 Dale Street, Roxbury (below). The Dorchester house was defaced by mindless redevelopment and the Huse house torn down for turn-of-the-century three-decker housing.

Whether designed by its owner like the William Bellamy House (left), or stamped with the signature of a well-known architect like Samuel J. F. Thayer who designed the Mallon House (below), residences of the 1880s sprawled with asymmetrical grace around Mount Bowdoin Green in the street-car suburb of Dorchester in the early 1880s. The Mallon House, later a home for unwed mothers, was demolished in the twenties. The Bellamy House was razed in 1940.

Fin-de-siècle finish and formal gardening marked the high style of the Larz Anderson Estate in Brookline on the Jamaica Plain line of Boston. Here, after 1899, the well-traveled millionaires had Little and Browne add to the original home designed by Edmund March Weelwright in 1885, fashioning rooms filled with artifacts from India, Tibet, and less exotic points. The building was demolished in the 1950s by an era that called such lavish estates white elephants.

–*CHAPTER 10*–

Muted Hurrahs, 1900–1930

What primarily differentiates Boston from all other cities is this: It is finished, I mean complete; of the great cities, while admitting their actual achievement, one would say, "They will be." Boston is.

— ARNOLD BENNETT

"THE TWENTIETH century ought to begin as the eighteenth began," Edward Everett Hale wrote. Without benefit of megaphone, the venerable Bostonian read psalm and hymn atop the State House balcony to start off the new century at midnight on December 31, 1899. His voice traveled all the way to Winter Street to mingle with the bells of King's Chapel and the trumpets' blare.

Such ancient echoes could not carry into the new century, though. The ring of the telephone and the blast of the first automobile horn attested to another day. The world was moving "from horsecar to electrics, from the dimness of a world lighted by gas to the blazing illumination of electricity," the Boston *Globe* proclaimed. Tellingly, it was not the steady pace of construction but the mounting speed of transportation that would define Boston in the decades that "opened with the horsecar and the herdic and closed with the Cadillac and the airplane."

No wonder that visionary of space-age architecture R. Buckminster Fuller saw changing times symbolized by a change in mobility. As a boy living just outside Boston, Fuller's first memories were of walking down to the end of his driveway, then to the world beyond "through an almost continuous tunnel of trees." Fuller grew up in Milton, where trolley and train had only recently stretched the range of horse and carriage to carry him downtown. One hundred years and more had passed since Paul Revere's Boston with its smell of animals, living and dead, of whales and fish, of "the sea, tar, soapboiling, brewing, spice and humanity." Still the workaday odors of Victorian life lingered in Fuller's youth.

You could smell the different districts of the town, as you could in many other big cities like New York. The shoemaking areas with very strong leather smells and the smells of linen, the smells of tea, coffee, and so forth were prominent. One of the pleasantest smells came from the ship chandlers on the waterfront where the smells of rope and tar and other sea-going equipment add a particular pleasing aroma to my childhood settings.

That was the old Boston. Fuller projected the future city otherwise: from its faster transit — the elevated that began to zip from Cambridge and Roxbury to Boston, and the tunnels that allowed an unimpeded race toward suburban Dorchester. Older Bostonians could well remember the progress from "hourlies" (stages), to steam railroads, to horsecars, to trolleys. Fuller, futurist from the first, compared his era's speedier transit with his ancestors' day-long trips from Cambridge to Boston and "realized intuitively" that the subway

Overleaf:
Fogg Art Museum, a symbol of the era's cultural blooming encased in a classical facade by Richard Morris Hunt, rose in 1893 and fell in 1973 for prefabricated college dormitories.

linking Cambridge to Boston in eight minutes in 1912 was "a harbinger of an entirely new space-time relationship of the individual and his environment." That change, seen in hindsight, held as much threat as promise for the city on the hill.

Early-century enthusiasts had a shorter range. They could see only the continued greening of their city. "There is a saying," writer Claude Bragdon told the Boston Architectural Club, " 'To be young, to be in love, to be in Italy.' I would paraphrase it thus: 'To be young, to be an architect, to be in America.' " Boston's version of this lively expansion meant designing branch libraries and baths, police and fire stations, City Hall Annex and courthouse, playground and recreational facilities, aquarium and zoo. New sewers, streets, a high-pressure water system, and the inching subway helped keep the city's infrastructure intact.

Above all, Bostonians maintained their civic concern and their pleasure in urban celebration in the new century. Crossing the Common, Mayor Honey Fitz overheard a tramp's lament, "This is Christmas Eve, but there is no Christmas for me." He promptly installed an official city tree and annual celebration. Carolers, among them architect Ralph Adams Cram, set out one Christmas to serenade their neighbors — and the annual carol singing on Beacon Hill began. Even in the depths of the Depression, a young man named Arthur Fiedler, son of the first violinist in the Boston Symphony, would promote the first free open-air concert by the Charles.

Did the ongoing exodus to the suburbs bother city-lovers? "The population which 'sleeps out of town' is immense and increasing," George Curtis wrote in his book *Easy Chair*. He worried about the fell hand of improvement. "The law steps forward, cuts down your trees, plows up your lawn, lays a gutter under your window, destroys your home." Curtis was ahead of his time — and of *our* time — in warning that newcomers would de-rusticate suburban life. For most Bostonians, development could not destroy their country idyll, and dispersion was no dilemma. Using the phrase "Greater Boston," the city tallied in more than a million people in the population around the Boston basin, twice that of the center city. Metropolitan Boston was more than mere verbiage, however. The political and administrative linkages of the Metropolitan system sired by Charles Eliot's park plan reflected political power based on the physical and topographical reality. Early in the century, city and state cooperated in their parks and joined to build metropolitan trunkline sewers and a magnificent metropolitan water system to slake the endless thirst. To do so, Boston spent more on its municipal housekeeping per capita than any other city in America.

273

Bostonians also breathed deep the Progressive and muckraking impulses in the early decades of the twentieth century. Edward A. Filene, a public-spirited merchant willing to turn his department store into a worker-owned cooperative, launched a plan for the city called Boston 1915. Olmsted's firm designed for it. In times past, Filene had shared in the formation of the Good Government Association. Mayor James Michael Curley, "last of the political buccaneers," mocked what he called "googoos," but in 1908, Filene went so far as to import Lincoln Steffens, famous for his muckraking *Shame of the Cities,* to uncover the depths of Boston's corruption and to plan afresh. The Boston 1915 movement had the energy, and the same cast of activists, as had the Battle of the El. It partook of the zeal for reform while looking to shape a brighter future. Fighting merger and monopoly, the causists dreamed of making city life rational and responsive to the population under Euripides' motto "Thou has heard men sworn by the city . . . Go forth, my son, and help."

In the end, Steffens's report went unfinished and unpublished, nonetheless, and the movement failed. "Boston was corrupt," the muckraker wrote. The city "has carried the practice of hypocrisy to the nth degree of refinement, grace, and failure." Planning was futile, Steffens said, for "the city was accepted as all done."

Was Boston finished? Certainly, the construction and building projects completed by the city seemed to stem less from the old broad vision and urge for urban betterment than from the handout style of Big Boss politics. The dirty streets defaced by advertising signs, the dangerous tenements, the noise and "cloud of soft coal smoke" appalled the Boston Society of Architects in 1907. But the starry-eyed plans by the Society's designers and city-beautifiers failed too. Their dream to thrust a Beaux-Arts boulevard down Arlington Street, construct a Mount Olympus around the State House with a new city hall atop Beacon Hill, and create a manmade island on the widest portion of the Charles didn't have a chance. These plans, though not one whit more daring or visionary than the land schemes of other days, never became more than paper dreams published by the Society.

At the same time, construction did not totally halt. The two terms of Mayor Honey Fitz, who chorused his way to success with "Sweet Adeline," saw the building of the City Hall Annex, City Point Aquarium, Franklin Park Zoo, and random public toilets. James Curley, who would reign five times — once as governor, four terms as mayor — continued the spending spree, for tunnels, transit, city hospital, bathing beaches, and Strandway. Staffing the "sleepy hollows" of municipal government with his cohorts, the political "Vox of Roxbury"

Mayor Curley in a 1930 tickertape parade for Admiral Byrd in front of the First National Bank.

John F. Fitzgerald.

built up the city and employed the jobless by hook or by crook. With great aplomb, Curley opened the streets, enlarged Boston City Hospital, bought property, and lengthened tunnels and expanded transit everywhere. Four million dollars went to extend the East Boston rapid transit tunnel and five million to stretch trolley lines under the Back Bay and out at Kenmore Square. A passage from Joseph Dineen's *The Purple Shamrock,* describes the momentum of construction in Curley's day:

Trucks rumbled night and day over city streets. Bright floodlights at night made daylight over tunnel excavations, work going on night and day, girders and stringers went high into the air.

If ripped up and torn down streets, multiplying payrolls, and contracts "with liveried chauffers" showed political shenanigans, they also revealed an enduring concern with citymaking and serving a new constituency. Even through World War I, Curley's Yankee successor, Mayor Andrew J. Peters, oversaw the building of seventy-five miles of artificial stone sidewalks and the extension of Stuart Street and Huntington Avenue. During Curley's mayoral rule, in 1913, the city's first planning board was named. Yet, the mayor's flight to a costly and controversial house on the suburban Jamaicaway showed another trend: It reflected the search for trees and greenery and mimicked the widespread passion to plunder and dwell within the past. Behind the white shutters with the shamrocks, Curley installed a staircase lifted from an old Connecticut mansion along with its Waterford crystal chandeliers, paneled dining room, mantels, twenty-eight carved mahogany doors, columns, and balustrades — an entourage culminating in a downstairs "crowded, almost enveloped, with expensively inappropriate geegaws," and a vestibule that held "a marble statue of St. Joseph holding his arm out as if to take one's hat or umbrella," author Francis Russell wrote.

The same hunger for the colonial past characterized the booming suburbs. What some called "Bull Market Georgian" plus some stucco English tudor and cottage styles covered the leftover landscape on the city's periphery. Often mannered, the mode sought to recapture the colonial flavor lost in the ethnic diversity of the tumultuous downtown. "A girdle of inflammable and dangerous tenements surrounds the city," the Boston Society of Architects report labeled the ethnic city. No wonder new monuments honored the Puritans, Paul Revere, Lafayette, and like heroes of bygone Golden Ages. The hunger for this distant grail sent preservationists to restore the Old State House once again in 1908 and to rip the eighteenth-century aspects off Paul Revere's house in favor of a seventeenth-century look. Love of the past encouraged Henry Ford to salvage the remains of the Wayside Inn in Sudbury and inspired many a simpler Boston household to display its "antique" spinning wheel.

Some devotees of old architecture banded together more formally. While Jewish immigrants bent to their pages in the West End branch library (made over from Asher Benjamin's West Church), the descendants of Yankee sea captains and mill owners formed the Society for the Preservation of New England Antiquities in the Harrison Gray Otis house next door. Under founder William Sumner Appleton, the preservationists began to collect threatened old houses on the landscape the way the Museum of Fine Arts amassed their interiors in its exhibit halls. Such zeal did not attend the making of new forms, however. It did not mean a respect for Victorian architecture. The immediate past was pariah. Let it fall; for as Ralph Adams Cram put it, its architecture was based on "false principles, horrid methods and shocking bad taste."

All was not re-creation or fossilization in the larger plans of the early decades of the modern century, however. The period of Filene's planning dream coincided with the fruition of Charles Eliot's conservation vision. The Metropolitan Park Commission had plotted out its own tomorrow. H. G. Wells would praise its plan for readying the radius within fifteen or twenty miles of the State House for civilized growth. Olmsted's disciple Sylvester Baxter had given the visiting English author a map of the tinted areas that would become great reservations of woodland and hill. It showed streams and rivers secured for public park and garden, and big avenues of young trees with driveways, ridingways, and a central grassy band for electric tramways. "The fair and ample and shady new Boston, the Boston of 1950, grows visibly before one's eyes," Wells exclaimed. It is "a fresh and more deliberate phrase in this Great American symphony, this symphony of growth."

A still expanding Boston desperately needed this creative planning — and nowhere more so than on the Charles River where Eliot's vision of a pondlike basin at last became a reality. More than a decade had passed since Eliot drummed up popular support for the Charles with this eloquent — and enduring — plea:

Dressmaker's shop in the bygone West End.

Here is a rapidly growing metropolis planted by the sea and yet possessed of no portion of the sea-front except what Boston has provided at City Point. Here is a city interwoven with tidal marshes and controlling none of them; so that the way is open for construction upon them of cheap building for the housing of the lowest poor and the

nastier street trades. Here is a district possessed of a charming river

*already much resorted to for pleasure, the banks of which are con-
tinually in danger of spoilation at the hands of their private owners.
Here is a community which must have pure drinking water, which
yet up to this time has failed to secure even one water basin from
danger of pollution.*

The $2 million Charles River Dam that finally transformed the pol-
luted tidal estuary into a contained lake was his response in 1910.

Taming the river this way had its drawbacks. No more would Cambridge naturalists hunt wild ducks. No future Longfellow could pen
odes to the marshy view. Moreover, the saltwater vegetation of Olmsted's Fens would suffer from the change in ecology. Happily, though,
a city lagoon was born. The row houses on the north side of Beacon
Street became rooms with a view. Along the edges, new buildings
traveled eastward parallel to Charles Street. Westward, more row
houses marched down Bay State Road. Boston was rid of the river
whose rise and fall of fifteen feet had made it an "ungodly neighbor," in Eliot's words. The Brighton lowlands, the Cambridge
marshes, and the rotting wharves became tidy shorelines. So groomed,
the made land soon became the locale of today's university row.

The newly solid banks by the Charles allowed not only building
sites but open space. A gift of $250,000 from the patrician banker
and politician James Storrow provided a promenade; later, the handsome Charles River embankment was funded by his widow. All along
the shores, Sunday leisure-takers took advantage of the firmed ground
and freshwater lake, turning them into a citydwellers' peninsula for
recreation. The Charles River between Newton and Waltham could
hold 3000 canoes on a summer day. Norumbega Park, a ride down
the new Commonwealth Avenue trolley line, sprang to life with zoo
and amusements. It was a superb playground at the turn-of-the-century
city's edge. Horseback riders traveled special routes on the riverbank
and the Emerald Necklace. Bicyclists took new footpaths, parked in
Norumbega's thousand spaces and the fad grew:

*In 1906 a bicycle was the dream of a 10-year-old boy in a quiet Bos-
ton suburb. Almost all the older kids had bikes. The automobile
hadn't yet taken over the roads, trolleys ran on tracks but kept to their
place. The roads were safe enough so the police seldom interfered
with coasting on them in winter, sometimes protecting the best coasting hill. All it took was a cop at the bottom to blow a warning whistle
if a coal wagon was starting up.*

For now, the automobile's roar was still a distant murmur. When
the city painted the first fresh white lines to separate traffic lanes, Bos-

A lamppost on the Charles River Esplanade.

277

tonians viewed it as an act of vandalism. Irate citizens accused the politicians of extravagance and blamed the brushwielders for disfiguring the historic streets. Still others like the prolific Boston author Mark A. DeWolfe Howe damned the street widening that moved the hallowed Charles Street Church and flattened the Eye and Ear Infirmary for a monstrous garage in 1922. He found it all a somber portent. Sylvester Baxter complained that parkways and boulevards had "become the primary factor in the scheme of the park system."

Nonetheless, the great Victorian transit network stayed more or less intact. Ferry, train, trolley, foot sufficed to carry Bostonians back and forth. The new South Station, the largest in the world when it appeared in 1900, and the salt-and-pepper-shaker-shaped Longfellow Bridge with rails running down its middle, dominated the landscape in 1912. In the next eight years, the suburban population served by the new Cambridge subway came close to doubling. Rapid transit had its faults, of course. Both the El that took the Atlantic Avenue loop and the train that shadowed the South End's Washington Street had been clamoring, yammering beasts. No better than highways, they sacrificed urban amenities to a swift suburban exodus. Then, too, the 1920s saw Bostonians step off the piazza into the automobile. They turned quiet arborways into roads. Yet few who spun off in some merry Oldsmobile sensed what would come when car and motorcoach sluiced across the city and countryside. In 1929, some 1266 miles of rail still laced a compact metropolis.

Boston's skill in creating urban design forms did not vanish. For one hundred years, the city had dappled its landscape with the most advanced architecture and planning styles — from the tree-shaded square to the bowfront row house, from land tailored for the commercial builder's need to buildings shaped for cultural institutions. Now with one last flourish, Boston's builders blessed their city with a design on the mass scale: The three-decker dwelling was ready for the city's final ring of land.

Boston had always embraced a dense lifestyle. Even in its spacious suburbs, a happy mix of housing types went beyond the narrow option of the lone house on the lone lot. Two-, three-, and even four-family houses allowed a choice of lifestyles and a close-knit community. Apartment houses on the Fens and suburban outskirts went beyond what critics disparagingly called "a hive of hearths." Some of the apartments began to experiment with community kitchens and day-care rooms; others were laid out like palaces around an airy courtyard. The boarding house, though deplored by some, was, in Russell Lynes's retrospective, "home for the rootless . . . home of those who were waiting." Reformers and snobbish critics might say its in-

Alexander Wadsworth Longfellow Jr.'s sprawling complex for Dudley Station.

The interior of South Station, after 1899.

278

habitants had roots no deeper than the pile of its Brussels carpet, but Lynes, in his book *The Domestic Americans,* describes a boarding house of many uses, "both springboard and safety net, a place from which to leap into the future and to fall back into the past."

The three-decker widened all these options. Turning to house vast numbers in the beckoning suburbs, Bostonians found the stacked three-family dwelling the answer to reform dreams. With the turn of the century, the flicker of three-deckers built since 1880 spread across the suburbs. Here, said social workers, "the air is brighter, cleaner, and more vibrant; sunshine falls in floods rather than in narrow shafts; there is less congestion and more freedom of movement." Individual builders put up a fleet of the three-tiered wooden dwellings at a production-line pace, naming them, some say, for the three-decker steamers that they resembled. Airier than the row house, the three-decker house had windows on four sides, and small yards and tidy porches. Enthusiasts of the new form found them far superior to Boston's brick tenements "where the buildings are set close up to the sidewalk, where there is no way of painting up or rejuvenating the brick structure to give it an appearance of youth and freshness, and where there are few trees, backyard gardens or front lawns."

What later generations would call "economies of scale" added to the appeal and growth of the three-decker. One cellar, one water and gas main, one plumbing shaft served three families, dividing the cost by three for each family. Add to that the less expensive flat roof, the front and back piazza, a hot-air furnace, electricity, hardwood floors, ample yards behind, the chance for one family to own and collect rent in a place they might build themselves . . . and you explain the outpouring of families to the three-decker world of the inner suburb. A "rational structure," said its advocates, though "it would never be able to boast of either beauty or variety."

To those comparing the three-decker to the mansion estate in established neighborhoods, three-deckers and their dwellers seemed "undesirable elements." They "made the street look mean and narrow," one Dorchester resident observed. Yet houseowners and renters found them gift enough. Their bay windows, corner towers, built-in cabinets and stained-glass windows had individuality. Their airy rooms provided a spacious and civil way of life. Rolling across the hills of Dorchester or hop-stepping along on scattered sites within and outside Boston in a staccato rhythm, the three-decker created an inviting streetscape not unlike that of its urban ancestors. Multicolored paint jobs and fancy trimming by the carpenter-builders of the day gave them the spry life and flavor of the suburb's finest. Blending city and country best, this working-class house has yet to find

279

a peer. By 1920, some 15,000 such dwellings, housing more than three times that number of people, had spread across Boston. Neighboring towns and cities added to the count.

While this humble building rat-a-tatted across the city, Boston architects aimed for something more imperial in their major work. They sought a dignified avenue of approach fit to hold grandiose designs reminiscent of the Chicago fair's "congregation of brides." The new Museum of Fine Arts was typical. A few hundred yards away from Isabella Stewart Gardner's palace on the Fenway, the Boston Museum of Fine Arts prepared the site for still another massive excavation in the first decade of the twentieth century. "The new building was not deliberately planned as an architectural monument," one of its builders noted, "but inevitably became one from the dignity of its purpose and the necessary amplitude of its extent."

If a bigger America didn't exactly *need* bigger buildings, its expansive urges, untempered by restraint, produced them. The urge for "culture by contagion," as Walter Muir Whitehill put it, topped the need for growth; made Harvard build a monumental flight of stairs to reach its new Widener Library or stage a Renaissance courtyard on the path to classrooms. A vast limestone edifice with a dome served Mary Baker Eddy's Christian Science Church in 1906. A marble Middle Eastern monolith held Temple Israel on the lengthened Commonwealth Avenue the next year.

Whether heft made waste was no issue in these booming decades any more than in the 1880s, which launched the classical revival. The Roman look suited enlarging institutions that needed grander schemes. Educational and public institutions — hospitals, universities, libraries — were transforming the city into the hub of learning for America. "Boston's business ceased to be cotton and became higher education," Harvard architecture professor John Coolidge has recalled, "so that the appalling Back Bay I remember as a child — grandfather's stuffy mansion and dentist appointments — now filled with life. For the first time, Boston's music and medicine and scholarship achieved the highest international standing," Professor Coolidge wrote.

Let us reflect that standing, the buildings seemed to say. By moving from the city and planting themselves on the Fenway or Charles River with spacious symmetry, by borrowing a grandiose way from abroad, the architecture responded to the urge. Why even the public bathroom on the Common copied the elegance of Versailles.

All Boston's buildings did not stand as stony symbols of restraint in the flashy decade. The twenties roared here too. Boston boasted new hotels, stores stretching toward the Back Bay and lavish theaters

The Chamber of Commerce Building at 80 Federal Street by Parker, Thomas and Rice lasted less than fifty years.

Mitchell Woodbury Corporation at 55
Summer Street.

— this era's extravagant palaces for the people. The city's architects sired gaudy playhouses, concert halls, and picture palaces that earned the label the Boston Rialto. Tremont and Boylston streets were blazoned with lights. The Metropolitan Theater, today's Music Hall, designed by Clarence H. Blackall, was the biggest of the lot. More than 4000 people watch each show, passing by fresh flowers in a dazzling lobby that offered everything from six lounges to Ping-Pong tables.

On a more traditional note, there was All Saints' Church at Ashmont, Dorchester, a masterwork by Ralph Adams Cram and Bertram Goodhue. Work for the Roman Catholic Archdiocese by Charles Maginnis and Timothy Walsh soon brought national renown to their creators. Rich adornment gave designs for school or home an opulent air: heroic sculpted doors enriched the Salada Tea Building, classical or Georgian detail adorned the universities. Dapper and delightful street-floor shops lined new office buildings and pocketed them with arcades. As if to mark the crest of the twenties, the spring of 1927 saw three new hotels open in muted but elegant versions of the streamlined mode called art deco. The irrepressible Mayor Jimmy Walker, in from New York, joined the gala opening of one, the Ritz-Carlton Hotel.

Yet some saw signs of civic weakness as well as civic splendor in the city's growth. Expansion rode roughshod over the old Massachusetts General and City hospitals and their graceful grounds. Beaux-Arts urges could lead to bulbous and mannered monuments — a bombastic classicism trumpeted by overwrought statuary and stiffly ceremonial layouts. The Museum of Fine Arts held superb collections, but its building by Guy Lowell seemed an isolated and swollen affair. Lowell's product looked pallid compared to its terra-cotta predecessor sitting so urbanely in Copley Square. In front of Lowell's new Museum, Cyrus F. Dallin perched his 1913 sculpture of an Indian, seated on a well-fed carriage horse. Making an Appeal to the Great Spirit, the piece beckoned city-bred art lovers with more comic than spiritual flair. Inside, the murals by John Singer Sargent, inserted in the rotunda's dome at great cost, displayed twin aspects of humor and elegance in the classical figures modeled by the Ziegfeld Follies showgirls on a whiz-stop tour through town. Harvard, though more robust, was still lodged in the tradition of what a contemporary called "mildly gladiatorial spectacles." It did its darndest to imitate the ancient models by welcoming in the modern age of concrete in a Roman coliseum. This Portland cement stadium bore the garb of ancient times. In further *recherche du temps perdu,* Harvard's campus stretched along the river lyrically in Georgian Revival style.   *281*

All Boston's books were antiques and its statuary was nothing but casts of the Nike of Samothrace in her ancient robes, H. G. Wells declared in a more critical mood. The statue's headless frozen stride was typical of Boston's retrospective stance, he wrote:

I remember Boston as a quiet effect, as something a little withdrawn, as a place standing aside from the throbbing interchange of East and West. I think . . . that Boston tries to remember too much.

A bit "aside," perhaps, but Boston's vaunted conservatism held elements of strength as well as irony. Elsewhere across the continent, the sky might be the architectural limit, but the Hub could never quite forsake its orderly building heritage. While New York and Chicago adventured upward long before the century's turn, Boston didn't take to the skyscraper. For decades, the tall building had held scant appeal. Even now it won no more.

Some cite the economic slowdown and stagnation of the period to explain the city's low skyline. Yet the reason Boston, like Europe, forbade the skyscraper went beyond the lessened impulse to build downtown. Perhaps the Hub was indeed what Lincoln Steffens labeled "a common city of superior people," for Boston did not yet succumb to the lure of the elevator. It resisted the urge to maximize value on every lot. Perhaps some lingering sense of urban civility and scale blessed the cityscape and bred its aversion to the light-snatching style of the hour.

Even the first structure to be called towering — the handsome Ames Building designed by Richardson's successors Shepley, Rutan and Coolidge in 1889 — had risen a mere fourteen stories. A Romanesque palace with lower walls four or five feet thick, it was admired more for style than size. Five years later, the city's first steel-frame structure, the Winthrop Building by the prolific architect Clarence H. Blackall, became "the source of curiosity and doubting amazement," as Ralph Adams Cram wrote in his *Autobiography*. But it likewise stayed in scale. So too the most ambitious State Street houses of finance moved into offices that sought dignity in girth not height. The National Shawmut Bank Building, right in the middle of the financial district, need not use height to garner high praise in 1906. It was a magnificent structure of New England granite without a peer. A contemporary guidebook praised it as "a fitting monument."

The more profit-minded may have disagreed. One such soul criticized the Kidder Peabody Building — a two-and-a-half-story Greek temple on busy Devonshire Street — as "conspicuous for its wasteful use of high land values in disdain of utilizing even the normal build-

ing height of the area." The Boston Society of Architects criticized

Hotel Westminster by Henry E. Cregier and detail of its sculpted exterior by Max Bachman.

the "too restrictive building laws." All the same, such structures as the Shoe Machinery Building, symbol of a prosperous industry, chose to boast of horizontality and "terraced altitudes," and not mere height.

Bostonians fought vigorously to rule out an architecture of canyons. Let buildings across America burst old bounds; no darting "apotheosis of commerce" here. The city had set a 125-foot limit downtown in 1892 and a 90-foot ceiling on the edge of Copley Square came just six years later. This last measure stemmed from a petition signed by more than 3000 citizens to scale down buildings within 500 feet of the new square or any park ground. "What of value the public creates, the public has the right to control," a petitioner had argued to the legislature. "It was the city that made the square so beautified," the city's largest taxpayer, William Minot, agreed. A celebrated case came to confirm his view of Copley Square in the new century.

The nationally famous Westminster Chambers case arose with the construction of the hotel by that name on the corner between Trinity Church and the old Museum of Fine Arts (at today's Copley Plaza Hotel). Slowly, as the steel beams and ornamental superstructure of the hotel passed beyond the legislated height, Bostonians saw its threat to shadow church and museum. The museum and MIT, which had property on or near the square, took the owners into court. Heated suits and countersuits blazed a trail up to the Supreme Court. Who had shaped the beauties of Copley Square and raised its land value? The public asked, Who then should benefit? Piracy, the defenders of the hotel replied. What the public has created, the public has a right to control, the suing parties countered. The Massachusetts court concurred and, in 1903, the Supreme Court decreed. In this landmark case, the nation's highest court endorsed the city's right to hold the building to 90 feet. The superstructure was cut down. Though the institutions so tenacious for their environment soon deserted the neighborhood of Copley Square, the opinion sealed the lid. A year later, in 1904, Boston once more took a pioneer role, zoning separate heights for commercial and residential areas. Again the ruling held.

Saving the skyline of the city's most splendid ensemble and capping the ceiling downtown restrained speculators for two decades or more. Both conservative and constructive, such restrictions suffered few lapses.

"Boston held out against the skyscraper longer than most cities and even now nothing excessive or egregious is possible — barring the Custom House Tower, which after all was the affair of the authorities

283

at Washington," Ralph Adams Cram, now a member of the city
planning board, observed. Plopped atop Boston's most grandiose
Greek Revival building in 1914, this Custom House Tower by Peabody and Stearns was "a vast chimney stack rising from a Roman
Temple," said one of many critics. As for its ornament, a fifty-ton
eaglelike bird, it was "a dark-billed platypus from the River of
Doubt," another wrote. More than that, the tower's rise foretold the
city's loss of scale and evidenced "the will to grow everywhere written
large, and to grow no matter what or to whose expense," as Henry
James noted in his *American Scene.* All the same, the old restraints
held down the Hotel Statler and the Ritz-Carlton. They needed special legislation to go some fourteen floors. The Batterymarch and elegant Park Square buildings, bulking large, if not high, were more in
keeping with the streamlined era across America.

If the twentieth century had become space, speed, and the skyscraper, this Boston did not succumb. Somewhat crabbed and altogether low-rise, the city could have fit that new image only by a
rampage of destruction and defacement.

Some sharpened their axes to do just that. "There is probably no
city in the United States where traffic conditions on the streets of the
downtown business section are so near the saturation point as they
are here in Boston," a city planner fretted in the late twenties. He re-
peated the age-old plea to widen the crooked streets. Boston was
idling in the economic slough of the Depression, though. Happily, the
city could not afford to swing a deadly blade or to build aloft. Poverty proved an ironic blessing in these dark days.

"Boston is a good city to come from; but not a good city to go to,"
Joseph P. Kennedy, founding father of the political dynasty, observed
in 1926, chafing from his cool treatment by Boston Brahmins. Her
mills in decline, her port slipping, her financiers cautious, Massachusetts lived out the Depression on bygone glories, not great expecta-
tions.

"These, in a word, are not the spacious days of 1880," Mark A.
DeWolfe Howe put it dolefully in the history for the tercentenary of
September 17, 1930. Dorothy Parker, fined for "loitering and saun-
tering" on the Common during her trip to seek mercy for Sacco and
Vanzetti, must have agreed. So might Hemingway, O'Neill, or
Dreiser, whose censored works made "banned in Boston" a national
joke. No wonder Cornhill was down to "four dusty tunnels" and the
Old Corner Book Store was falling into ruin. Lengthening bread lines
and corner apple sellers did not augur well for Boston's three hundredth birthday jubilee.

284   Yet the plucky city could not let such an anniversary pass unsung.

Bostonians celebrated the tercentenary of
their city by marching down Federal Street
past the Chamber of Commerce Building
(left) and hanging over the edge of the
old John Hancock Building (right). The
buildings proved more precarious than the
observers' perches. Nearly all had disappeared before the city's three hundred and
fiftieth birthday.

Its values might seem to languish along with its landscape, but the visitor to the three hundredth birthday celebration would find it as exuberant as festivals before. For a year the city staggered celebrations, from air meets and evening illuminations to placing twenty historic tablets on city landmarks. The end of the year saw the city decked with glory for a final "Boston Week." An "electrical parade" filled the nighttime hours "with the gold and amethyst fires of the Tercentenary." By day the buildings of Post Office Square dripped banners to match the flags of marching legionnaires. Day after day for much of the week, Bostonians of all stripes were on parade. Foreign-born citizens had their moment. Marchers from the Sons of Italy to St. Mary's Polish School joined Chinese delegations, Spanish-American War veterans in uniform, high school girls in middy blouses, and fish pier troops in slickers grouped between the dancing floats. The Boston Tea Party display bobbed by with its smudge-faced "Indians" and a shack-sized float depicting the early life of the colonists slid down the street not far from a rolling Faneuil Hall and a rocking *Arbella.*

The ten thousand Bostonians who had held a town meeting in the Public Garden were a small band compared to the multitude that packed the streets: In procession, 40,000 marchers, 100 units, and 200 floats passed the classical reviewing stand with its court of honor where officials tried not to flinch at the blare of firefighters' horns. In the final tally, more than one million Bostonians had massed for their moment of cheer, pacing the still tortuous streets, grouping inside the granite and castellated buildings, and peering down from window ledges atop the neoclassical concoctions of the hour. Not the glory days, perhaps, but celebration notwithstanding. For was this not a city worthy of a festival, a glorious old town upon its rolling hills, an exuberant citizenry whose unflinching ancestors, the tercentenary poet, Edwin Markham, wrote,

> *. . . fetched red bricks from ever smoking kilns,*
> *Timber from Maine, granite from shattered hills,*
> *And built long wharves and stretched out sheltering piers*
> *To draw great ships from all the world of man*
> *Until it seemed that Carthage had come again.*

God Was in the Details

A myriad of minute touches gave a human dimension to the grandest and most lofty building. Doors with elegant trim accented the sense of welcome. Windows gazed generously at the passersby, and facades, framed with careful carving, made the streets of an earlier day avenues of delight. Even the billboards and signs dotting the surface of such structures had a restrained animation, while their lights twinkled through the city night. Vandalized by blank-faced modernization or totally wiped out in our zeal for the sanitized surface, these buildings no longer provide the detail that humanizes city life.

The Building as Billboard

Form really did follow function on these buildings in the Scollay Square area. Stripes declared that a barber dwelled within, embossed stamps showed a stampmaker, and more straightforward letters spelled out their calling. The Scollay Building (left) fell for a street widening in 1871. The S. M. Spencer Manufacturing Company on Corn-hill and Washington Street (below right), and the battered leftovers of the buildings that housed F. W. Woolworth on Tremont Row (above right) came down through modern urban renewal's agents of destruction in the early 1960s.

A competing barrage of insurance agency placards somehow enlivened the Old State House in the 1870s (left) and signs of the building trades—plumber, carpenter, glazier, cabinetmaker — give a buoyant air to Province Court off Province Street (below) in a late-nineteenth-century view. The Old State House lost its signs as well as its Greek Revival porch by Isaiah Rogers in an 1881 restoration. Its neighboring buildings had vanished altogether by late 1912. Province Court was leveled to widen Province Street and provide for new construction earlier in the twentieth century.

Never the flashiest of American cities, Boston still dazzled the night with light works on Tremont Street. Here the department store Houghton and Dutton (above), designed by Horace Burr and Lyman Size, celebrated Christmas 1912 with 22,000 light bulbs, and lower Washington Street showed the art deco ribbon of light that flashed at the Paramount Theatre (below) from 1936. Houghton and Dutton's building was torn down in 1967 for a high-rise; the Paramount has lost its sign and movie house tenant.

Art of Adornment

Columns provided more than structural support as the voluptuous columns of the old John Hancock Mutual Life Insurance Building on Franklin Street show. The 1910 building designed by Shepley, Rutan, and Coolidge, became the offices of Stone and Webster and was lost for a parking lot in 1966. The high-rise Shawmut Bank Building now occupies the site.

A door was more than a mere point of entry to nineteenth-century Bostonians. "The Gothic" (above) built circa 1900, disappeared in the taking of the West End in the 1960s. Its design by the famous firm of McKim, Mead, and White, builders of the Boston Public Library, did not deter developers from turning the 1906 New England Trust Company at Devonshire and Milk (below) into a parking lot in 1972.

Twenty-six years of imposing life was all that was allotted before the ponderous eagle and curving facade of the 1953 Federal Reserve Bank of Boston designed by Paul Philippe Cret was torn down for a high-rise at Post Office Square.

The lions that stood guard at the Hotel Kensington and its successor occupants on Boylston Street near Copley Square moved after the building was torn down for a parking lot. How long the peripatetic kings of the wild will endure on their patch of urban jungle is not known.

Picture Credits

Bibliography

Index

Detail, former Jordan Marsh Company
building

Page

255 Franklin Park, shelter. *Bostonian Society*
256 Norumbega Park, boathouse. *S.P.N.E.A.*
256 Norumbega Park, open-air theater. *Norton D. Clark*
257 Charles River Esplanade. *Metropolitan District Commission*
258 Marine Park, City Point, 1900. *Boston Public Library Print Department*
258 Head House, City Point. *Bostonian Society*
259 *Maid of the Mist*, Public Garden. *S.P.N.E.A.*
259 Sculpture by George Aarons at Old Harbor Village Housing Project. *Private collection*
260 Washington Street railway, Roxbury, 1901. *Norton D. Clark*
260 Beacon Street line, Cleveland Circle. *Norton D. Clark*
261 North Station turntables. *Sydney F. Towle*
262 Union Station. *Boston Public Library Print Department*
263 Fitchburg Depot. *Bostonian Society*
263 Boston and Providence Railroad Station, Park Square. *Boston Public Library Print Department*
264 Highland Street Station, West Roxbury. *Norton D. Clark*
264 Hyde Park Station. *Norton D. Clark*
265 Haymarket Square. *Boston Athenaeum*
266 Alvah Kittredge House, Roxbury. *Photograph by A. H. Folsom. Boston Public Library Print Department*
266 Gleason House, Dorchester. *Photograph by A. H. Folsom. Boston Public Library Print Department*
267 Walnut Street, Neponset, Dorchester. *S.P.N.E.A.*
267 119 Dale Street, Roxbury. *S.P.N.E.A.*
268 Bellamy House, 17 Bowdoin Avenue, Dorchester. *Photograph by William Bellamy. Bostonian Society*
268 Mallon House, Bowdoin Avenue, Dorchester. *Photograph by William Bellamy. Bostonian Society*
269 Larz Anderson Estate, Brookline, interior. *S.P.N.E.A.*
269 Larz Anderson Estate, Brookline, exterior. *S.P.N.E.A.*
270 Fogg Art Museum, Hunt Hall. *Harvard University Archives*
274 Mayor Curley. *Boston Athenaeum*
274 John F. Fitzgerald. *Private collection*
276 Dressmaker's shop, West End. *Photograph by Jules Aaron*
277 Lamppost, Charles River Esplanade. *Metropolitan District Commission*
278 Dudley Station, Roxbury. *Courtesy of Robert Severy*
278 South Station, interior. *Private collection*
280 Chamber of Commerce Building, 80 Federal Street. *Courtesy of Robert Bayard Severy*
280 Mitchell Woodbury Corporation. *Boston Globe*
283 Hotel Westminster, exterior detail. *Photograph by Irene Shwachman*
283 Hotel Westminster. *Boston Public Library Print Department*
284–85 Tercentary parade, Federal Street, 1930. *Bostonian Society*
286 Scollay Building. *Bostonian Society*
287 Woolworth's, Tremont Row, 1912. *S.P.N.E.A.*
287 Spencer Manufacturing Company, Cornhill. *Photograph by Irene Shwachman*
288 Old State House, 1860s. *Bostonian Society*
288 Province Court. *S.P.N.E.A.*
289 Houghton and Dutton, Tremont Street. 1912. *S.P.N.E.A.*
289 Paramount Theater, 1932. *Boston Globe,* February 26, 1932
290 Columns, John Hancock Mutual Life Insurance Building, Franklin Street. *Photograph by Irene Shwachman*
291 "The Gothic," Allen Street. *Photograph by Cervin Robinson, 1959. HABS photo, Library of Congress*
291 New England Trust Company. Devonshire Street, doorway, 1972. *Photograph by Steve Rosenthal*
292 Federal Reserve Bank, Milk Street, 1979. *Photograph by Robert Bayard Severy*
293 Lions, Hotel Kensington, near Copley Square. *The Negative Side*
294 Jordan Marsh Co. *Bostonian Society, Severy Collection*

American Architect and Building News. 191 vols. Boston, 1876–1938.
Antin, Mary. *The Promised Land.* Boston, 1969.
Austin, William D. *A History of the Boston Society of Architects from 1867 to Jan 4, 1901.* Boston, 1942.
Back Bay Boston: The City as a Work of Art. Boston, 1969.
Bailyn, Bernard. *The Ideological Origins of the American Revolution.* Cambridge, 1967.
Baxter, W. T. *The House of Hancock.* Cambridge, 1945.
Bentley, William. *Diary, 1784–1819.* 4 vols. Salem, 1905–1914.
Blodgett, Geoffrey. *The Gentle Reformers: Massachusetts Democrats in the Cleveland Era.* Cambridge, 1966.
Bowen, Abel. *Picture of Boston.* Boston, 1833.
Brandeis, Louis Dembitz. *The Social and Economic Views of Mr. Justice Brandeis.* Edited by Alfred Lief. New York, 1930.
Bridenbaugh, Carl. *Cities in Revolt; Urban Life in America, 1743–1776.* New York, 1955.
———. *Cities in the Wilderness; The First Century of Urban Life in America, 1625–1742.* New York, 1955.
Brooks, Van Wyck. *The Flowering of New England, 1815–1865.* New York, 1936.
———. *New England: Indian Summer.* New York, 1965.
Bryan, John Morrill. "Boston's Granite Architecture, c. 1810–1860," Ph.D. dissertation, Boston University, 1972.
Bulfinch, Ellen Susan. *The Life and Letters of Charles Bulfinch, Architect.* Boston, 1896.
Bunting, Bainbridge. *Houses of Boston's Back Bay.* Cambridge, 1967.
Bunting, William Henry. *Portrait of a Port: Boston, 1852–1914.* Cambridge, 1971.
Cambridge Historical Commission. *Survey of Architectural History in Cambridge.* Nos. 2, 3, 5. Cambridge, 1966–1977.
"Carleton." *The Story of the Great Fire.* Boston, 1872.
Chamberlain, Allen. *Beacon Hill; Its Ancient Pastures and Early Mansions.* Boston, 1925.
Clarke, Bradley H. *The Boston Transit Album.* Cambridge, 1977.
Copeland, Robert Morris. *The Most Beautiful City in America; Essay & Plan for the Improvement of the City of Boston.* Boston, 1872.
Corwin, Emil, "Cogswell's Great Fountain Crusade," *Yankee,* March 1971, p. 71.
Craven, Wayne. *Sculpture in America.* New York, 1968.
Cummings, Abbott Lowell. *The Framed Houses of Massachusetts Bay, 1625–1725.* Cambridge, 1979.
Curley, James Michael. *I'd Do It Again.* Englewood Cliffs, N.J., 1957.
Cutler, John Henry. *"Honey Fitz": Three Steps to the White House; The Life and Times of John F. (Honey Fitz) Fitzgerald.* Indianapolis, 1962.
Damrell, Charles S. *A Half Century of Boston's Buildings.* Boston, 1895.
Dineen, Joseph Francis. *The Purple Shamrock.* Boston, 1949.
The Dorchester Book. Boston, 1899.
Dow, George Francis. *The Arts and Crafts in Early New England, 1704–1709.* Topsfield, Mass., 1927.
———. *Every Day Life in the Massachusetts Bay Colony.* Boston, 1935.
Eliot, Charles William. *Charles Eliot, Landscape Architect.* Boston, 1902.
Fein, Albert. *Frederick Law Olmsted and the American Environmental Tradition.* New York, 1972.
Fitch, James Marston. *Architecture and the Esthetics of Plenty.* New York, 1961.
Glaab, Charles Nelson, and A. Theodore Brown. *A History of Urban America.* New York, 1967.

Goody, Marvin E, and Robert P. Walsh, eds. *Boston Society of Architects, The First Hundred Years, 1867–1967*. Boston, 1967.

Hamlin, Talbot Faulkner. *Greek Revival Architecture in America*. London & New York, 1944.

Handlin, David, P. *The American Home*. Boston, 1979.

Handlin, Oscar. *Boston's Immigrants 1790–1865*. Cambridge, 1941.

Harrel, Pauline Chase, and Margaret Supplee Smith. *Victorian Boston Today: Ten Walking Tours*. Boston, 1975.

Harvard College Library, Dept. of Graphic Arts. *H. H. Richardson and His Office*. Cambridge, 1974.

Herndon, R. *Boston of Today*. Boston, 1892.

Hitchcock, Henry-Russell, Jr. *A Guide to Boston Architecture, 1637–1954*. New York, 1954.

Homer, Rachel Johnston. *The Legacy of Josiah Johnson Hawes*. Barre, Mass. 1972.

Howells, John Mead. *Lost Examples of Colonial Architecture*. New York, 1931.

Huse, Charles Phillips. *The Financial History of Boston from May 1, 1822 to January 31, 1900*. 1916. Reprint. New York, 1967.

Jackson, John Brinckerhoff. *American Space*. New York, 1972.

James, H. *Charles W. Eliot, President of Harvard University, 1869–1909*. Boston, 1930.

Journal of the Society of Architectural Historians, May 1973.

Kilham, Walter H. *Boston After Bulfinch*. Cambridge, 1946.

King, Moses. *Handbook of Boston*. 7th ed. Cambridge, 1885.

Kirker, Harold. *The Architecture of Charles Bulfinch*. Cambridge, 1969.

———, and James Kirker. *Bulfinch's Boston, 1787–1817*. New York, 1964.

Kirkland, Edward C. *Men, Cities, and Transportation*. Cambridge, 1948.

Koren, John. *Boston, 1822–1922*. Boston, 1922.

Krim, Arthur J. *Three-deckers of Dorchester: An Architectural Historical Survey*. Boston, 1977.

Leavitt, Percy M. *Souvenir Portfolio of Universalist Churches in Massachusetts*. Boston, 1906.

Lodge, Henry Cabot. *Early Memories*. New York, 1913.

Lord, Robert Howard, John E. Sexton, and Edward T. Harrington. *History of the Archdiocese of Boston in the Various Stages of Its Development, 1604 to 1943*. New York, 1944.

Lynes, Russell. *The Tastemakers*. New York, 1961.

———. *The Domestic Americans*. New York, 1957.

Marquand, John Phillips. *The Late George Apley*. New York, 1940.

Marr, Thomas E., and Son. *A Collection of Views of Fenway Court*. Boston, 1902–1904.

Morison, Samuel Eliot. *Builders of the Bay Colony*. Rev. and enlarged. Cambridge, 1964.

———. *The Founding of Harvard College*. Cambridge, 1935.

———. *Harrison Gray Otis 1765–1848*. Boston, 1969.

———. *The Maritime History of Massachusetts 1783–1860*. Boston, 1961.

———. *Three Centuries of Harvard, 1636–1936*. Cambridge, 1936.

New England Magazine and Bay State Monthly. Boston, 1886–1916.

O'Gorman, James, *H. H. Richardson and His Office*. Cambridge, 1975.

Old-Time New England: The Bulletin of the Society for the Preservation of New England Antiquities. Boston, 1910 to present.

Olmsted Papers. Washington, D.C., Library of Congress.

Pemberton, Thomas. *A Topographical and Historical Description of Boston*. Boston, 1794.

Pierson, William Harvey, and William R. Jordy. *American Buildings and Their Architects*. Vols. 1–4. Garden City, N.Y., 1970–1978.

Place, Charles A. *Charles Bulfinch Architect and Citizen*. Boston, 1925.

Proceedings of the Bostonian Society. Boston, 1882 to present.

Quincy, Josiah. *Figures of the Past from the Leaves of Old Journals*. Boston, 1926.

———. *Municipal History of the Town and City of Boston During Two Centuries*. Boston, 1852.

Reps, John William. *The Making of Urban America; a History of City Planning in the United States*. Princeton, 1965.

Rettig, Robert Bell. *A Guide to Cambridge Architecture: Ten Walking Tours*. Cambridge, 1969.

Roper, Laura Wood. *F. L. O.*, Baltimore, 1974.

Ross, Marjorie Drake. *Colonial Boston; Federal Boston; Victorian Boston*. New York, 1960, 1961, 1964.

Santayana, George. *The Last Puritan*. New York, 1936.

Shaw, Charles. *A Topographical and Historical Description of Boston*. Boston, 1817.

Shurtleff, Nathaniel Bradstreet. *Topographical and Historical Description of Boston*. Boston, 1871.

Sinnott, Edmund W. *Meetinghouse and Church in Early New England*. New York, 1963.

Smith, Margaret Supplee. "Between City and Suburb: Architecture and Planning in Boston's South End." Ph.D. dissertation, Boston.

———, and Pauline Chase Harrell, eds. *Victorian Boston Today: Ten Walking Tours*. Boston, 1975.

Solomon, Barbara Miller. *Ancestors and Immigrants, a Changing New England Tradition*. Cambridge, 1956.

Stanley, Raymond W., ed. *Mr. Bulfinch's Boston*. Boston, 1963.

Stanwood, Edward. *Boston Illustrated*. Boston, 1878.

Stevenson, Elizabeth. *Park-Maker: A Life of Frederick Law Olmsted*. New York, 1977.

Sturges, W. Knight. *The Origins of Cast Iron Architecture in America*. New York, 1970.

Tharp, Louise Hall. *The Appletons of Beacon Hill*. Boston, 1973.

Thwing, Annie Haven. *The Crooked and Narrow Streets of the Town of Boston, 1620–1822*. 1920. Reprint. Detroit, 1970.

Tucci, Douglass Shand. *Built in Boston: City and Suburb, 1860–1940*. Boston, 1978.

———. *Church Building in Boston, 1720–1970*. Concord, N.H., 1974.

———. *The Second Settlement, 1875–1925*. Boston, 1974.

Van Brunt, Henry. *Architecture and Society*. Edited by William A. Coles. Cambridge, 1969.

Van Rensselaer, Mariana G. *Henry H. Richardson and His Works*. 1888. Reprint, New York, 1969.

Vose, George Leonard. *Sketch of Life and Works of Loammi Baldwin*. Boston, 1885.

Warden, Gerard B. *Boston, 1689–1776*. Boston, 1970.

Warner, Sam Bass. *Streetcar Suburbs: The Process of Growth in Boston, 1870–1900*. Cambridge, 1962.

Wells, Herbert George. *The Future in America; A Search After Realities*. New York, 1906.

Weston, George F., Jr. *Boston Ways: High, By and Folk*. Rev. ed. Boston, 1967.

Whalen, Richard J. *The Founding Father*. New York, 1964.

Wheildon, W. W. *Memoir of S. Willard*. Boston, 1865.

Whitefield, Edwin. *Homes of Our Forefathers in Boston, Old England, and Boston*. Boston, 1889.

Whitehill, Walter Muir. *Boston Museum of Fine Arts: A Centennial History*. Cambridge, 1970.

———. *Boston Statues*. Barre, Mass., 1970.

———. *Boston: A Topographical History*. 2nd ed. Cambridge, 1968.

Winsor, Justin. *The Memorial History of Boston Including Suffolk County, Mass. 1630–1880*. Vols. I–IV. Boston, 1880–81.

Woods, Robert A., and Albert J. Kennedy. *The Zone of Emergence*. Cambridge, 1962.

Zaitzevsky, Cynthia. *William Ralph Emerson, 1833–1917*. Cambridge, 1969.

———. *Frederick Law Olmsted and the Boston Park System*. Ph.D. dissertation, Cambridge, 1975.

Index

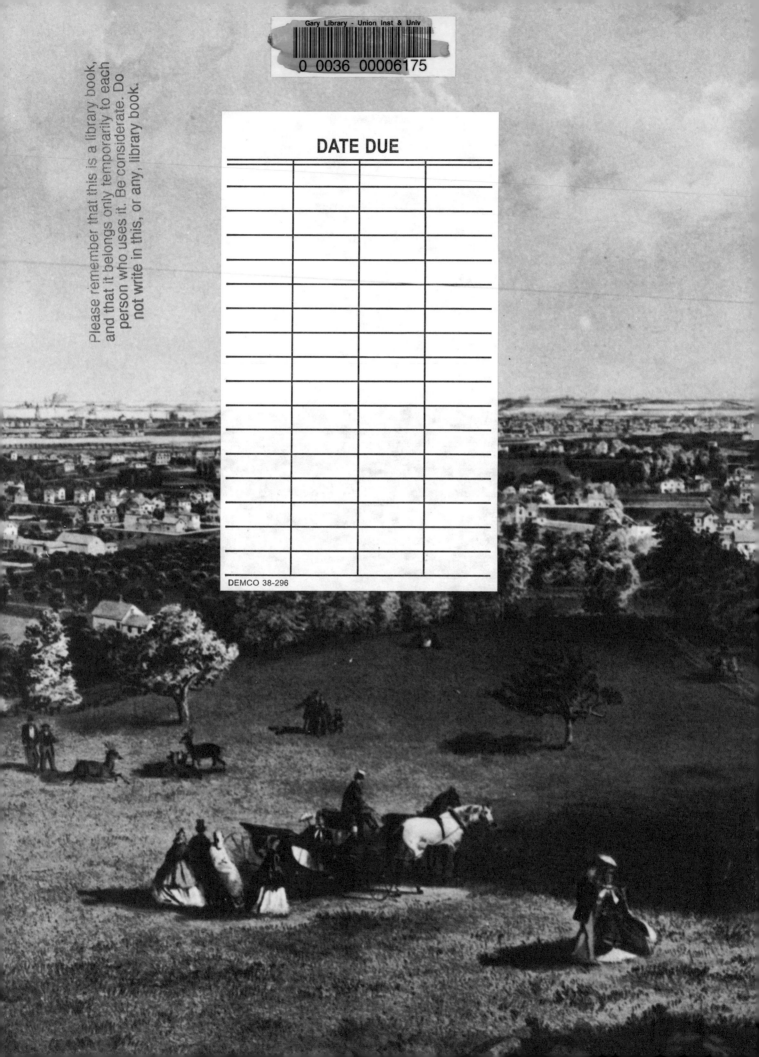

Gary Library - Union Inst & Univ

0 0036 00006175

Please remember that this is a library book,
and that it belongs only temporarily to each
person who uses it. Be considerate. Do
not write in this, or any, library book.

DATE DUE

DEMCO 38-296